Marketing Planning for Services

Malcolm McDonald and Adrian Payne

Published on behalf of
The Chartered Institute of Marketing

Butterworth-Heinemann
Linacre House, Jordan Hill, Oxford OX2 8DP
225 Wildwood Avenue, Woburn, MA 01801-2041
A division of Reed Educational and Professional Publishing Ltd

A member of the Reed Elsevier plc group

OXFORD   BOSTON   JOHANNESBURG
MELBOURNE   NEW DELHI   SINGAPORE

First published 1996
Paperback edition 1996
Reprinted 1997 (twice), 1998

British Library Cataloguing in Publication Data
McDonald, M. H. B.
    Marketing Planning for Services -
    (Marketing Series)
    I. Title II. Payne, Adrian III. Series
    658.802

ISBN 0 7506 3022 1

Typeset by Keyword Typesetting Services Ltd, Wallington, Surrey
Printed and bound in Great Britain by MPG Books Ltd, Bodmin, Cornwall

Contents

Preface

This is one of a trilogy of Butterworth-Heinemann books on marketing planning:

Marketing Plans: How to prepare them; how to use them (1995, 3rd edn)
Retail Marketing Plans (1993)
Marketing Planning for Services (1995)

This latest addition to the series is in recognition of the growing importance of the service sector in Western economies and of the significant differences between product and service marketing.

The original text, *Marketing Plans: How to prepare them; how to use them*, has sold over one hundred thousand copies around the world. It is recommended that this latest text be used in conjunction with the original text by those working within the service sector. Taken together, the two books represent an extremely powerful contribution to understanding the domain of marketing planning, which has its own special challenges.

The two authors work with many of the world's leading service organizations in their role as professors of marketing at one of Europe's most prestigious business schools. We have sought to combine the experience of Europe's first full-time professor of services marketing (Adrian Payne) with the acknowledged leadership of Cranfield University in the domain of marketing planning (Malcolm McDonald) to produce a unique text for those who are faced with the special challenge of producing marketing plans for services where there are no tangible products.

The approaches outlined in this book have been used extensively by us in a large number of services organizations.

We believe you will find, in the pages of this book, the answer to the challenge of creating marketing plans that produce significantly improved bottom-line results.

Malcolm McDonald
Adrian Payne
Cranfield University

The structure of the book and how to use it

This book consists of eight chapters, some examples of marketing plans and a glossary of terms used in marketing planning.

Chapter 1 provides a broad view of marketing as it relates to services. It describes the marketing concept, some key misunderstandings about marketing and the nature of services and relationship marketing.

Chapter 2 provides an overview of the four key phases of the marketing planning process and looks at the barriers that can prevent a service organization being successful in introducing marketing planning.

Chapters 3 to 6 provide a detailed examination of each of the four phases in the marketing planning process and an explanation of the frameworks and techniques which are useful in undertaking these tasks.

Chapter 7 examines some of the key organizational aspects relating to marketing planning. These issues, although not directly part of the marketing planning process itself, have an important and profound impact on its ultimate effectiveness. Here we discuss the role of marketing intelligence systems; market research; to what extent the introduction of marketing planning is appropriate at the different stages of development of an organization; and finally the issue of how a service organization can develop or improve its marketing orientation.

Chapter 8 provides structures for a three-year strategic marketing plan, a one-year detailed marketing plan and a headquarters consolidated plan of several strategic businesses unit (SBU) strategic marketing plans. These structures will help with implementing the processes and frameworks outlined earlier in this book. Also, in the appendices, are a number of marketing plans which illustrate what strategic marketing plans actually look like in different types of service organizations.

> **For those readers who are new to marketing planning, it will be beneficial to skim-read Chapter 8 and the marketing plans in the appendices before starting at Chapter 1.**

Those readers who have read widely on the services sector and are familiar with the services marketing literature can start at Chapter 2.

We suggest that all readers should undertake a close examination of the process aspects in the text, covered in Chapters 3 to 6. We also recommend that Chapter 7 is read thoroughly as, although not directly about the marketing planning process, it addresses many of the issues which are critical to successful implementation of a marketing planning system.

> **However, it should be recognized that a little learning is a dangerous thing. Whilst Chapter 8 and the examples of marketing plans provide a clear overview as to how a marketing plan is structured, we advise a thorough examination of the detailed discussion of each of the key steps. For those seriously interested in either initiating marketing planning or in improving the quality of their marketing planning, we strongly recommend them to study the whole book before attempting to use any of the systems and plans provided at the back of the book.**

Best of luck – and happy and profitable marketing planning.

1 Marketing and services

The growing importance of the service sector

Since the Second World War, Western Europe has seen a steady and unrelenting decline in its traditional manufacturing industries. Their place has been taken by numerous service-based enterprises, who were quick to spot the opportunities created by both organizational needs and by the increased personal affluence and the consequent raised lifestyle expectations of the population.

> **So successful has been this transition from an essentially industrial society, that today, more than 60 per cent of Western economies are now in the service sector, whether measured in terms of income or numbers employed.**

The service-led 'second industrial revolution' This shift in emphasis has been so pronounced that some observers refer to it as the 'second industrial revolution'. As individuals spend greater proportions of their income on travel, entertainment and leisure, postal and communication services, restaurants, personal health and grooming and the like, so has the service sector responded by creating businesses and jobs. In addition, the growing complexity of banking, insurance, investment, accountancy and legal services has meant that these areas of activity showed a similar inclination to expand, in terms of their impact on the economy as a whole.

In the UK, government employment statistics (Table 1.1) provide a telling picture of this silent revolution.

> **Whereas employment in the service sector accounted for roughly 50 per cent of the total workforce in 1968, by 1990 this figure had increased to 70 per cent.**

This pattern has been repeated in most of the developed countries, as Table 1.2 shows.

Table 1.1 Total UK employees in employment (thousands)

	Service employees	All others	Total
1968	11 242	10 944	22 186
1975	12 545	9 668	22 213
1980	13 384	9 074	22 458
1985	13 769	7 151	20 920
1990	15 609	6 771	22 380
1995	15 418	5 616	21 034

Source: *Monthly Digest of Statistics and Employment Gazette*, February 1991.

Table 1.2 Civilian employment by sector: international comparison, 1992 (%)

	Services	Industry	Agriculture
UK	70.7	27.1	2.3
Australia	70.1	23.8	5.2
Austria	57.4	35.6	7.1
Belgium	69.7	27.7	2.6
Canada	73.1	22.7	4.4
Denmark	67.6	27.4	5.2
Finland	63.5	27.9	8.6
France	65.8	28.8	5.2
FR Germany	58.5	38.3	3.1
Irish Republic	57.3	28.9	13.8
Italy	59.6	32.2	8.2
Japan	59.0	34.6	6.4
Netherlands	71.4	24.6	4.0
Norway	70.9	55.3	11.6
Portugal	55.3	33.2	11.6
Spain	55.7	32.4	10.1
Sweden	70.1	26.5	3.3
Switzerland	60.6	33.9	5.6
United States	72.5	24.6	2.9

Source: *Monthly Digest of Statistics and Employment Gazette*, August 1995.

Although there is a realization that it is essential for a country to have some kind of industrial base, there is little to suggest that this trend towards the service sector is slowing down.

> **Indeed, the manufacturing industry itself is showing a greater propensity to subcontract out a wide range of activities which at one time were carried out in-house.**

For example, outsourcing is increasing in areas such as cleaning, catering, recruitment, deliveries, computer services, advertising, training, market research, and product design. These are all areas where it has been found that external specialists can provide a cost-effective alternative to a company's own staff. More and more companies are choosing to contract out for specialist services and concentrate attention on their core activities.

Service industries and marketing effectiveness

Throughout roughly the same period, business schools and consultancy firms have been emphasizing how important it is for companies to develop a marketing orientation. At first sight this message would appear to have hit home, because today many companies claim to be market-led and customer-focused. However, from our position of working with senior managers and marketing staff from a wide range of companies, we can see that this so-called 'marketing orientation' has, for most of them, not been accomplished.

Marketing has not yet stormed the citadels of service organizations

> **There is more emphasis on rhetoric than transactions. In fact, we estimate that less than one service organization in five has a marketing plan worthy of the name.**

One of the major UK banks has recruited hundreds of consumer goods trained marketing personnel, yet still has no observable differential advantage in any of its operations. It is clear that such organizations have confused marketing orientation with selling and promotion. The result is that they have merely succeeded in creating a veneer and a vocabulary of marketing.

Recent research by one of the authors into the marketing effectiveness across a variety of service organizations suggested that many of the companies studied operated well below their potential marketing effectiveness.

> **With organizations paying only lip-service to being marketing orientated, the results suggest a dramatic need for improvement in marketing effectiveness.**

What is clear is that many service companies are misdirecting their energies and resources and thereby are failing to create competitive advantage and capitalize on market opportunities.

The purpose of this book

This book sets out to demonstrate how a service organization can formulate a strategic marketing plan which contributes to the establishment of competitive advantage. It examines the marketing planning process in some detail and shows how successful companies tackle its difficult elements. Where necessary, relevant marketing theory, techniques, and research results are introduced so that the reader can better understand the implications of taking particular actions at various stages of the process. In addition, it is important to consider the demands a new approach to planning places on the organization.

> **For marketing planning to take root, not only must new skills be learned, but often new attitudes have to accompany them. Indeed, many of the barriers that hamper the acceptance of marketing planning can be attributed to outmoded or inappropriate organizational behaviour.**

The purpose of this opening chapter is briefly to examine the marketing concept and explore to what extent the marketing of services differs from the marketing of products. We will also look at the diverse range of services in terms of establishing some threads of 'commonality'. In doing this, it makes it possible for the service manager to learn from other companies who may not necessarily be in the same business field.

This chapter will also develop reasons why the service marketer must formulate an enlarged and more sophisticated marketing mix than has traditionally been the case, and why focusing solely on customer markets will not prove to be enough for a guaranteed long-term marketing success.

The marketing concept

Marketing as a source of competitive advantage

The central idea of marketing is to match the organization's capabilities with the needs of customers in order to achieve the objectives of both parties. If this matching process is to be achieved, then the organization has to develop strengths, either from the nature of the services it offers or from the way it exploits these services, in order to provide customer satisfaction.

Since very few companies can be equally competent at providing a service for all types of customers, an essential part of this matching process is to identify those groups of customers whose needs are most compatible with the organization's strengths and future ambitions. It must be recognized that the limitations imposed by an organization's resources, and the unique make-up of its management skills, make it impossible to take advantage of all market opportunities with equal facility. Companies who fail to grasp this fundamental point, which lies at the heart of marketing, are courting commercial disaster.

The matching process is complicated by the ever-changing business environment

This matching process is further complicated in that it takes place in a business environment which is never stable for any length of time. External factors continue to have a major impact on the company's attempts to succeed. For example, new competitors might enter the business, existing ones may develop a better service, government legislation may change and as a result alter the trading conditions, new technology may be developed which weakens their current skills base – the possibilities are almost endless. However, not every external factor will pose a threat. Some environmental developments will undoubtedly provide opportunities.

Figure 1.1 provides a visual summary of the matching process, which is the essence of marketing. As it shows, the environment has an impact not only on the matching process, but also on the 'players'. So, for example, local labour conditions might limit the company in recruiting a workforce with the appropriate skill levels. Equally, changed levels of unemployment can have a drastic impact on customer demand, making it either much greater or much less.

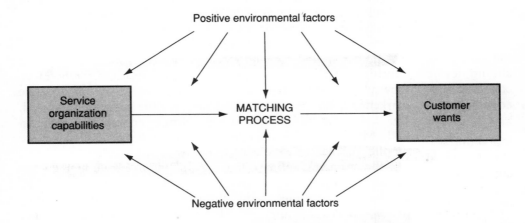

Figure 1.1 Marketing: a matching process

Misunderstandings about marketing

One of the biggest areas of misunderstanding is that concerned with customer wants. Many people, unfortunately some of them in marketing, have a naive concept of customers. They see customers as people, or organizations, who can be manipulated into wanting things that they do not really need.

In the long run, customers always have the final say

However, commercial life is not really that simple. Customers are not prepared to act so unthinkingly at the request of the supplier, as evidenced by a very high proportion of new products and services that fail to make any impact in the marketplace. All the evidence suggests that it would be foolish to deny that the customer, in the end, always has the final say. Moreover, customers invariably have a choice to make about how they satisfy their particular requirements.

> **In the final analysis, they will choose these services that they perceive to offer the benefits they seek, at the price they can afford.**

Marketing should not be confused with sales

Another area of misunderstanding is the confusion of marketing with sales. Some ill-informed organizations actually believe that marketing is the new word for what was previously called sales. Others perceive marketing to be a mere embellishment of the sales process, a sort of 'selling with knobs on'. That such companies exist is a sad reflection on the standard of management and suggests that marketing education has been less than effective. By failing to recognize that marketing is designed to provide a longer-term strategic, customer-driven orientation rather than a short-term tactical triumph, such an organization is certain to under-achieve. Not surprisingly, the chief executive of one such company was overheard to say: 'There is no place for marketing in this company until sales improve!'

Marketing should not be confused with advertising

A similar misunderstanding occurs which confuses marketing with advertising. Here, gloss is seen as the magic formula to win business. However, without integrating advertising into an overall strategic marketing plan, hard-earned budgets can be completely wasted. Throwing advertising funds at a problem is no way to resolve an underlying issue which might have its roots in the fact that the service on offer has been superseded by another superior offer.

Marketing should not be confused with having a good product or service

Another misconception is that it is enough to have a high-quality service or product to succeed. Sadly, this has proved not to be the case time and time again. No matter how good the service or product, unless it is appropriately priced and promoted, it will not make any lasting impact.

Marketing should not be confused with customer service

The final area of confusion, and one to which we will return in more detail later, is to think that marketing is synonymous with customer service. With misguided enthusiasm, many organizations subscribing to this belief have rushed into organizing 'customer service' programmes for their staff.

> **Had they bothered to find out what their customers really wanted, perhaps they would have responded differently.**

Train passengers might have travelled in less dirty and cramped conditions, and might have arrived at their destination on time more frequently. Those using banks might have found them open at more convenient times, and with more than one cashier on duty during the busy lunch period (the only time working customers can get there!). Instead, customers have been treated to cosmetic 'smile campaigns', where, regardless of their treatment, they were thanked for doing business with the supplier and encouraged to 'have a nice day'. Most people can recall an incident of this nature.

This is not to say that 'customer care' programmes are not important. What we contend is that, unless the core service and the associated intangibles are right, such programmes will fail. Such programmes ought to be part of the overall integrated set of marketing activities, not a substitute for them. The warning signs are there for those who care to look for them.

> A recent US study showed that, while 77 per cent of service industry companies had some form of customer service programme in operation, less than 30 per cent of chief executives in these companies believed that it had any significant impact on profit performance.

The nature of services marketing

So far, much of what has been said could be equally applicable to either a product or a service. So, is there anything special about services marketing? Our answer is: 'it all depends'.

A negative answer could be justified because, at one level, the theory of marketing has universal application – the same underlying concerns and principles apply whatever the nature of the business. However, since the nature of some types of services may dictate a need to place more emphasis on certain marketing elements, which in turn could lead to different approaches, a positive answer is also appropriate.

The more obvious differences between a product and a service listed below only serve to underline that some differences in marketing approach will often be required.

> 1 A service cannot be patented and specified with drawings in the same way that a product can.
> 2 Service quality cannot be guaranteed in the same way as that of a product, which can be controlled accurately at each stage of its manufacture, which in turn is accomplished in controlled conditions.
> 3 A service cannot be stored on a shelf to be taken down and used at a later time in response to customer demands.

> 4 An indifferent salesperson does not necessarily obscure the inherent value and quality of a tangible product, whereas with an intangible service the salesperson is often perceived as an integral part of the offer.
> 5 The value of a product can be assessed at the time of purchase, whereas the true value of a service can only be assessed on its completion. Thus, the purchase of a service is characterized by a much higher component of trust than a product.

However, it must be borne in mind that the explosive and some-times erratic growth of the services sector means that there is a diversity of types of businesses, some of which do not readily fit into any neat definition.

> **One of the problems of defining a service is to do with the fact that, whereas a product is seen to be tangible and a service intangible, there are in reality many variations on the degree of tangibility.**

Kotler[1] has identified four categories, varying from a 'pure' product to a 'pure' service.

(a) A pure tangible product	A tangible offer, such as sugar, coal, or tea. No services are bought with the product.
(b) A tangible product with accompanying services such as commissioning, training, maintenance.	Here, the offer has built-in services to enhance its customer appeal, e.g. computers, machine tools.
(c) A service with accompanying minor goods (or services)	Here, the offer is basically a service but has a product element, e.g. property surveyors, whose expert inspection is encapsulated in a report. Similarly, airlines offer in-flight meals, or entertainment.
(d) A pure service, where one buys expertise	Here, the offer is a stand-alone service such as psycho analysis.

These categories can be placed on a continuum which embraces all possible degrees of intangibility.

Figure 1.2 identifies the continuum of tangible–intangible possibilities. Point (a) on the left-hand side of this figure illustrates an offer where there is no service element and so the product is highly tangible. At the other end of the continuum, point (d) illustrates a product which is entirely a service and is therefore highly intangible. Points (b) and (c) show varying mixes of tangibility/intangibility. For example, point (b) illustrates the mix of tangibility and intangibility for a computer company. Computer hardware and programmes are highly tangible and can be regarded as commodities; however, the service elements of user training and troubleshooting are largely intangible.

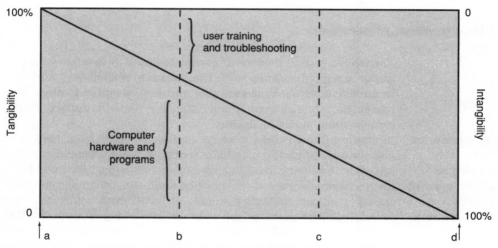

Figure 1.2 Continuum of tangible–intangible possibilities

Service marketing does not only apply to service industries

Viewed in this way, the difference between a product and a service becomes far less discrete.

It follows that to define services as being confined only to service industries is not strictly true.

There is an increasing trend towards differentiating what were once considered to be tangible products by exploiting the intangible service elements of the offer. The service elements can be added to provide unique features matching customer needs. For example, in the highly competitive photocopier business, service has become a major factor in the buying decision. Photocopiers are leased or sold with service contracts which tie customers to the supplier.

Nevertheless, it will be difficult to proceed without attempting to define a service in some way. Therefore, while recognizing that any definition might prove to be unduly restrictive, and that somewhere a service may exist which does not conform to what we say, our definition is:

> A service is an activity which has some element of intangibility associated with it. It involves some interaction with customers or property in their possession, and does not result in a transfer of ownership. A change of condition may occur and provision of the service may or may not be closely associated with a physical product.

Classification of services

There have been a number of approaches used to develop a classification scheme for services.[2,3] The intention behind this work was to provide service managers with a means of identifying other companies who, though operating in different types of industries, shared certain common characteristics.

Much can be learned by looking at other types of service organizations

Interesting though some of these approaches have been, they were not always sufficiently helpful in terms of aiding comparison with others or developing marketing strategies. Sometimes, the fault lay in the oversimplification of the classification used, which did not offer enough strategic marketing insights to be of much value. At other times, the blame could be laid at the service managers' door, for they were not open-minded enough to recognize where similarities with other industries could exist. For example, for some, providing service in a hospital was thought to be so specialized that there was nothing to be learned from considering, say, an airline or hotel business.

The fact that most attempts to classify services have done little to excite service managers has caused academic researchers to try new avenues. Lovelock[4] has developed a classification framework which yields valuable strategic marketing insights in response to five crucial questions, and he examines these in a series of two-dimensional matrices.

1 What is the nature of the 'service act'?
2 What style of relationship does this service organization have with its customers?
3 How much room is there for customization and judgement?
4 What is the nature of supply and demand for the service?
5 How is the service delivered?

Based on Lovelock's work, each of these questions and the associated matrices are now examined in more detail.

1 What is the nature of the service act?

The primary considerations here are whether or not the service is largely tangible or intangible and if it is addressed essentially to people or to 'things', be they property, systems or equipment. Not only can these factors be combined in the matrix shown in Figure 1.3, but they also raise further issues for the inquisitive service manager, such as:

- **What benefits does the service provide?**
- **Does the customer need to be present as the service is delivered?**
- **Is the customer changed as a result of the service?**
- **Does the customer have to come out to receive the service, or can it be provided at home (or at the office)?**

Exploring possible answers to these questions might enable the service manager to gain new insights, thereby repositioning the service by making it more beneficial or convenient to the customer. For example, a hairdressing salon might develop an 'at-home' service for customers who are incapacitated or who find travelling difficult. If this proved to be successful, it could reduce the need for having an expensive High Street establishment. Indeed, it might eventually lead to withdrawing from fixed premises entirely.

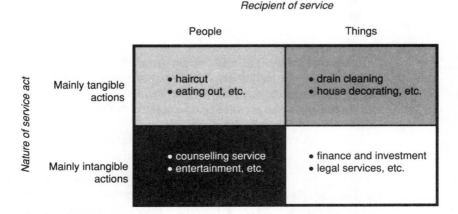

Figure 1.3 Nature of service matrix

2 What style of relationship does the service organization have with its customers?

The prime factors which underpin this question concern whether or not the customer has some type of formal relationship with the provider of the service, and whether the service itself is provided continuously or in discrete transactions. These considerations lend themselves to the matrix in Figure 1.4.

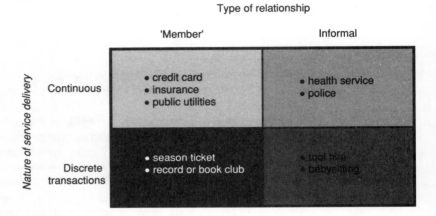

Type of relationship

'Member'   Informal

Continuous
- credit card
- insurance
- public utilities

- health service
- police

Discrete transactions
- season ticket
- record or book club

- tool hire
- babysitting

Nature of service delivery

Figure 1.4 Style of relationship matrix

Clearly, there are advantages for the service provider to have customers as 'members', whether this is done in a contractual sense or just by mutual agreement. By knowing personal details about the customers, it becomes easy to contact them via direct marketing and to tailor special offers around their particular needs. Thus, market segmentation becomes relatively straightforward and it is possible to build up customer loyalty by trading on the special relationship that membership brings.

In contrast, when the relationship is informal, next to nothing is known about the customer. Another problem is assessing how to charge for a continuous delivery, informal relationship type of service. In the examples provided in the matrix, they come 'free', but are of course funded by the taxpayer.

The key questions this matrix raises for service managers are:

- Can anything be done to move 'informal' into 'member' relationships (e.g. random cinema visitors become cinema club members; regular tool hirers get a privilege card; etc.)?

- Where can there be trade-offs between pr...
  rates (e.g. season ticket holders for th...
  entertainment; book clubs that give price...
  membership)?

3 How much room is there for customization and judgement?

Here, the issues centre on the degree to which the service can be tailored to meet specific needs, and the degree of judgement required by staff who come into contact with the customer. This is illustrated in Figure 1.5.

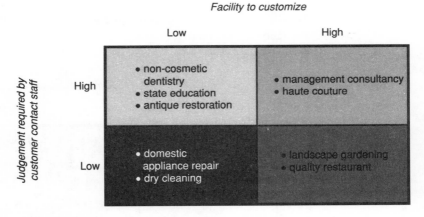

Figure 1.5 Customization and judgement matrix

The questions this matrix raises for the service manager are, on the whole, bound up with cost and the availability of the right calibre of staff. For example:

- Is it desirable to limit the degree of customization and thereby benefit from 'standardization' and economies of scale?
- Should customization be increased in order to reach a wider range of customers?
- Should services be simplified so that less judgement is required by contact staff?
- Should the service be updated in order to capitalize on the expertise of staff?

In answer to questions like these, a general management consultancy firm might start to specialize in just one or two specific areas. Similarly, the landscape gardener might focus on paths and patios.

The level of customization will often create friction between the marketing and operations function. Service market managers will often see the need for a high level of customization which poses greater demand on operational staff. Higher levels of service customization often require employees at the point of service delivery to make decisions based on their own judgement. This means that employees require greater levels of training and a wider skill base. For example, a waiter who prepares at the customer's table requires a higher level of training than one who delivers food from the kitchen to the table.

4 What is the nature of supply and demand for the service?

In other words, are demand fluctuations large or small, and can peak demands be met relatively easily? The matrix these questions provide is shown as Figure 1.6.

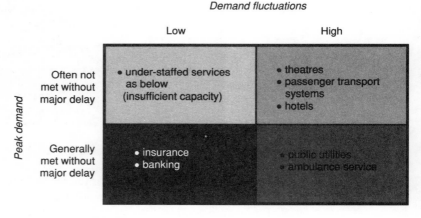

Figure 1.6 Supply and demand matrix

As was stated earlier, a service cannot be stored, so if demand exceeds supply, it is an invitation for another supplier to step in. This indicates that it is important for the service manager to understand demand patterns over time, knowing why and when peaks occur, and taking steps to work out what alternative strategies might be used for 'smoothing' them. Some examples of how this works in practice would be:

- The DIY store, whose busiest time is weekends, expands 'capacity' by employing temporary staff.
- British Rail provide reduced price 'off-peak' travel.

> ● Harvester Restaurants provide a reduction for early eve-
> ning diners during the week, but restore normal pricing at
> weekends.

Typical of the questions that supply and demand prompt in the minds of service managers are:

> ● How susceptible to peaks and troughs is the business?
> ● To what extent can peaks be coped with?
> ● Should alternative strategies be adopted for creating capacity?
> ● Should alternative strategies be adopted for introducing differential pricing?
> ● Should a new mix of strategies be experimented with, involving both capacity and pricing?

Coping with demand fluctuation can cause serious problems for service managers. Computer technology helps delivery scheduling for services. For example, on the underground train network in Singapore, the passenger flow is constantly monitored via a computer-linked ticketing system. If passenger flow suggests additional trains are required, the system will immediately trigger action to correct the situation.

5 How is the service delivered?

The method by which the service is delivered to customers can be another area where a change of marketing strategy could pay dividends. The factors to consider are shown in Figure 1.7.

This matrix raises another set of questions for the service manager:

> ● Should the service be delivered at a single site or through multiple outlets?
> ● What is the most convenient type of transaction for customers?
> ● If the type of interaction changed, would the service quality improve or deteriorate?
> ● Can suitable intermediaries be used in order to achieve multiple outlets? (e.g. franchises)?

Service delivery is of great importance to the customer's overall perception of service quality. Services that generally require the customer to come to the supplier have a greater opportunity to control

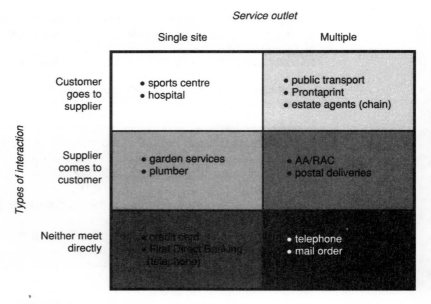

Figure 1.7 Service delivery matrix

the delivery experience. For example, a client visiting a lawyer's office will gain an impression of competence and professionalism from the 'atmosphere' of the waiting area and the friendliness and efficiency of the receptionist. However, increasingly, many services are being delivered without the customer and supplier meeting. Examples include telephone banking, the use of fax and EDI (electronic data interchange) that are being introduced within many service sectors.

Lovelock's five questions (and associated matrices) clearly raise a number of interesting and important issues for the service provider. The advantage of this particular method of classification is that it can cut across service industry barriers, thus enabling comparisons to be made with, and lessons to be learned from, service companies in other business fields. They also highlight key issues that need to be addressed in the marketing plans of service organizations.

The strategic value of services in manufacturing

As was shown earlier, the 100 per cent tangible product is a rarity. Apart from a few commodity items or foodstuffs, most products have an element of service attached to them.

> Many manufacturers have been quick to realize that, although their basic product might be in the 'me-too' category, they can bring about some differentiation from the way they manage the service element of the product.

The types of services that can feature in an expanded 'product package' are:

- Training
- Consultancy
- Service contracts
- Customization
- Fast-moving troubleshooting
- Help with financing
- Special delivery arrangements
- Stockholding or inventory control for the customer
- No-quibble guarantees

Adding services can become a major source of differential advantage in the manufacturing sector

As manufacturing companies become more sophisticated and as technological advantages become ever more transitory, services begin to represent an area of significant profit potential. This trend has even earned itself a new piece of jargon, 'servitization of business', coined by Vandermerwe and Rada.[5] Not surprisingly, manufacturing is now looking more and more at the service industry in order to learn from its experience. As a result, what was once a clear divide between two quite different types of businesses is becoming increasingly blurred.

This section on the nature of services was prompted by a seemingly simple question about the difference between marketing a product and a service. As we have seen, not only is it not easy to define where a product finishes and a service begins, but even the difference between manufacturing as an industry and the traditional notion of a service industry is becoming ever less clear.

This discussion was important, because it should help the reader to have a much clearer idea about how a business should be defined in terms of the intangibility of its service and the other characteristics that give it a particular identity. Knowing this makes it easier to recognize how the marketing planning process can be best adapted for particular circumstances.

The marketing mix

Earlier, marketing was described as being a process which matches the supplier's capabilities with the customer's wants. We also saw that this matching process took place in a business environment which could pose threats for the supplier, but which also created opportunities.

The marketing mix is, in effect, the 'flexible coupling' between the supplier and customer which facilitates the matching process. Traditionally it was said to consist of four elements, namely:

• *Product*	The product or service being offered
• *Price*	The price or fees charged and the terms associated with its sale
• *Promotion*	The communications programme associated with marketing the product or service
• *Place*	The distribution and logistics involved in making the product/service available.

From this, the shorthand term for the marketing mix became the 4Ps, for reasons which are obvious. However, it must be remembered that within each 'P' is subsumed a number of subelements pertinent to that heading. So, for example, promotion will include not only face-to-face communications provided by contact staff, but also indirect communications such as advertising, sales promotions, publications and direct mail.

Services and the marketing mix

In services marketing, the 4 Ps need to be expanded
In recent years, those charged with developing the application of marketing in the service sector have questioned whether the 4Ps approach to the marketing mix was sufficiently comprehensive.[6] As a result, there has been a marked shift of opinion which now advocates that the original concept should be expanded, as shown below. This new mix is more appropriate for service businesses and ensures that important elements are not overlooked.

Added to the original 4Ps are:

• *Customer service* As customers demand higher levels of service, this element becomes a competitive weapon with which a company can differentiate itself. In the longer term it helps to build closer and more enduring relationships with customers.
• *People* Since people are an essential element in the production and delivery of services, the quality of the service is largely determined by the quality and behaviour of the company's staff. This is particularly true in respect of those whose jobs involve high levels of customer contact.
• *Processes* The procedures, routines and policies, which influence how a service is created and delivered to customers, can clearly be instrumental in determining how 'customer friendly' the company is perceived to be.

This expanded marketing mix will be found to be robust enough to cover most service marketing situations.[7] Of course, with the diversity of services which exist, there could still be a few situations where it might be necessary to vary the constituent elements of this new marketing mix, but they will be relatively rare.

By introducing the marketing mix into the earlier diagram, it becomes possible to arrive at a far more accurate representation of how the marketing process for services really works (Figure 1.8).

The output of the supplying company results from the effort it puts into the marketing mix.

> **Just as a master chef will prepare food to a different recipe for customers he or she knows, so will the intelligent marketing organization split its customers into segments and provide a different marketing mix best suited to the needs of each one.**

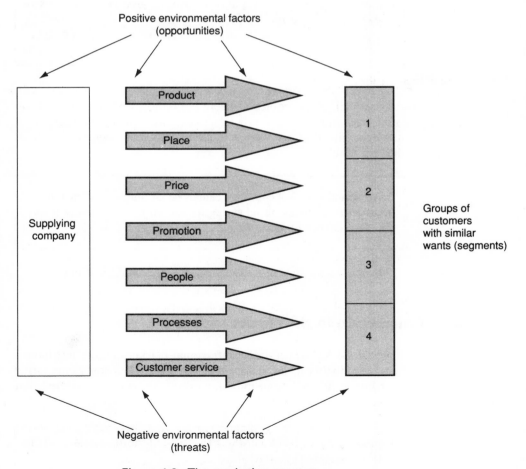

Figure 1.8 The marketing process

Perhaps the service product provided is slightly different, perhaps the financial transaction is varied from segment to segment, perhaps the promotion is different with, say, one segment influenced by indirect communications and another by face-to-face methods, perhaps the place element of the mix is different for each segment, or perhaps it is customer service which is differentiated.

Success depends on careful market segmentation

There is in reality a tremendous range of options open to the marketer who chooses to explore all of the marketing mix possibilities, but of course the whole marketing process really hinges on how accurately the wants of customers are known and how astutely they are grouped into segments which meet the following criteria:

> - They are adequate in size to provide the company with a good return for its effort.
> - Members of each segment have a high degree of similarity, yet are distinct from the rest of the market.
> - Criteria for describing the segments are relevant to the purchase situation.
> - Segments are capable of being reached through communications.

It goes without saying that a company should not try to work with too many different segments. There is a danger that some will be too small but, more importantly, the company will not be capable of managing its dealings with too many different segments without diluting its efforts.

> **Like an individual, a company cannot be all things to all people. It must learn to focus on its strengths and on markets where it has the best chance of succeeding.**

Market segmentation is discussed in more detail in Chapter 4.

A history of marketing in the service industry

It would be fair to say that professional marketing does not have a very long history in the service industry. In 1970, a study comparing four hundred service and manufacturing companies discovered that the service companies were:

> - less likely to have marketing mix activities carried out in the marketing department
> - less likely to do comparative analysis of service products

- less likely to use outside agencies for their advertising (they showed a preference to do it themselves)
- less likely to have an overall sales plan
- less likely to have sales training-programmes
- less likely to use market research firms and marketing consultants
- less likely to spend as much on marketing as a percentage of gross sales.

The service industry still lags behind in marketing

Nonetheless, in general, the service industry has demonstrated robust growth since then. However, with increasing globalization and de-regulation, competition has also become far more intense. Today, we find an industry that has grown, but in marketing terms still lags behind the consumer goods and industrial sectors. Even so, the picture is not universally bad, for many service companies have become very sophisticated in their marketing and would compare favourably with good examples of best practice anywhere in the world.

It was only in the 1980s that serious attention was given to service marketing. Some of the work developed since then has suggested that service companies alter their 'marketing' focus as they evolve and develop. These different phases are shown in Figure 1.9. However, it should be noted that this is a general pattern that companies follow. Some individual companies might have reached these focus points in a slightly different sequence, or indeed might have jumped some of the steps completely.

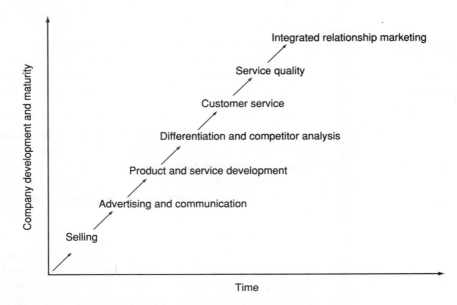

Figure 1.9 General development pattern of marketing approaches

In a sense, the pattern shown in Figure 1.9 is not too surprising, because it conveys something of a learning process, whereby each step is almost a natural extension of moving forward. In fact, it could be argued that this sequence closely follows the various phases of activity which exercised certain kinds of service companies from approximately 1960 to the present day.

Seeking to reach the final stage requires the service company to:

- Integrate all marketing activities
- Develop a realistic and focused approach to marketing planning
- Develop a marketing-orientated culture
- Recognize the importance of quality transactions both inside the company and with customers
- Capitalize on the use of database marketing techniques
- Increase profitability through improved customer retention.

This last point is not always fully appreciated by service companies and it merits some further elaboration.

Customer retention and profitability

Acquiring customers can be expensive. Usually it involves certain one-off costs, such as, for example, advertising, promotion, the salesperson's time, and even the cost of entering data into the company's data bank. Thus, every customer represents an investment, the level of which will vary from business to business.

Retaining customers is extremely profitable

If they are treated correctly and remain customers over a long period, there is strong evidence[8] that they will generate more profits for the organization each year they maintain the relationship. Across a wide range of businesses this pattern is the same (Figure 1.10).

> **For example, an industrial laundry almost doubled its profits per customer over five years. A car servicing business expects fourth-year customers to generate three times the profit of a first-year customer. A distributor of industrial products found that net sales per account continued to rise even into the nineteenth year of the relationship.**

This trend holds true for many types of service companies. As the relationship extends, the initial 'contact' costs, such as checking creditworthiness, no longer figure on the balance sheet. In addition, the more that is known about the customer as the relationship develops, the more offers can be tailored effectively to meet their needs.

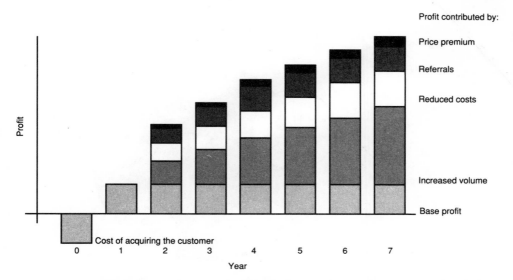

Profit contributed by:

Price premium

Referrals

Reduced costs

Increased volume

Base profit

Cost of acquiring the customer

Figure 1.10 Retaining customers pays off (*Source*: Based on Reichheld, F. R. (1994) Loyalty and the Renaissance of Marketing. *Marketing Management*, **12** (4), 17.

Thus, the customer gets greater value, which in turn encourages more frequent and larger purchases.

> **It follows, therefore, that when a company lowers its customer defection rate, average customer relationships last longer and profits climb. Viewed in this way, the costs of providing enhanced customer service could be seen as an investment in customer retention.**

Integrated relationship marketing

For an organization to reach this level of sophistication, it needs to reappraise the way it relates, not only to customers, but also to all other areas which have an impact on the business. It is a recognition that in order to achieve success, the organization is dependent upon the outside world for everything: its skills (through the workforce), its materials, the machinery or equipment it uses and, as we saw earlier, the trading conditions under which it operates.

There are six 'markets' that need to be managed

There are six 'markets' to be managed within this broader vision of relationship marketing, as shown in Figure 1.11. Only the central area, customer markets, is a market in the traditional sense and it is on this that the remainder of this book will focus. It is only in its

Figure 1.11 Relationship marketing – a broadened view of markets

customer markets that the services which are the raison d'être for the organization's existence have any currency.

> **All of the six markets are interrelated and influence each other, but it is the customer market which is the central focus of the organization's goal.**

Whilst it is important to understand this concept, it is equally important to understand that it is not the primary role or function of an organization's marketing department to prepare 'marketing plans' for these other five 'satellite' markets. (However, the tools and methodologies of marketing planning outlined in this book can be used to develop market plans for these other satellite markets.) Clearly, managing these other markets is the responsibility of the Board of Directors, through both the functional chiefs who manage each area and the management of cross-functional activities within the service organization. For example, the recruitment 'market' should be managed by the personnel department, with all the other 'markets' in mind, but particularly with what pertains to the customer market and corporate success, since this is the whole point of what we have called 'relationship marketing'.

Relationship marketing is more profitable than one-off transactions

With customers being the prime focus of the organization's marketing efforts, this new orientation calls for there to be a switch from seeking 'one-off' transactions with any customer who can be inveigled to buy, to building long-term relationships. This change from 'transaction marketing' to 'relationship marketing' has very real implications for the organization. Some of these are listed below.

Transactional marketing focus	Relationship marketing focus
• Single sale	• Customer retention
• Service features	• Service benefits
• Short timescale	• Long time-scale
• Little emphasis on customer service	• High emphasis on customer service
• Moderate customer contact	• High customer contact
• Limited customer commitment	• High customer commitment
• Quality is the concern of 'production'	• Quality is the concern of all

A similar shift in orientation needs to accompany this change of focus with respect to the other 'markets' shown in Figure 1.11. Thus, a more open, long-lasting and committed relationship is called for in the organization's dealings with what we have termed internal markets, referral markets, influence markets, recruitment markets and supplier markets.

> **By building longer-term quality relationships in this way, the organization can establish stability in the restless, ever-changing business environment.**

Not only is this mutually beneficial to the parties involved in the short term, but it also makes it easier to plan ahead with greater accuracy.

Not all 'satellite' markets are equally important

Clearly, not all of these satellite markets are necessarily going to be of equal importance to all companies. Therefore, each organization will have to make decisions regarding what levels of attention and resources they devote to each one. The corporate thinking process is likely to follow these steps:

1 Which of these areas has the greatest impact on our future success?
2 Who are the key participants in these markets?

> 3 What are the expectations and requirements of these participants?
> 4 To what extent is the company currently meeting these expectations and requirements?
> 5 What strategy needs to be formulated to bring these relationships to the desired level?
> 6 Are any of these strategies sufficiently complex or resource intensive to justify the need for a formal written plan?

As an aid to these deliberations, a relationship marketing network diagram or 'spidergram', as illustrated in Figure 1.12, can be used. This has two axes representing customer markets – existing and new – and five axes representing the 'satellite' markets. Each axis has a scale ranging from 0–10 on which it is possible to plot the current and desired levels of emphasis on each market.

In the example shown of the changing emphasis of the management of an international airline, the greatest improvement is required

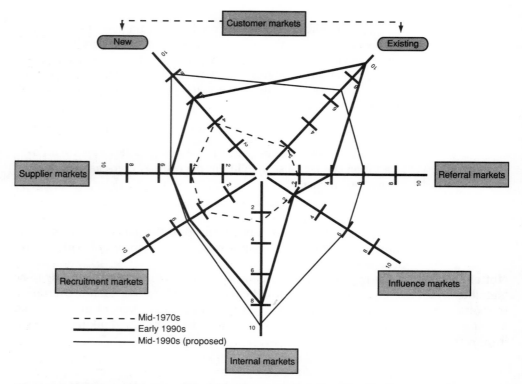

Figure 1.12 Relationship marketing network diagram for a major international airline (*Source*: Payne, A. F. T. (1993) Relationship Marketing: The Six Markets Framework. Cranfield School of Management Working Paper.)

in influence and internal markets, whereas the other markets call for more modest changes in emphasis.

> **Of course, the more the measurements on the spider diagram are based on research or objective criteria, the more accurate and useful the finished diagram becomes regarding policy-making.**

In conclusion, whilst this is not intended to be a book specifically about relationship marketing and strategies for customer retention,[9] it should be obvious that in preparing a strategic marketing plan, the only real justification for giving up resources to complete this task is if the final result spells out clearly how the organization is going to get and keep customers.

The plan, then, will show clearly what it is that the organization is offering its target customers that are intended to make them want to buy from this organization rather than from any other that happens to be in the market. This is true relationship marketing.

Summary

In this chapter, we have taken a broad-ranging review of marketing and of the special nature of services. Albeit there has been a spectacular growth in service businesses in the last two decades in the developed economies, much of this was to do with opportunism, which was possible in the largely favourable business environment which then prevailed. Today, the trading conditions, which are far more bleak and competitive, call for a more analytical and strategic approach that only marketing planning can provide.

Although products and services are on the surface quite different, closer inspection reveals that a 'pure' service or product rarely exists. Most services contain a tangible product element and most products have an intangible service element. The relative weight of tangibility to intangibility in a company's offer will indicate whether or not the service can be marketed much like a traditional product or if a new approach is required. Indeed, such is the range and diversity of services that service managers can often learn from other industries where services are provided which, although different, have some of the same inherent characteristics as their own.

Marketing was described as a matching process which tries to optimize the company's capabilities in the context of meeting customer needs. The 'flexible coupling' in this matching process is the marketing mix, which consists of the product/service, price, promotion, place, people, processes and customer service. While many organizations claim to subscribe to a marketing approach, there is considerable evidence to show that they do in fact misunderstand some of the basic principles that should be followed. Indeed, such has been the evolution of marketing over the last few years that only the more mature and sophisticated organizations have grasped the fact that the more traditional approach, which we called 'transaction marketing', is no longer likely to bring lasting success. Instead, 'relationship marketing' is more in keeping with the times in which we live.

However, in order to adapt to the principles behind relationship marketing, the organization needs to look afresh not only at its customer markets, but also at what we have termed satellite markets – the internal, influence, referral, recruitment and supplier markets. In fact, what this new approach demands is an entirely new kind of marketing orientation, which in turn often requires that there is a change in the organizational climate and the attitudes of staff throughout the company.

Finally, as we have seen, there is a potential problem of confusing customer markets with satellite markets, thereby causing a blurring of focus of the company's efforts. The satellite markets are aimed at supporting the initial customer market. This problem can be avoided by remembering that, whatever else might be provided, the organization's key output, the service(s) upon which its very existence depends, are directed and tailored to meet only the needs of customer markets. In order not to compound any confusion about this, for the remainder of this book we will use the term 'service product' to

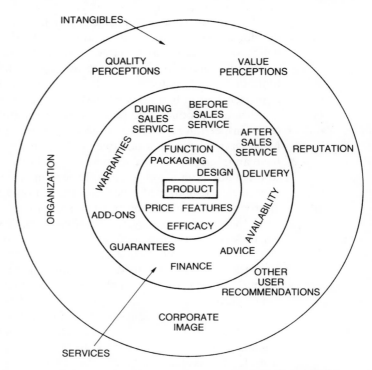

Figure 1.13 The 'service product' and the product surround

indicate the main output and to distinguish it from the array of other supporting services the company might provide. Figure 1.13 puts into perspective what constitutes the service product and the product surround.

Having discussed the specific nature of services and the need for services business to shift to a relationship orientation, we will now proceed to examine the processes and problems in developing marketing plans for service businesses.

References

1 Kotler, P. (1991) *Marketing Management: Analysis, Planning and Control*, 7th edn, Prentice Hall, Englewood Cliffs, NJ.
2 Bowen, J. (1990) Development of a Taxonomy of Services to Gain Strategic Marketing Insights. *Journal of the Academy of Marketing Sciences*, **18** (1), 43–49.
3 Grönroos, C. (1990) *Services Management and Marketing*, Lexington Books, Lexington, MA.
4 Lovelock, C. H. (1983) Classifying Services to Gain Strategic Marketing Insights. *Journal of Marketing*, **47**, Summer, 9–20. (The matrices shown in this chapter are based on those developed by Lovelock.)
5 Vandermerwe, S. and Rada, J. (1988) Servitization of Business: Adding Value by Adding Service. *European Management Journal*, **6** (4), 314–423.
6 For example, see Booms, B. H. and Bitner, M. J. (1981) Marketing Strategies and Organisational Structures for Service Firms, in J. H. Donnelly and W. R. George (eds), *Marketing of Services*, American Marketing Association Proceedings Series, Chicago, p. 48.
7 For a more detailed discussion of the services marketing mix see Payne, A. F. T. (1993) *The Essence of Services Marketing*, Prentice Hall, Englewood Cliffs, NJ. Chapter 6.
8 Reichheld, F. F. and Sasser, W. E. (Jr) (1990) Zero Defections: Quality Comes to Services, *Harvard Business Review*, September–October, 105–111.
9 For a more detailed discussion on this topic, see Christopher, M., Payne, A. F. T. and Ballantyne, D. (1991) *Relationship Marketing: Bringing Quality, Customer Service and Marketing Together*, Butterworth-Heinemann, Oxford.

2 Marketing planning for services – the process and the problems

The strategic marketing planning process for services

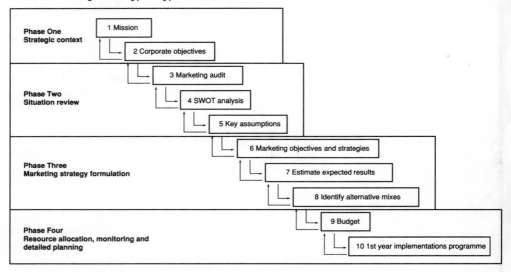

In this chapter, we will take an overview of the strategic marketing planning process for services, shown above, and also a brief look at some of its component parts. We will also consider some of the reasons why service organizations do not always manage to take advantage of the benefits that strategic marketing planning should bring. The following four chapters will then examine each of the four phases shown above in detail.

What is marketing planning ?

In essence, marketing planning is a series of activities which are tackled in a logical sequence in a way that leads to the setting of marketing objectives and the devising of programmes to meet them. Thus, the marketing plan becomes a framework for identifying where and why marketing resources are going to be allocated, when they are to come into play and how they are to be integrated in order to make maximum impact.

The output of this process is the strategic marketing plan, the contents of which will be spelled out later in this chapter.

Marketing plans are now an essential aspect of business

As we saw in the previous chapter, when business life was less volatile and complex than it is today, service companies were able to survive and sometimes prosper without paying very much attention to marketing planning. Indeed, there are no doubt a few fortunate companies who are still in growth sectors, or who happen to be in the right place at the right time and, as such, see little benefit in devoting resources to marketing planning.

> **However, for the vast majority, the more uncertain their prospects become, the greater their necessity to have the lifeline that a well-formulated marketing plan can offer.**

During periods of recession there is often an increased interest in marketing planning and how it can help organizations deal with economic downturn.

Research shows that, not only will a marketing plan bring about a better coordination of activities and individuals whose actions are interrelated over time, but it will also result in a discipline that will:

- Increase the likelihood of identifying external developments
- Prepare the organization to meet change
- Minimize non-rational responses to the unexpected
- Improve communications between executives and departments
- Reduce conflicts that inevitably arise when organizational direction is unclear
- Force management to think ahead systematically
- Balance corporate resources more effectively against market opportunities
- Provide a framework for the continuing review of operations
- Most telling of all, lead to a higher return on investment (as shown in evidence from the PIMS[1] study).

Marketing planning involves organizational change

At first sight, with all these benefits on offer, it is surprising that more service organizations have not invested in marketing planning.

> **However, what on the surface appears to be a fairly straightforward planning process, does, in fact, raise a number of deeper issues for the organization.**

To introduce marketing planning is more than a cognitive process because, inherent in this new approach, there are implications that can impact on all parts of the business, from the boardroom down. If the planning task is tackled properly, no organizational areas are immune. Marketing planning needs to permeate all parts of the organization, to the extent that even its structure and traditional power patterns have to stand up to scrutiny and change if they are found wanting.

Other approaches to marketing planning

This book is about the scientific, normative type of marketing planning described in many articles and textbooks during the past thirty years. There are, of course, other strategic decision-making models and it would be remiss not to mention what these different approaches are, together with their strengths and weaknesses.[2] There appear to be six accepted models of perspectives of strategic decision-making. These are:

1 *A planning model* Here, strategic decisions are reached by use of a sequential, planning search for optimum solutions to defined problems. This process is highly rational and is fuelled by concrete data.

2 *An interpretative model* Here, the organization is regarded as a collection of associations, sharing similar values, beliefs and perceptions. These 'frames of reference' enable the stakeholders to interpret the organization and the environment in which it operates. Information which does not fit with the dominant reference system is actively ignored or downgraded. The same could be said of people. In this way, a particular culture emerges which encourages individuals to lend themselves to self-fulfilling organizational prophecies, uncontaminated by deviant behaviour or information. Strategy thus becomes the product, not of defined aims and objectives, but of the prevailing values, attitudes and ideas in the organization.

3 *A political model* Here strategy is not chosen directly, but emerges through compromise, conflict and consensus seeking among interested stakeholders. Since the strategy is the outcome of negotiation, bargaining and confrontation, those with the most power have the greatest influence.

4 *A logical incremental model* Here, strategies emerge from 'strategic subsystems', each concerned with a different type of strategic issue. Strategic goals are based on an awareness of needs rather than the highly structured analytical process of the planning model. Often, due to a lack of necessary information, such goals can be vague, general and non-rigid in nature. The commitment to a firm's strategy for reaching the 'image of the future' is delayed as long as possible, as various 'first steps' are evaluated. As events unfold and movement towards the strategic goals proceeds, more information becomes known and strategic action can be adjusted and brought into sharper focus.

5 *An ecological model* In this perspective, the environment impinges on the organization in such a way that strategies are virtually prescribed and there is little or no free choice. In this model, the organization which adapts most successfully to its environment will survive in a way which mirrors Darwin's natural selection. In reality, restriction of strategic choice is not solely attributable to the external environment. Blinkered perception and the feeling of powerlessness by decision-makers also play their part.

6 *A visionary leadership model* Here, the strategy emerges as the result of the leader's vision. It is not necessary for the leader to have originated the idea, but his or her commitment to it, their personal credibility, and how they articulate it to others, can provide the necessary organizational momentum. However, to be successful, the vision has to have some resonance with the followers and the surrounding circumstances. In other words, it must be attractive and timely.

It is unlikely that a given service organization will use a pure version of any of these models. In all probability, its strategic decision-making model will be a hybrid of some of them. However, it is possible that one or two of these will predominate and thereby give strategic decision-making a distinctive 'flavour'.

It will be of interest for the service organization to be aware of the ways in which its strategy-forming processes are 'biased', because each of the models described above has inherent strengths and weaknesses (Figure 2.1).

The reason this book deals with the planning model, rather than the others, is that the authors' research has shown that this is the most effective way of coping with the turbulence and rate of change which now characterizes most service businesses. Also, it is a model that can easily be adapted to take account of organizational size and complexity.

The marketing planning process

In the opening chapter, it was explained how the marketing perspective has to change from being essentially concerned with short-term transactions to longer-term relationships. This being the case, the marketing planning process needs to be considered over a reasonably long time-frame and in a strategic context.

> **Indeed, the blame for the failure of so many companies in recent years can be firmly traced to short-term, financially-dominated objectives; and to being over-concerned with immediate sales performance and profit ratios which reflected historical and current conditions, rather than long-term growth.**

A strategic approach is essential

A reasonable compromise between short-termism and looking so far ahead as to render it meaningless is to consider a planning period of about three years. Of course, for some types of services, this might still prove to be too long (for example, in computer services) or too short (for example, in energy utilities), but these companies will have to establish a planning window which is appropriate for their particular businesses. Thus, right from the outset, the emphasis is on a three-year (or longer, where necessary) marketing strategy rather than on a one-year tactical plan.

> **It has been shown that many of today's organizational problems stem directly from a historical over-emphasis on short-termism. Many organizations that were tactically efficient died because they did not have an effective strategy towards their markets. Doing things right (tactics) is not an effective substitute for doing the right things (strategy).**

Strengths	Weaknesses
Planning Model	
• Systematic	• Assumptions are made that the environment is predictable over the strategic time-span
• Unemotional	
• Clear analysis of problems	• It is implied that the organization is not directly affected by the environment over this time
• Various strategic options are considered before selecting the most appropriate one	
• It provides a framework which can be communicated and understood through the organization	• There is separation between those who make decisions and those in possession of the most useful information
• It provides a discipline of review and evaluation for managers	• It can become bureaucratic and ritualistic, e.g. the annual numbers game
	• It assumes that people are rational and have the skills to handle information in an unbiased way
	• It is impossible to assemble all the data required to make a truly rational choice
Interpretative model	
• There is a conscious effort to establish shared values or beliefs through the organization	• Symbols and mythology assume greater importance than hard data
• Individuals contribute in a way which is congruent with personal values, therefore their commitment is high	• Strategy is not related to defined aims, but common perceptions held by the organization
	• Information which does not confirm the model is rejected or downgraded
	• If change becomes necessary, a radical shake-up and readjustment programme is rquired, in order to kill off the old paradigm and those who promoted it
Political model	
• There is a recognition of the realities of power	• Strategies, coming as they do from conflict and compromise, are rarely unanimously accepted doctrines
• Only serious issues get put on the agenda, i.e. those with bargaining power	• There is an over-emphasis on jockeying for position, at the expense of 'keeping an eye on the ball'
• Strategic decisions are acceptable to dominant interest groups	
	• Personal success takes precedence over organizational success
	• The 'out-voted' minorities will often subvert strategies to meet their own ends
Logical incremental model	
• There is widely shared consensus for action among top management	• The formal processes of the organization cannot analyse and plan all possible strategic variables concurrently
• The organization is open to learning from the environment	• Strategic goals are arrived at by a 'muddling' process, rather than analysis
• Key players are encouraged to view issues dispassionately	• The process does not allow much scope for creative options
• Tentative strategic options are tested before being adopted fully	• Strategies seem to focus on 'no lose' and organizational health, rather than 'winning'
• Ongoing assessment of the environment enables strategy to be modified if necessary	• New problems can disrupt the 'up and running' strategy in a disproportionate way
• Resources are generally allocated to those parts of the organization which promise most	
• Change is evolutionary not revolutionary	
Ecological model	
• Organizational variations which match the environment produce definite advantages	• Decision-makers mistakenly believe that they are powerless to develop strategy options, whereas they could exercise choice in terms of market segmentation, product differentiation, and so on
Visionary leadership model	
• It simplifies complex organizational issues	• The process is heavily dependent on the visionary's dream
• It communicates at a 'gut' level	• Visions might be inadequate or out of synchronization with the times
• It can generate high levels of commitment and motivation among 'believers'	• The organization can remain too committed to an out-of-date vision.

Figure 2.1 Strengths and weaknesses of alternative marketing planning models

It is crucial to do the right things as well as to do things right

'Doing the right things', in the context of strategic marketing, simply means ensuring on a continuous basis that customers have good reasons to want to do business with one's own organization rather than with any other competitor who happens to be around. This, in turn, requires an on-going dialogue with specific groups of customers, whose needs are understood in depth, and for whom offers are developed that have differential advantages over the offers of competitors.

To do this effectively means predicting the changes that are taking place in the business, economic, legislative, technical, market and competitive environment, setting objectives and strategies for a period of around three years and then setting in motion the necessary tactical changes in the first year of the plan (the tactical plan). In the absence of a strategic marketing plan, it is simply impossible to do this by means of only a one-year tactical plan. In its turn, of course, a strategic marketing plan is likely to be more effective if appropriate strategic tools are utilized, such as scenario planning, as well as the methods outlined in this book. The really crucial document, however, will always be the strategic marketing plan.

Because research has shown that it is effective strategic marketing planning that is so difficult and elusive, this book focuses solely on this form of planning – the strategic marketing plan.

The planning process which follows is one that has been tried and tested at the Cranfield University Marketing Planning Centre for over fifteen years. The framework provided originates from research carried out by one of the authors, Malcolm McDonald.[3] In outline there are four major phases:

Phase One	Establishing the strategic context
Phase Two	Conducting a situation review
Phase Three	Formulating marketing objectives and strategies
Phase Four	Allocating budgets and developing a detailed first-year implementation plan.

In turn, these four phases can be broken down into a series of steps, as shown in the figure at the start of this chapter. For the sake of clarity, the ten steps in the marketing planning process are shown as quite distinct activities.

In practice, many of the steps are interrelated and the whole process is highly interactive.

Thus, instead of starting at Step 1 and pushing on relentlessly to the end, it is likely that there will be quite a lot of interaction and doubling back, as the 'feedback' loops indicate.

The next four chapters focus on each of the four phases in the planning process in some detail. However, at this point we will briefly explain what each of the ten steps involves before expanding on each of them so as to turn them into actionable propositions.

Step 1 Mission

It is important for all companies to have a sense of mission. By encapsulating this into a brief, highly personal and meaningful statement, it gives the various stakeholders in the service organization a clear purpose and sense of direction.

The mission statement is an important device that can provide an understanding for staff working in different parts of the organization, enabling them to pull together and uphold the corporate values and philosophy. However, it is essential that the mission statement is communicated clearly to all stakeholders and is perceived to be both relevant and realistic. Unless these requirements are met, the mission statement is unlikely to have any real impact on the organization. This is explained in detail in Chapter 3.

Step 2 Corporate objectives

The purpose of corporate objectives is for the stakeholders to measure the success of the mission. Seen in this light, the only true objective of a company is what is stated as being the principal purpose for its existence. In most commercial service companies, this is expressed in terms of profit, since profit is the one universally accepted criterion by which efficiency can be evaluated. It is profit which provides the means of satisfying shareholders and owners alike. It is also profit which provides the wherewithal to reinvest in the business to make it grow. For non-profit-making service organizations such as government departments or charities, objectives such as economic efficiency, funds raised or projects completed might be more realistic measures of performance.

From this, it follows that stated desires such as to 'expand market share', 'increase sales' or 'improve productivity' are not objectives, but are actually *strategies* at a corporate level, since they are the means by which the company will achieve its profit objectives.

Some typical corporate objectives and strategies for a commercial organization are shown in Figure 2.2. From this, it can be seen that, at the next level down in the organization, i.e. at the functional level, 'what services and what markets' become *marketing objectives*. In turn, the *marketing strategies* for meeting these, such as using advertising or personal selling, become *departmental objectives* for those particular parts of the business.

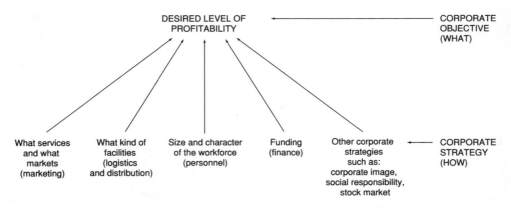

Figure 2.2 Relationship between corporate objective and strategies

When viewed in this way, it can be seen that within the whole organization is a hierarchical chain of interlinking objectives and strategies.

> **With such a protocol in operation, an objective or strategy set at even the lowest reaches of the organization should be capable of being traced upwards in order to discover how it contributes to the overriding corporate objective.**

This, then, is how, when taken together, the mission statement and corporate objectives provide the strategic context for what follows in the marketing planning process.

More about this stage of planning is given in Chapters 4 and 5.

Step 3   Marketing audit

> **The purpose of the marketing audit is to gather all the relevant data which can determine how well equipped the service organization is to compete in its chosen marketing arena now and in the future.**

Much of the data collected comes from external sources, and is concerned with the business and economic environment, together with market and competitor analysis. Not only is the current situation analysed, but also future trends and their significance are considered. Internal sources provide additional information and help to identify the company's strengths and weaknesses.

In its search to understand the business environment, the sensible service organization will be selective in terms of what it strives to uncover, knowing that 20 per cent of relevant data will provide it with 80 per cent of the answers it needs to know. Unless it is practical in its approach to the marketing audit, the task can become extremely time-consuming, with huge volumes of data which over-whelm the process of identifying key relevant information.

This is discussed in more detail in Chapter 4.

Step 4 SWOT analysis

The purpose of the SWOT (Strengths, Weaknesses, Opportunities and Threats) analysis is to identify the key components of marketing information from the vast amount of data generated by the audit. By grouping all the salient information under these four headings, it becomes possible for the organization to highlight the external opportunities and threats, and to weigh them against its current internal strengths and weaknesses. Once in possession of this information, the way forward becomes clearer.

Detailed guidelines on how to complete a SWOT analysis are given in Chapter 4.

Step 5 Key assumptions

The marketing audit and the subsequent SWOT analysis can only reflect reality if some assumptions are made about the future. These might concern the number of competitors, the political climate, the general economic well-being of certain markets, and so on.

> **Such assumptions, or educated guesses, should be few in number and be addressed only to key factors that have a bearing on the planning period.**

They should also be committed to paper so that everyone involved in the planning process understands how the 'playing field' might be expected to change over time. Key assumptions also identify areas which may need to be addressed through 'contingency plans'.

Assumptions are discussed in more detail in Chapter 4.

Step 6 Marketing objectives and strategies

The SWOT analysis and key assumptions steps provide the marketing planner with the data with which to set marketing objectives and strategies. The marketing objectives will be concerned about which services are provided for which markets. The possible combinations

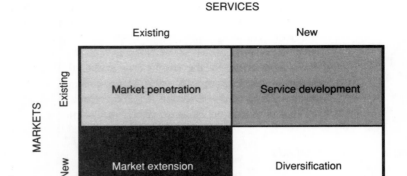

Figure 2.3 Ansoff matrix

of these are illustrated in a neat way by the matrix developed by Ansoff,[4] shown in Figure 2.3.

Clearly, the quadrant representing current business (existing services to existing markets) reflects the arena about which the company knows most. In that sense, it is the area of least risk, unlike new services to new markets (diversification) which represents the least known, hence most hazardous, way forward.

As Figure 2.3 shows, marketing objectives bring with them a strong sense of what the marketing strategy should be to achieve them. In Chapter 5 we will explore strategy formulation in more detail. For now, it is enough to recognize that the marketing strategy has its roots in an analytical process.

Step 7 Estimate expected results

Because the marketing objectives and strategies have to contribute to the corporate objectives in the way shown earlier, the financial outcome of Step 6 has to be calculated as accurately as possible. If the expected results far exceed the corporate objective, then it could be that the corporate objectives need to be set at a higher level. Conversely, if the expected results fall short of the corporate objectives, the next step considers if they can be met by a revised alternative marketing mix.

This is further considered in Chapter 5.

Step 8 Identify alternative mixes

In this step, the SWOT analysis and key assumptions are reappraised in order to identify if there are other, more productive, mixes of marketing objectives and strategies which get closer to achieving (or exceeding) the corporate objectives. If, after considerable creative experimentation, there is still a shortfall, it has to be considered that the original corporate objectives were unrealistic and they should be adjusted accordingly.

Even if the first attempt at marketing objectives and strategies yields the right level of expected results, it is still recommended that some alternative mixes are considered, as the first solution is not always the best one. The step of alternative mixes helps identify the most appropriate and rewarding marketing objectives and strategies.

This is further considered in Chapter 5.

Step 9 Budget

Once the marketing objectives and strategies are agreed, it becomes possible to cost out the various programmes for the contributing marketing activities. The nature of the advertising input, sales staff, distribution and so on can be determined and budgets allocated accordingly.

Step 10 First-year detailed implementation programme

With the three-year strategic plan as a guide, the detailed implementation programme or one-year tactical plan can be developed. In effect, this one-year tactical plan propels the company towards its strategic goals. Of course, the sensible marketing planning system has a monitoring and control procedure in order to ensure what was planned actually happens – and if it doesn't happen, to know the reason why.

Steps 9 and 10 are dealt with in more detail in Chapter 6.

With the ten-step planning process we have just outlined, it becomes a relatively easy task to monitor progress and to identify the root causes of any 'derailments'. By taking whatever corrective action is shown to be necessary, and by learning from its mistakes, the company does, in fact, develop a stronger and more effective planning process for the future.

We have found only a relatively few service organizations whose planning 'systems' possess all of these steps linked in this way.

> **Those whose marketing planning closely follows this approach do, on the whole, manage to cope with their environment much more successfully than those who rely mainly on a 'sales forecasting and budgetary control' approach.**

Moreover, the genuine marketing planners are more prepared and so have less need to 'fire-fight' ongoing events. In short, they suffer fewer operational problems and, as a result, tend to be more effective organizations.

Marketing planning and services

Having reviewed the ten key steps in the marketing planning process, we will briefly review some studies on the use of marketing planning by service companies and make some summary comments on usage and implementation of marketing planning by them.

The need for effective planning in the services sector has been recognized for a considerable time. For example, in 1975, Chisnall[5] pointed to the growing services sector and emphasized that in planning services, whether it be in the commercial or public sector, greater attention should be given to input/output measurement to ensure that resources used reflect their contribution to the efficiency of the organizational output. He described the relevance of marketing techniques such as marketing research, strategic planning and marketing control to help improve the development of service organizations, but argued that there was an institutionalized reluctance of service industries to develop a more realistic and market-oriented approach to marketing planning.

There is little evidence that marketing planning is widely used in the service sector

There is little evidence that service organizations in the UK have adopted marketing planning on a widespread and successful basis. Hooley[6] and his colleagues found that 43 per cent of their sample of 529 service firms claimed to have both one-year and long-range marketing plans but noted that their mailed surveys were skewed towards more successful companies. No attempt was made to evaluate formally how comprehensive the marketing planning was.

Greenley[7] examined marketing planning practices in 50 UK service companies from a number of industries including: banking and insurance; freight forwarding and transport; management and market research consultancy; technical consultancy; catering; television entertainment; and the gas and electricity sector. He compared the headings of the major sections of marketing plans of these service companies with a typical list of headings suggested in the marketing literature, which included: situation analysis; objectives; strategy statement; action programme; budget; and control.

> **The study found that, although 62 per cent of the companies claimed to prepare a marketing plan, only 12 per cent disclosed a format considered to be comprehensive. (This represented 25 per cent of total companies prepared to divulge the contents of marketing plan headings.)**

He concluded that marketing planning in service companies was not well developed.

The research on marketing planning in service organizations follows more general research on marketing planning. Despite the obvious and theoretically supported benefits of marketing planning, a review of empirical studies that have been carried out suggest that as few as 10 per cent of companies actually use a comprehensive marketing planning process and even the most optimistic of these studies only offered a figure of 25 per cent. A further study of 385 medium and large firms in the UK[8] found that just over half attempted to prepare marketing plans. Of these, 73 per cent were described as 'having a go at the entire marketing planning model, whilst doing little of it comprehensively'.

Research in the USA[9] shows that marketing planning tends to be seen, at best, as a 'rough action guide' (Figure 2.4). This figure shows that the status of marketing planning is worse in service companies, with only 18 per cent taking it 'very seriously'.

There are signs of an improved approach to marketing planning in the service sector

Despite the slow start, there has been a growing emphasis on and acceptance of marketing planning over the past ten years and an increasing body of literature focusing on the preparation of marketing plans has started to appear. However, it is true to say that development of marketing planning in UK industry appears to lag behind the USA. Given the evidence in Figure 2.4, much remains to be done in asserting the role of marketing and marketing planning in the boardroom.

Effective marketing is enhanced greatly by a well thought-through and developed marketing plan. Such a plan helps bring all the service firm's marketing activities together in an integrated manner and helps create a positive future for the firm. However, a number of problems create barriers to the development and implementation of marketing planning.

What gets in the way of marketing planning ?

Service organizations currently facing difficulties in their markets have instinctively recognized a need for an integrated approach to marketing planning. Indeed, many have attempted to adopt a new planning approach. However, it is clear that any attempt to introduce a formalized marketing planning system, like the one described in this book, carries with it serious organizational and behavioural implications for the company. It is not a quick remedy for a service organization's problems.

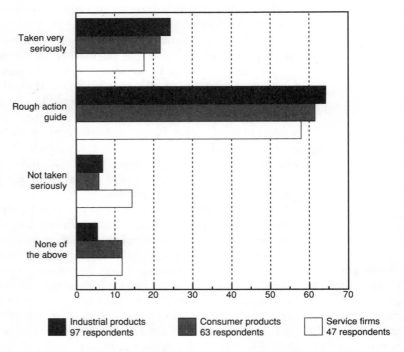

Figure 2.4 Status of marketing plans in US companies (*Source*: Sutton, H. (1990) *The Marketing Plan in the 1990s*, The Conference Board, New York)

> **The introduction of this type of approach strikes at the very heart of how the organization is managed and unless it recognizes this and faces up to the new problems which surface, then real improvements will not take place.**

Research in the USA undertaken by the Conference Board[10] shows that the three most critical problems facing service organizations in their marketing planning are (in order of importance):

- Hard to get consensus/cooperation
- Company isn't market-oriented
- Plans not taken seriously enough.

Our research and experience agree with these findings, but suggest there are other common barriers which get in the way of successful marketing planning.

Here are some of the common barriers which prevent genuine change taking place and an effective services marketing plan being developed in service organizations. There are other barriers which will be described throughout this book.

1 Short-termism

Too many service organizations are so engrossed in what is happening today that they neglect the future of the company. Managers who are evaluated and rewarded on the basis of current operations will naturally enough find it difficult to concern themselves with the corporate future. Decisions are, therefore, based on short-term results.

> **It is obviously safer and easier for managers to concentrate on managing current services and customers in order to achieve their current budget rather than concerning themselves with the future.**

Similarly, there is a reluctance to invest in tomorrow's services, technologies, and even managers. Of course, there are always cogent arguments why such investment must be delayed, but the truth is that for most managers, tomorrow never comes.

2 Weak support from the chief executive and top management

Senior managers are extremely influential in establishing a corporate climate or culture. While top management might not deliberately set out to do this, subordinates are quick to spot what excites and interests the 'culture carriers'. These areas then become the unwritten agenda for corporate politics, which is all about getting noticed, getting resources and getting on.

> **Unless the chief executive understands marketing planning, sees the need for it, and, above all, shows an active interest in it, then it will be virtually impossible for a senior marketing executive to make any real progress in improving marketing planning.**

Figure 2.4 shows that marketing planning is taken less seriously in service firms than in the consumer foods and industrial products sector.

Where the chief executive pays only lip-service to marketing planning and starves it of adequate resources, it is not likely to flourish and be a successful value-adding activity for the organization. Moreover, other managers will see the low level of priority given to marketing planning and judge for themselves if it is worth getting associated with an out-of-favour activity. Thus, the notion that marketing planning is not really important becomes a self-fulfilling prophecy.

In contrast to this restrictive scenario, the chief executive who champions marketing planning will ensure that it is regularly on the agenda of management meetings, will be chasing up for progress reports, will be seen frequently talking about marketing planning, will see to it that marketing planning skills figure in criteria for recruiting or promoting managers, and so on. There would be no doubt whatsoever in the minds of the staff in this company that marketing planning is *really* important.

3 Lack of a plan for planning

It is one thing to establish a marketing planning system on paper, yet another to make it come alive. As with any significant organizational change process, there has to be a plan for introducing the new system in a way that it becomes part of the service organization's fabric, rather than an élitist, peripheral activity. Several issues need to be addressed:

- There is a need to mobilize top management support (for reasons explained above).
- There is a need to communicate throughout the company why a new approach to planning is required.
- There is a need for training programmes to equip people for the new roles they have to play.
- There is a need to set up the subsystems which are required to provide the data to fuel the planning system.
- There is a need to ensure that adequate resources are available and in place to make the new system work.
- There is a need to make a 'dummy run', or small-scale trials, before plunging headlong into the new approach.
- There is a need to tailor the process so that it fits the specific needs of the organization.

All of these things take time. They cannot just be ignored or glossed over, otherwise marketing planning will be ineffective. By planning the introduction of planning, companies are more likely to get it right first time. In our experience, it can take two to three years from making a decision to introduce strategic marketing planning to getting it right at an operational level.

4 Lack of line management support

> Line managers, that is to say those with a responsibility for delivering the service product, are often knowingly or unknowingly the repositories of exceedingly valuable marketing information, be it about particular customers or trends they have spotted. For this reason, they have a significant role to play in terms of contributing to the formulation of the marketing plan.

At the same time, these managers are already likely to be very busy doing their 'real job', as they would probably describe it. Therefore, it is essential for those responsible for coordinating marketing planning to win such staff over to their cause and thereby gain access to the information they possess. How this is achieved will vary from company to company. It might be through training, it might be through getting the line managers involved in designing the way data is collected, or it might be through redesigning their jobs. Whatever the chosen method, one thing is certain. Unless there is the committed support from these managers to the marketing planning process, it will be fatally handicapped.

5 Confusion over planning terms

Those charged with setting up a marketing planning system are frequently well-qualified in this field. For them, marketing terminology and jargon are convenient verbal shorthand with which to communicate to fellow professionals. However, in order to win over the hearts and minds of others in the organization, the planning terminology used must be understood by all managers. Too much talk to non-marketing managers about missions, matrices, strategic thrusts, positioning, and so on, is inappropriate and may well 'turn off' those we seek to influence.

Companies with successful planning systems have used terminology which is acceptable to operational managers, and, where terms like 'objectives' and 'strategies' are introduced, these are clearly defined. To help with this definition a glossary of marketing terminology is provided at the end of this book.

6 An over-reliance on numbers

Many managers are highly numerate. Quantities, percentages, discounts, success rates, sales revenue, costs and the like are the bread and butter of their everyday lives. It is numbers that make their world turn round. They are evaluated on the basis of numbers and, not surprisingly, in turn, judge others in much the same way.

However, when they are asked (as marketing planners often do) to elaborate on causal factors for past performance, to assess expected results, to highlight external opportunities, or to provide a critique of the key issues facing them, they have difficulty doing this.

> **They appear to be far happier extrapolating numbers and project-ing current performance into the future, rather than expressing the logic of how they perceive their current business situation and how that impinges on their objectives and strategies.**

A 'numbers-driven' mentality may encourage parochial and short-term thinking, whereas the required approach needs creative analysis. There has to be a new balance between quantitative data and quali-tative thinking, if there is to be effective services marketing planning.

7 Too much detail, too far ahead

Associated with the issue above is an alternative response from man-agers. If they are short of the analytical skills to isolate the really key marketing issues, they may over-react and identify far more problems and opportunities than the company can ever hope to cope with. When this happens, the really important strategic issues can get buried deep in a deluge of useless information and over-elaborate detail. Not surprisingly, the ensuing plan will lack focus and confuse those for whom it was supposed to provide guidance. There is also a danger that the company could become over-extended, heading off in too many directions at once.

> **Companies and individuals must learn that it is high-quality intel-ligence they seek, not a high quantity of data. Systems that gen-erate too much information are not only ineffective, they are also demotivating for those who have to struggle to use them.**

Organizations that have overcome these types of problems have done so by ensuring that all levels of hierarchy are clear about the nature of the contribution they are expected to make. At each suc-cessive level of management, lower-level analyses are synthesized in ways that ensure that only key decision-making information reaches the next level up. Thus, in effect, there is a hierarchy of audits, SWOT analyses, assumptions, objectives, strategies and plans, each pertinent to the level and sphere of influence that go with its position in the total enterprise.

Such a scheme of things ensures that top management of a service organization is charged with addressing mainly macro-issues and lower management concentrates more on key micro-issues. In this way, everyone plays more to their strengths.

Too much misleading and unreliable data can also be generated if the company's time-frame for planning extends too far into the future. Although anticipating the future is vital, if the time-frame is too long, then judgement becomes less reliable and realistic and the credibility and usefulness of the marketing plan then come into question.

8 Once-a-year ritual

In companies where marketing planning is not properly understood, rather like the seasons, 'marketing planning time' comes round once a year. Its arrival is signalled by thick sets of proforma sheets arriving on managers' desks, accompanied by a memo proclaiming the urgency of returning the same by a given deadline. The weeks which follow are characterized by a flurry of activity as managers investigate and compete for information. Once the forms are returned, organizational life can get back to normal and managers can relax in the comfort of knowing that their peace will not be disturbed for another twelve months.

One bank we have worked with has a planning process which has a close resemblance to what we have described.

> **Managers of this bank would make painstaking and diligent inputs to the system, then hear nothing more.**

Any plans which did emerge were, apparently, filed away, never to be referred to again. Not surprisingly, in this bank, 'involvement' in the planning process was seen to be a demotivating chore, and marketing is quite rightly interpreted as relatively unimportant.

Companies who tackle marketing planning seriously do not fall into this trap. They have a planning calendar which operates *throughout the year*, as will be explained in Chapters 7 and 8. By tackling the task in this way, marketing planning becomes an integral part of the service manager's job, not a temporary 'bolt-on' extra.

9 Confusion between operational and strategic marketing planning

From what has been said so far, it should be obvious that we advocate that a service organization should consider all the strategic implications of its position and set marketing objectives and strategies for about three years hence. Having done this, the company can then devise the one-year operational marketing plan, which in effect represents the first steps towards reaching those objectives.

Many companies do not do this. Instead, they argue that because the future is so uncertain, they can only look ahead for the next year. Accordingly, they prepare a marketing plan and operational plan rolled up into one. From this, they will extrapolate forward to arrive at their longer term 'strategic' objectives. Clearly, this approach fails to grasp the fact that the future is not likely to be the same as today, and it avoids looking at the real strategic issues which face the company.

> **Successful service companies understand that their operational marketing plans are derived from their strategic marketing plans, not vice versa.**

By operating with this protocol, both the operational and strategic plans will be integrated and mutually supportive.

10 Failure to integrate marketing planning into the corporate planning system

It is clear that the marketing plan should be an integral part of the total corporate planning process. However, it is implicit in this relationship that both are operating over the same time-scale and have a similar level of formalization. Indeed, other major functions such as information systems, finance and personnel should also be planned in a similar way over the same period. The linkages and integration between corporate planning, strategic marketing and other functional planning are illustrated in Figure 2.5.

By having all the planning processes integrated in this way, the fullest advantage can be taken of the company's multifunctional strengths, weaknesses, opportunities and threats, and trade-offs can be made at a functional level between what is needed and what can be afforded.

When marketing planning operates in isolation, it will find it more difficult to gain the participation of other key functions in the company which might be major determinants of success. For example, the marketing plan might call for more manpower and skill levels than personnel can deliver in time. This is why the creation of cross-functional linkages, shown in Figure 2.5, is so important.

11 Delegation of planning to a planner

Most of the literature sees the marketing planner basically as a coordinator, not as an initiator of goals and strategies. In many companies where there is a person with the title of Marketing Planning Manager, the appointment was made to resolve some significant marketing problems and to take the pressure off the marketing direc-

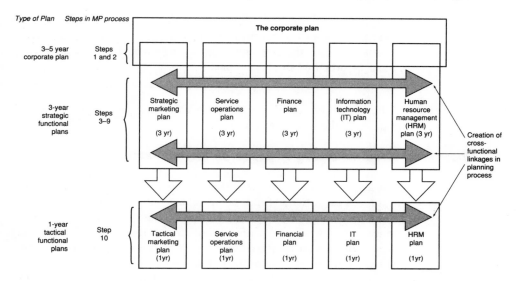

Type of Plan | Steps in MP process

Figure 2.5 Integration of corporate planning, strategic marketing planning and tactical marketing planning

tor (or CEO). As a result of this, the newcomer, who is often young and highly qualified, is given a (frequently remote) staff position responding directly to the marketing director or CEO.

Such new managers are then told that their task is to design a marketing planning system, coordinate the inputs and formulate overall objectives and strategies for the board.

> **This puts the marketing planner in an invidious position of having uncertain status and power, yet being expected to make impact on organizational behaviour at all levels.**

Some individuals have the personality, tenacity and political skills to operate from such an unpromising position and eventually win through. Most, however, never earn the respect or cooperation of line managers and, as a result, try to do more and more of the planning themselves.

Understandable though this situation might be, the resulting plan, deprived of crucial line management input, is usually critically flawed. Not surprisingly, those who resented the planner's attempts to establish some sort of order in the first place will happily pick holes in the plans produced, and be heard to make comments about the problems of 'not living in the real world'.

The problems for the marketing planner raised above occur directly as a result of the abdication of top management in giving thought to the formulation of overall marketing strategies.

> However, when market pressures call for a more robust or radical response from the company, top management must get involved and be prepared to play its part.

Planners, by themselves, are relatively impotent to make an impact on the organization.

12 Uncertainty about what should appear in the marketing plan

Just as an architect's working sketches and rough calculations would never appear on the final blueprints, even though they played a crucial part in the design, so should a marketing plan be free of unnecessary detail. Like any good report, the finalized marketing plan should be authoritative and easy to understand. Its major function is to determine where the company is, where it wants to go and how it can get there. It lies at the heart of the company's revenue-generating activities, such as the timing of cash flow and the size and nature of the workforce. It is in effect a 'selling document' for the service organization's marketing strategy.

What should appear in a written strategic marketing plan is shown in Figure 2.6. The items mentioned in this figure will be elaborated on in later chapters.

Summary

In this chapter we defined marketing planning and identified the benefits it could bring to an organization. We went on to outline a marketing planning process for service organizations which consists of four phases: establishing the strategic context; conducting a situation review; formulating marketing objectives and strategies; allocating budgets and devising a detailed first-year implementation plan.

These four phases can be further broken down into ten interactive and interrelated process steps. Each of the steps was described briefly as an introduction to what is to follow in the next four chapters. However, the amount of text devoted to each step in the following chapters will vary considerably, based on their complexity, importance and the amount of detail with which they need to be addressed.

Although the planning process looks straightforward when considered in the abstract, it actually presents a number of problems when considered in an organizational context. This is because the introduction of marketing planning is more than a cognitive process. It strikes at the heart of how a company is managed and structured. For this reason, there are a number of barriers which prevent a service organization from taking full advantage of marketing planning or introducing it successfully. We considered some of the more common barriers, which were:

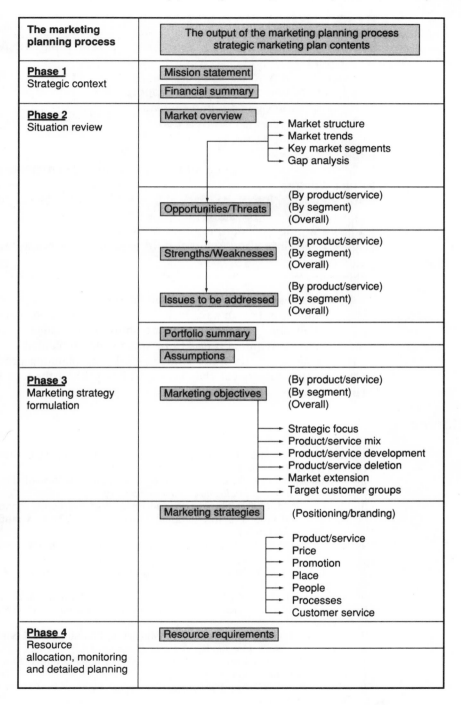

Figure 2.6 What should appear in a services strategic marketing plan (Source: Based on McDonald, M. (1995) *Marketing Plans: How to prepare them; how to use them,* 3rd edn, Butterworth-Heinemann, Oxford

1 Short-termism
2 Weak support from the chief executive and top management
3 Lack of a plan for planning
4 Lack of line management support
5 Confusion over planning terms
6 An over-reliance on numbers
7 Too much detail, too far ahead
8 Once-a-year ritual
9 Confusion between operational and strategic marketing planning
10 Failure to integrate marketing planning into the corporate planning system
11 Delegation of planning to a planner
12 Uncertainty about what should appear in the marketing plan.

All of these issues serve to underline the point that strategic marketing planning is not an easy task. Its introduction needs careful consideration and, sometimes, nothing short of a change of corporate culture is required if it is to be successfully implanted.

Having discussed the broad strategy marketing planning process in this chapter, subsequent chapters expand on each of the four key planning phases.

References

1 Buzzell, R. D. and Gale, B. T. (1987) *The PIMS Principles: Linking Strategy to Performance*, The Free Press, New York.
2 McDonald, M. (1992) Strategic Marketing Planning: A State-of-the-Art Review. *Marketing Intelligence and Planning*, **10** (4).
3 McDonald, M. (1982) The Theory and Practice of Marketing Planning for Industrial Goods in International Markets. PhD Thesis, Cranfield Institute of Technology.
4 Ansoff, I. (1957) Strategies for Diversification. *Harvard Business Review*, Sept/Oct.
5 Chisnall, P. (1975) Marketing Planning in a Service Economy. *Long Range Planning*, December, 43–52.
6 Hooley, G. J., West, C. J. and Lynch, J. E. (1984) *Marketing in the UK: A Study of Current Practice and Performance*, Institute of Marketing, London.
7 Greenley, G. (1983) An Overview of Marketing Planning in UK Service Companies. *Marketing Intelligence and Planning*, **1** (3), 55–68.
8 Cousins, L. (1991) Marketing Plans or Marketing Planning? *Business Strategy Review*, Summer, 35–54.
9 Sutton, H. (1990) *The Marketing Plan in the 1990s*, The Conference Board, New York.
10 *Ibid.*

3 Marketing planning Phase One – the strategic context

The strategic marketing planning process for services

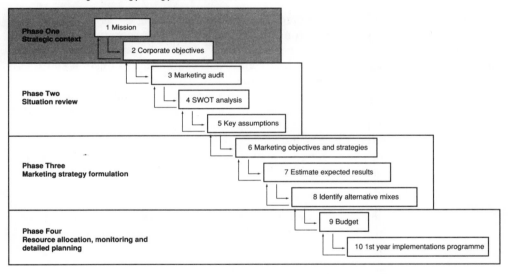

In each chapter, we will stress the difference between the *process* of marketing planning and the *output* of this process – *the strategic marketing plan*. What should appear in the written output of the strategic marketing planning process was shown in Figure 2.6 in the previous chapter.

We have seen that the first phase of the marketing planning process involves determining (or re-examining) the mission statement and setting corporate objectives. In this chapter, we will look at both of these issues in some detail, using examples from the service industry to illustrate how some companies have set about these tasks. These two steps form the strategic context and provide the pivotal link between the corporate plan and the marketing plan, as outlined in Figure 2.5.

Step 1 Mission

A mission for services

As briefly explained in Chapter 2, the mission statement, or mission, encapsulates the company's identity in terms of what it is, what makes it special, what it stands for, and where it is heading.

> **This would appear to be an eminently sensible starting point for moving the business forward, for if the organization has no notion about its identity and values, it may be in a quandary regarding the way forward.**

Mission statements must not be so broad as to make them meaningless

Yet, logical though the reasons for having a mission might be, a study[1] derived from 181 of the top 1000 corporations in the USA showed that 50 per cent had not developed a formal mission. Another study by Byars and Neil[2] examined 157 mission statements from 208 members of the Planning Forum (the world's largest membership organization on planning and strategic management) and concluded that most of these were so broadly written that they had little meaning.

Both of these investigations back up our own empirical evidence, which also suggests that relatively few service organizations have developed effective mission statements.

> **In contrast, service companies that have taken the development of a mission seriously have benefited from the discipline and direction it has provided.**

It seems that, as with marketing planning itself, there is confusion regarding how to define a mission. As a result, instead of a mission that reflects a unique commitment to corporate values and direction, what emerges is a bland set of generalizations and meaningless statements. Not surprisingly, such missions are greeted at best with scepticism, at worst with derision.

Whilst recognizing that different service organizations might use other terminology such as business definition, credo, statement of business philosophy, belief statement, vision statement, statement of purpose, and so on, we define a mission as follows:

> A mission is an enduring statement of purpose that provides an animated vision of the organization's current and future business activities, in service and market terms, together with its values and beliefs and its points of differentiation from competitors. A mission helps determine the relationships with each of

the key markets with which the organization interacts, and provides a sense of direction and purpose which leads to more correct independent decisions being made at all levels of the organization.

Before we go on to consider how to develop an effective mission statement, it has to be recognized that some organizations might have a mission which, although strongly embedded in their culture, does not appear in writing. Such might be the case in smaller organizations, or in those with a strong, charismatic leader.

> **Thus, while it is not essential for the mission to appear in writing, we would recommend that it should be, in order that it does not run the risk of being misinterpreted or of losing its impact at lower levels within the organization.**

The nature of corporate missions

An examination of what has been written about missions suggests that a number of key issues are important and need to be taken into consideration. They are:

> 1 It is dangerous to define the mission too narrowly or too broadly.
> 2 The audience for the mission should be considered carefully.
> 3 It is crucial to understand the business one is in.
> 4 The mission should be unique to the organization preparing it.
> 5 The mission should be market, rather than service, orientated.
> 6 Within any organization, there will need to be a hierarchy of mission statements.

Each of these issues gives rise to a number of interesting questions which need to be addressed.

1 How does one get the balance between too narrow and too wide?

One of the classic examples of a services sector business which defined its mission too narrowly was the railway industry in the USA. In his seminal paper on the topic, Levitt[3] argued that by defining themselves to be in the locomotive business, rather than helping customers solve their transportation needs, the industry as a whole failed to identify and capitalize on opportunities, and thereby hastened its own demise.

A more contemporary example would be Football League clubs in the UK, whose narrow focus on the game itself obscured the fact that their customers' needs for entertainment could be met by other more sociable and comfortable alternatives. They just did not perceive themselves to be in the entertainment business and, with only a few exceptions, attendance figures fell dramatically.

The mission statement has to provide some focus to the activities of an organization

> **However, just as there are dangers in defining the business too narrowly, to have no bounds can be equally ruinous.**

Indeed, this might be the more common of the two faults. For example, in recent years, the deregulation of the financial services sector has led to banks diversifying away from their core business into stockbroking and investment banking, with disastrous results. Similarly, retailers have undertaken diversification away from what customers perceived to be their traditional realms. Finding they were unprofitable in these areas, they are now struggling to get back to their core retailing business. The retailer Laura Ashley provides a good example of this.

Sometimes, their identity gets lost in the process. For example, the attempts of Woolworths to diversify might now be looked back on as a fit of corporate folly, where all its old strengths were thrown away and nothing of substance put in their place. Equally, some years ago Boots and W. H. Smith were taking routes which made them increasingly similar and were damaging their individuality. Fortunately, both have reasserted their market identity.

> In these cases, if *effective* missions had been formulated, with the requisite strategic focus that this implies, it is questionable if some of them would have diversified into the non-core, non-profit-making, non-integrated business areas that they entered in recent years.

2 Who is the target audience for the mission and what are their expectations?

The reasons for writing a mission statement can vary. Some organizations might do it for public relations purposes; some might do it because they see that other companies have them. As we said earlier, however, it should be for the purpose of strategically focusing the business activities. By being clear about the mission's purpose, it

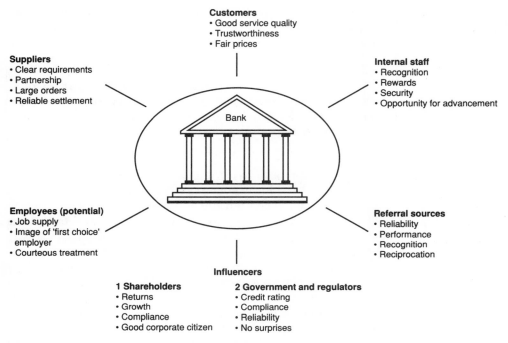

Figure 3.1 Key audiences and their expectations in a bank

becomes easier to define the target audience and to know the level of sophistication of their requirements.

Figure 3.1 identifies how a bank might consider its key audiences and their expectations, in terms of formulating a mission. This is based on a consideration of all the stakeholders described in the opening chapter. For some types of business, like water services, there might be additional stakeholders to consider, such as environmentalists, whose concerns will be about issues like the extraction of water from rivers and the effluent pumped back into rivers or the sea.

It is important that the mission statement is not too long

While this framework can be extremely useful for identifying and mapping the relative importance of each of these groups, clearly a mission which tried to embrace every group and issue equally could end up exceedingly long. Therefore, some decisions have to be made regarding which target audiences the company wants to recognize within the mission. The context for such decisions will be the nature of the service product, the current position of the firm in its industry sector, and who are the key players among the stakeholders.

> There is a view in many service organizations that the key messages in the mission should be concerned primarily with providing a sense of strategic direction and motivation of the *internal staff*.

When necessary, a modified version of this statement can be used for external purposes and reflect the considerations of other stakeholders.

> **There is, however, an obvious danger that, in producing an internally focused mission statement, the interests of two other principal stakeholders – the shareholders/owners of the business and the customer – are neglected.**

Perhaps the approach to recruitment attributed to Bill Marriot of Marriot Hotels puts this in context. When he interviews prospective managers he says, 'There are three important groups we need to satisfy – shareholders, customers and our employees. Which is the most important one to focus on?' To get the job you have to answer 'the employees'. Marriot argues that it is only by focusing on employees that he will have happy customers and only through happy customers will he provide good return to his shareholders.

3   What business are we in?

This question is closely related to the earlier one about defining the business too narrowly or too broadly. While many companies might claim that the answer is obvious, we have found that when asked to write it down without conferring, senior managers from the same service organization rarely come up with the same answer. This then poses another question: 'If *they* are confused, how must those at lower levels feel?'

The trap managers fall into is that they are guided by the nature of their output rather than the company's specific competences. Thus, the claim that their company was in the 'retail business' could, on deeper analysis, be found to be actually in the 'getting latest fashions into the High Street quickest' business. Similarly, the company that claims that it is in 'computer software' is likely to be really in the business of helping other companies to resolve managerial control problems, perhaps of a very specific nature.

Too often, companies fail to recognize their distinctive competences and, as a result, miss valuable opportunities to play to their strengths.

4   How unique is the mission statement?

Service organizations are in different sectors, have different facilities, staffing, levels of morale, geographic locations, track-records, management styles, expertise, values, hopes and ambitions. Taking these into account, it is unlikely that all these areas of potential difference should lead to one company having a mission much the same as any other. Yet, in our dealings with many service companies, that is what we find. This is especially true of banks and professional service firms.

> **It is as if the mission has been bought off the shelf rather than made to measure.**

All service organizations are different and this should be reflected in the mission statement

Not only may a service organization have specific competences, but it should also seek some differential advantages over its competitors. It might be closer to markets, be more efficient, be more aggressive, and so on. Any of these things ought to make the mission somewhat different. (Of course, the corollary of this statement is that, if the company genuinely cannot identify any differential advantages, it should seek to establish some.)

The underlying philosophy in striving for uniqueness is that success lies in obtaining a competitive advantage, in a preferred way, with a selected customer base. The acid test which discloses whether or not this has been achieved is to substitute a competitor's name into your mission. If it still makes sense, then you are implying that both companies are the same – something which is usually untrue.

5 Is the mission market orientated?

Organizations that focus too closely on their service product rather than market needs can have an inclination to develop new improved services or spin-offs which, brilliant though they might be, may not be required by the market. The message is clear. In order to avoid this, the mission should be market orientated and focus on customer needs.

Increasingly, organizations such as airlines, hotels and banks are considering customer needs and using this knowledge to make an input into the design of the services they offer.

6 At what level in the service organization is the mission statement being prepared?

Service organizations may have international headquarters, several national headquarters, divisional headquarters and, almost certainly, a number of individual service product, or business, centres. Clearly then, it is unlikely that one central mission statement will suffice in providing the direction to these several hierarchical levels in the organization. It is suggested, therefore, that all the guidelines provided in this section of this chapter can be applied equally well to any organizational level.

This issue is expanded on later in this chapter.

From what we have said here, there are two predominant types of mission statements – good ones and bad ones!

Type 1   These are generally found inside the annual reports and are designed to make shareholders feel good. They are invariably full of 'motherhood' statements and organizational puffery. As missions, they have little practical use and should not be confused with Type 2.

Type 2   The real thing. A meaningful statement, unique to the organization, that impacts on behaviour at all levels of the company. The following should appear in this type of mission:

---

1 *Role or contribution*
   For example, charity, profit seeker, innovator, opportunity seeker.
2 *Business definition*
   This should be done in terms of benefits provided or needs satisfied, rather than the services offered.
3 *Distinctive competences*
   These are the essential skills, capabilities or resources that underpin whatever success that has brought the company to where it is now. All of these should be considered in terms of how they confer differential advantages.
4 *Indications for the future*
   This will briefly refer to what the firm *will* do, what it *might* do and what it will *never* do.

In order that the mission is succinct, it is good practice to ensure that it can be written on a single A4 page.

Examples of service organization mission statements

In examining actual mission statements for service companies, it is clear that there are vast differences in the length and content of them. Some are more general statements of philosophy, whilst others are much more specific. In this section, we will review some examples of different approaches to the development of service organization missions and illustrate the wide range of approaches that are adopted which, in the view of the authors, represent good practice.

Although attention to missions is relatively recent in the management literature, some service organizations have had mission statements for a long time. The 'mission statement' developed in 1888 for the Northwestern Mutual Life Insurance Company is shown in Figure 3.2.

The Northwestern Mutual Way

The ambition of The Northwestern has been less to be large than to be safe; its aim is to rank first in benefits to policy owners rather than first in size. Valuing quality above quantity, it has preferred to secure its business under certain salutary restrictions and limitations rather than to write a much larger business at the possible sacrifice of those valuable points which have made the Northwestern pre-eminently the policy owners' Company.

Figure 3.2 Mission statement for the Northwest Mutual Life Insurance Company

---

This mission, developed by their Executive Committee in 1888, has helped the company exist and flourish for over a hundred years in the highly competitive insurance industry.

Thomas Watson, IBM's founder, articulated his company's philosophy in the phrase 'IBM means service'. IBM defines itself as a *service* company and the corporate philosophy articulated by Watson was not just to be a good service company, but to be the best service company in the world. The IBM mission espoused by Watson in the 1960s is shown in Figure 3.3.

IBM
- Respect for the individual
- Provide the best customer service of any company in the world
- Pursue all tasks with the idea that they can be accomplished in a superior fashion

---

Figure 3.3 Organizational statement of philosophy for IBM

Watson argued that the basic philosophy of the organization was more concerned with its performance than with technical or economic resources, organizational structure, innovation or timing. Some twenty years later, the then IBM chairman stated: 'We've changed our technology, changed our organization, changed our marketing and manufacturing techniques many times, and we expect to go on changing. But through all this change, Watson's three basic beliefs remain. We steer our course by those stars.'

No doubt the problems suffered by IBM in the early 1990s stemmed from a lack of focus on these basic beliefs. The plethora of books written in the early 1990s on IBM's problems provide much evidence that in their later years they began to focus more on technology than on customer needs.

Missions which are statements of business philosophy, such as this, give overall guidance in terms of values, but do not give much focus to service and product areas on markets. Clearly, in the case of IBM, this eventually proved to be a weakness.

Today, many service organizations are seeking to spell out their mission in more detail. The British Airways mission outlined in Figure 3.4 focuses on a number of key themes which include corporate charisma, creativity, business capability, competitive stance and training philosophy.

Ultimately, the company's mission needs to reflect the shared values which are held within the organization as part of its strategic focus. Within the industry sector in which it competes, British Airways aims to be 'the world-wide symbol of creativity, value, service and quality'. This mission statement is one of a series of missions

---

THE BRITISH AIRWAYS MISSION

To be the best and most successful company in the airline industry

OUR GOALS

- Safe and Secure
To be a safe and secure airline

- Financially Strong
To deliver a strong and consistent financial performance

- Global Leader
To secure a leading share of air travel business worldwide with a significant presence in all major geographical markets

- Service and Value
To provide overall superior service and good value for money in every market segment in which we compete

- Customer Driven
To excel in anticipating and quickly responding to customer needs and competitor activity

- Good Employer
To sustain a working environment that attracts, retains and develops committed employees who share in the success of the company

- Good Neighbour
To be a good neighbour, concerned for the community and the environment

To achieve these goals, we must:

Deliver friendly, professional service consistently through well-trained and motivated employees

Search continuously for improvement through innovation and the use of technology

Employ planning and decision-making processes that provide clear direction and sense of purpose

Foster a leadership style throughout the organisation which encourages respect for individuals, teamwork and close identification with customers.

Strive constantly to achieve agreed standards of quality at competitive cost levels.

Figure 3.4 British Airways mission statement

WORLDWIDE MISSION STATEMENT

DHL will become the acknowledged global leader in the express delivery of documents and packages. Leadership will be achieved by establishing the industry standards of excellence for quality of service and by maintaining the lowest cost position relative to our service commitment in all markets of the world.

Achievement of the mission requires:

☐ Absolute dedication to understanding and fulfilling our customers' needs with the appropriate mix of service, reliability, products and price for each customer.
☐ An environment that rewards achievement, enthusiasm, and team spirit and which offers each person in DHL superior opportunities for personal development and growth.
☐ A state of the art worldwide information network for customer billing, tracking, tracing and management information/communications.
☐ Allocation of resources consistent with the recognition that we are one worldwide business.
☐ A professional organisation able to maintain local initiative and local decision making while working together within a centrally managed network.

The evolution of our business into new services, markets, or products will be completely driven by our single-minded commitment to anticipating and meeting the changing needs of our customers.

Figure 3.5 Mission statement for DHL

which have been developed over a period of time to articulate progressively BA's view of their business.

The mission for DHL in Figure 3.5 focuses on many of the key issues we consider should be addressed in a mission statement for such a firm. It also illustrates the need to develop corporate objectives which are highly integrated with the mission statement.

Without a strong linkage which provides a means of measuring whether the mission can be achieved, much of the potential value of a mission can be dissipated. The relationship between corporate objectives and mission has been well summed up by the Chairman and CEO of General Mills:

> We would agree that, unless our mission statement is backed up with specific objectives and strategies, the words become meaningless, but I also believe that our objectives and strategies are far more likely to be acted upon where there exists a prior statement of belief (i.e. a mission) from which specific plans and actions flow.

It is a focus around shared corporate values and customer needs that signals the likely commitment by staff to its strategy. Figure 3.6 shows the mission statement for the Royal Trust Bank, a Canadian bank based in London.

ROYAL TRUST BANK
MISSION STATEMENT

We aim to strengthen and focus our role in the United Kingdom as a leading relationship bank offering our clients selected lending and investment products together with fiduciary and advisory services designed for developing companies, wealth-producing entrepreneurs and professional individuals.

We will create wealth for our clients, employees and shareholders.

Our aim will be achieved by:

Earning the loyalty of our clients and their recommendation of our people through:
- quality products and good advice
- dependable delivery
- efficient administration

Giving our employees purpose and pride through:
- training
- authority commensurate with responsibility
- recognition for performance

Maintaining the confidence and support of our shareholders through:
- prudence
- foresight
- progress

Figure 3.6 Mission statement for Royal Trust Bank

The strategic process of development of a mission statement involved detailed consideration and input from the board and senior management team. In the Royal Trust Bank, this led to a reappraisal of the key business areas. In particular, the bank recognized the importance of customer service at the strategic level and its role 'as a leading relationship bank'.

> **Mission statements can be an empty statement on a piece of paper, or can reflect and underpin fundamental values of an organization in pursuit of its strategy.**

In Royal Trust Bank's case, the importance of a relationship strategy was emphasized as the primary means by which their basic business objectives will be achieved. However, unfortunately the profitability of all the target segments selected by the bank for implementation of this strategy all turned down during the early 1990s.

Marks and Spencer were once quoted by Peter Drucker as being the best company in the world. Their mission statement is shown in Figure 3.7. Whether one likes or dislikes this particular mission statement, there is no question that Marks and Spencer have continued to thrive and prosper by espousing these particular values and philosophies.

Mission statement of Marks and Spencer Plc

Our three great assets are:

1　The goodwill and confidence of the public.
2　The loyalty and devotion of management and staff throughout the system.
3　The confidence and cooperation of our suppliers.

The principles upon which the business is built are:

1　To offer our customers a selective range of high-quality, well designed and attractive merchandise at reasonable prices.
2　To encourage our suppliers to use the most modern and efficient techniques of production and quality control dictated by the latest discoveries in science and technology.
3　With the cooperation of our suppliers, to enforce the highest standard of quality control.
4　To plan the expansion of our stores for the better display of a widening range of goods and for the convenience of our customers.
5　To foster good human relations with customers, suppliers and staff.

Figure 3.7　Marks and Spencer mission statement

Levels of mission statement

It is unlikely in most large organizations that one mission statement will suffice

Just as companies have different levels of objectives, ranging from strategic objectives through to tactical objectives and action plans, a service organization should consider to what extent it should develop mission or purpose statements at lower levels of the organization. For example, a bank with diverse financial services operations could have a mission statement for the bank as a whole, as well as individual missions for each business unit. Thus, it might develop missions for retail banking, corporate banking, international banking, investment banking, and its insurance and stockbroking activities.

> **Many multibusiness service organizations are in a similar position of needing to develop missions for their constituent parts.**

It may also be appropriate to have missions at individual functional levels. For example, missions could be developed for internal service functions. An example of a mission for a human resource department is shown in Figure 3.8. Some organizations develop a range of missions for internal service activities and departments. A customer service mission statement, for example, expresses the company's philosophy and commitment to customer service and the need for it follows from the increasing recognition that service quality is an important means of gaining competitive advantage. In some cases, customer service and quality missions are stated separately. In others, they may be combined as part of the statement of a firm's overall mission.

To develop and promote the highest quality human resource practices and initiatives in an ethical, cost-effective and timely manner to support the current and future business objectives of the organization and to enable line managers to maximize the calibre, effectiveness and development of their human resources.

This will be achieved through working with managers and staff to:

- Develop an integrated human resource policy and implement its consistent use throughout the organization
- Enhance managers' efficient use of human resources through the provision of responsive and adaptable services
- Be the preferred source of core strategic HR services
- Provide high quality tailored HR consultancy
- Introduce methods to plan for the provision of required calibre and quantity of staff
- Ensure consistent line accountability throughout all areas within the organization
- Assist the organization in becoming more customer aware and responsive to changing needs.
- Define and encourage implementation of an improved communications culture throughout the organization
- Maintain an innovative and affordable profile for HRM.

Figure 3.8 Human resource mission statement

In each case, the 'mission' should focus the company, business unit, or functional service activity. Where missions are formulated, for example, at the departmental level, they should be consistent with higher level missions within the organization.

Developing a service mission

Time must be devoted to the mission statement

All of the examples of missions we have provided have the advantage of being short and simple. However, it must be remembered that the few words on a piece of paper represent the end result of a 'distillation' process which has extracted the essential few key elements from a mass of raw material.

> **To arrive at a meaningful mission statement is, therefore, a time-consuming and sometimes painful experience, not something that can be rushed.**

Bearing this in mind, the organization must be genuinely committed to developing its mission if it is going to get any lasting value out of the investment of time and energy it puts into it. Speed and compromise are not legitimate in the mission formulation process.

Producing the mission statement should be a group process

While the mission can be developed by the chief executive in isolation, or by a management consultant, such approaches miss the vital part of the process – that of creating ownership and gaining organizational acceptance of the outcome.

> **The more managers and staff are involved in formulating the mission, the more committed they will be to it.**

There are a number of ways by which the desired level of involvement can be accomplished. Here are two approaches we have used with success:

Workshops

These can be held in the context of a broader marketing planning exercise, or as stand-alone events. Typically, the participants would be senior executives, but there is no reason why a representative cross-section of other members of the organization could not produce valuable inputs.

How the workshop unfolds will vary from company to company, but it is likely to follow these general steps:

1 *Introduction*   The chief executive explains why it is important for a mission to be formulated. The top-level support the CEO brings leaves participants in no doubt that they are working on a real task.

2 *Orientation*   Time is spent explaining the purpose of missions and what they contain (much as we have done in this chapter). Examples from other companies can be used as visual aids. Participants are encouraged to critique such examples.

3 *Syndicate work*   Small groups of 4–6 people are charged with developing a first draft of the company's mission.

4 *Plenary session*   The individual groups present their missions and all contributions are analysed and discussed regarding their strengths and weaknesses.

5 *Pulling together*   Either by further syndicate work, or through the mechanism of a specially constituted task group, the draft mission takes shape.

6 *Testing*	The draft mission is tested out in other parts of the organization and amended when it is sensible to do so. Thus, the final mission is developed.

Top team approach
This would involve working with the Board of Directors and so the total group size is only about eight, thereby precluding syndicate work. Here, we adopt a slightly different methodology:

1 *Orientation*	This operates in much the same way as described above.
2 *Individual*	Team members work in isolation to formulate a working mission.
3 *Clarification and review*	Individual contributions are put onto flip charts (without attribution) and posted around the room. Team members then circulate, either: (a) studying all flip charts unaware of the author; or (b) each author in turn answers *only* questions seeking clarification (there is no critique made).
4 *Reformulating the mission*	Working individually, team members, building on the previous phase, reformulate a second draft of the mission.
5 *Clarification and review*	Step 3 is repeated, but this time missions that are essentially the same are grouped together.
6 *Discussion*	The team, through detailed discussions, review the missions, and seek to develop a mission that is both realistic and one to which they are all committed. (In some cases this process extends over several meetings.)

Both of these broad approaches have worked well for us, because we played a catalyst role and were not involved in corporate politics, as well as being unbiased regarding what the outcome should be. We were also able to challenge corporate assumptions which were suspect or just not true, hence establishing a more permissive, and therefore creative, learning environment. As a result of our experiences, we would strongly recommend that a company following the routes we have outlined seeks out an experienced third party, either a consultant or someone from a business school, to facilitate the event. Furthermore, such a person might also be able to help further develop the final mission and improve its potential as a communications aid. Those wishing to examine mission statements in more detail should see Falsey[4]; Campbell *et al.*;[5] and Campbell and Yeung.[6]

Once established, the mission should not be susceptible to frequent change, because what the company wishes to become should remain more or less the same. The exception to this general rule is if a fundamental change takes place, such as, for example, if new technology develops and renders the company's current technology redundant, or a new strategic direction is determined. Nevertheless, whilst the mission will not be changed very often, it should be re-examined for its relevance on a fairly regular basis.

Step 2 Corporate objectives

Corporate objectives and strategies

Once the mission has been developed, attention needs to switch to the corporate objectives and strategies. By way of recapitulation, how these are related is illustrated by Figure 3.9. From this, we can see that the corporate objectives and strategies need to be consistent with the sense of identity and direction provided by the mission statement.

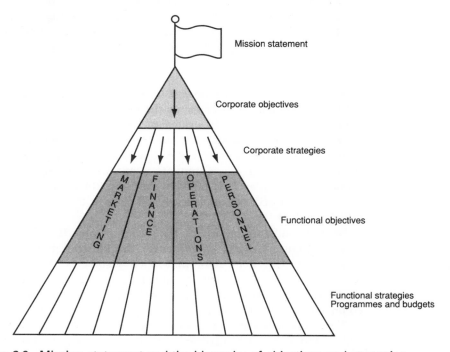

Figure 3.9 Mission statement and the hierarchy of objectives and strategies

As we saw earlier, the language of the corporate objectives will, in most cases, be in terms of profitability or return on capital invested, for these measures are universal yardsticks of organizational efficiency.

How these objectives will be achieved gives rise to the corporate strategies which impact on the various functional areas of the business. While there can be no absolutes in terms of what corporate strategies should address, it is likely that they will cover much of the following:

1 *Market standing*	e.g. sales and market share by market segment and the nature of services provided.
2 *Innovation*	e.g. new avenues of development.
3 *Productivity*	e.g. productivity of employees; effective use of capital and resources.
4 *Financing*	e.g. the nature of funding; levels of investment in fixed assets.
5 *Staff performance and development*	e.g. management and worker attitudes; preparedness to change.
6 *Public responsibility*	e.g. to the environment; to the local community; legislative requirements.

From Figure 3.9, it will be seen that what is a *strategy* at a higher level may become an *objective* at the next level down, so giving a hierarchy of objectives and strategies.

Service companies need to consider which specific functional areas will make the largest contribution to achieving the corporate objectives and, in doing this, formulate a mix of strategies which are mutually supportive. It is unlikely that any functional area can be completely ignored, because, clearly, all parts of the organization are interdependent.

Service companies approach the setting of objectives in different ways, as Figure 3.10 shows. Of course, this illustration is fairly general. However, it does show that when a company focuses on its services at the expense of its customers, a certain type of organizational 'culture' almost naturally follows. This is equally true when the company focuses on customers.

That this happens is supported by looking at British Airways before and after its privatization. In its earlier life, it saw itself as being in the business of flying planes. A consequence of this was that

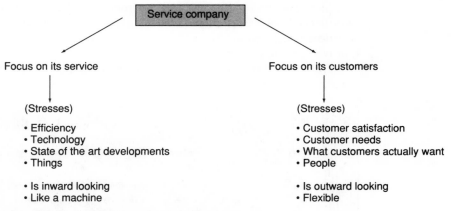

Figure 3.10 Different types of organizational focus

it was led by objectives which stressed technical efficiency and customers came a poor second to the pursuit of operational excellence. A major turnaround in profitability was brought about by privatization, which forced the company to modify its objectives and recognize that its future success lay in satisfying passenger requirements. However, to switch from one type of culture to another is never easy.

> **The more deep-rooted the original corporate beliefs, the more difficult it is to change them. British Airways, to its credit, addressed the issue of changing the culture as it restructured and slimmed down to become the world-class company it is today.**

As we have said before, only customer-focused objectives and strategies (and organizations) hold the prospect of corporate success in the longer term. Those readers wishing to examine corporate objectives in further detail should consult a strategy text such as Richards,[7] Steiner,[8] or Schellenberger and Boseman.[9]

Quantitative vs qualitative objectives

> **While objectives may sometimes be of a qualitative nature for internal company purposes, they must always be capable of being measured.**

Thus, they should be clear and provide specific targets to be achieved in a given time. If imprecise objectives are allowed, the organization will never have proper yardsticks against which to measure its performance. Thus, if a hotel decided that one of the objectives was to provide the best bedrooms in the area, it would have to spell out the criteria by which it expected to be judged. Then, surveys could be conducted to benchmark competitors and to ascertain whether these criteria were being met.

Here is how a financial services company phrased its objectives in quantitative terms:

• *Profit*	Double group earnings over the next five years.
• *Growth*	Treble revenues over the same period.
• *Innovation*	At least one new product or service to be launched every two years, with the intention of its accounting for 10 per cent of total sales revenue within two years of launch.
• *Corporate image*	To improve unprompted recognition (as measured by external research) from 30 per cent to 50 per cent over three years.
• *Services*	Improve advisory and value-added services from 15 per cent to 20 per cent of total revenue over four years.
• *Staff*	Reduce staff turnover by 60 per cent over three years.

Managers working in this organization are left in no doubt about what they are expected to achieve. Everything can be measured.

However, for broad statements of intent that are made public, such as in the annual report, qualitative objectives may be justified.

> **Finally, it must be stressed that for corporate objectives to have any real meaning, they must be based on a deep understanding of customer needs. Consequently, the marketing process has to take place where the customers are, so that a mutual interdependency develops between marketing planning at the operational level and the setting of corporate objectives and strategies.**

Summary

In this chapter, we have looked at the first phase of the planning process, which we called the 'strategic context'. It consists of two steps: formulating the corporate mission and setting corporate objectives and strategies. We went on to define the mission statement and to discuss its strategic value. Companies who had trouble in formulating their mission did so partly from ignorance and partly because they fell into some common traps – they made it too broad or too narrow, were unclear about the audience to which it was addressed, were confused about the nature of their business, the mission was not sufficiently unique and representative of the company, or it focused on the service rather than on the customers.

Being clear about what the mission means is one thing, formulating it so that it is both realistic and acceptable is something else. We looked at two participative methods for arriving at a mission which had organizational value. Methods such as these not only utilized organizational creativity, but also initiated the communication process which is so essential if the mission is to impact on the hearts and minds of managers and staff.

Corporate objectives and strategies are designed to make the mission come alive. We saw that the organization also had to align its objectives and strategies towards meeting customer needs and that, sometimes, this could have profound implications for the corporate culture. Although objectives could be qualitative or quantitative in nature, the latter must be capable of being measured, because they remove ambiguity. However, we did see that there was a role for qualitative objectives in terms of providing a broad backdrop to the organization.

The success of the whole marketing planning process is determined to a large extent by the way these first two steps are tackled. That is why it should be done very thoroughly. No marketing plan can be written properly until these elements of the overall corporate strategy are in place. That they should be in place is the responsibility of top management, not the marketing department.

However, as it will be seen, these corporate objectives must inevitably be driven by a deep understanding of customer markets, which entails getting marketing planning done where the customers are. Thus, both top-down corporate objectives and bottom-up, customer-driven marketing plans are mutually interdependent.

References

1 David, F. R. (1989) How Companies Define their Mission. *Long Range Planning*, **22** (1), 90–97.
2 Byars, L. L. and Neil, T. C. (1987) Organisational Philosophy and Mission Statements. *Planning Review*, July/August, 32–35.
3 Levitt, T. (1960) Marketing Myopia. *Harvard Business Review*, July–August, 45–56.
4 Falsey, T. A. (1989) *Corporate Philosophies and Mission Statements*, Quorum Books, Westpoint, Connecticut. p. 55.
5 Campbell, A., Devine, M. and Young, D. (1990) *Sense of Mission*, Economist Books/Hutchinson, London.
6 Campbell, A. and Yeung, S. (1990) *Do You Need a Mission Statement?* Economist Publications Management Guides, London.

7 Richards, M. D. (1986) *Setting Strategic Goals and Objectives*, West Publishing, St. Paul, MN.
8 Steiner, G. (1979) *Strategic Planning*, The Free Press, New York.
9 Schellenberger, R. E. and Boseman, G. (1982) *Policy Formulation and Strategy Management*, 2nd edn. Chapter 2, Wiley.

4 Marketing planning Phase Two – the situation review

The strategic marketing planning process for services

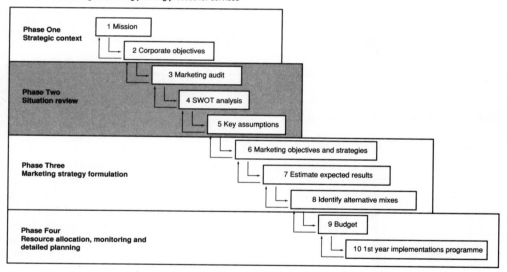

Once again, we should like to emphasize the difference between the *process* of strategic marketing planning described here, and the *output* of this process, the *strategic marketing plan*. What should appear in the written output of the strategic marketing planning process was shown in Figure 2.6 in Chapter 2.

In this chapter, we will consider in some detail the component steps of Phase Two of the marketing planning process – the situation review. We will look at ways of tackling each of these process steps, and also outline some of the tools such as market segmentation, positioning, life cycle analysis and portfolio analysis that service companies can use to help address them.

> Once again, we must stress that, for the purposes of clarity, we deal with each of the steps in Phase Two in a linear sequence. In reality, they are highly interactive and far less obvious as 'stand-alone' activities.

Service organizations need to evaluate their future prospects

While the purpose of the previous chapter, the corporate strategic context, was to provide marketing planning with a sense of strategic direction, the situation review is concerned with evaluating the future prospects of the service enterprise. Depending upon the outcome, the company may well be placed to face the future, or, alternatively, it might be found to be lacking in certain areas. Another possibility is that, because of the current circumstances facing the organization, the original corporate objectives of the plan may have to be modified considerably.

> **The first step of the situation review phase, the marketing audit, provides the information which shapes the subsequent elements of the planning process.**

Step 3   The marketing audit

A marketing audit provides the means to enable the service organization to understand how it relates to the environment in which it operates. It also enables internal strengths and weaknesses to be identified in terms of how they match external opportunities and threats. The audit should be a systematic, critical and unbiased review and appraisal of the company's marketing operations. Thus, it provides management with the information to select a position in its particular environment based on known facts. In short, it provides the answer to the question: 'Where is the company now?'

The marketing audit should be kept separate from the marketing plan

> **It needs to be stressed here that the marketing audit is an essential part of the strategic marketing planning process and that the results of the marketing audit constitute a separate document.**

The marketing audit itself is not a marketing plan and only some of the details contained in it should appear in the plan itself. We recommend that a marketing audit be carried out by all commercial managers in their area of responsibility and that this should be a required activity.

By carrying out an audit on a regular basis, e.g. once a year (rather than just at those times when things go wrong), management is more likely to recognize trends and spot underlying problems of a fundamental nature. This means that, instead of responding to symptoms, managers, in fact, address the root causes of organizational and marketing problems.

Such is the complexity of operating in rapidly changing market conditions that it makes good sense to carry out a thorough situation analysis at least once a year at the beginning of the planning cycle.

Indeed, in many leading organizations, a marketing audit is a *required* activity, which has an equivalent status to a financial audit.

Who should do it?

Sometimes, outside consultants are hired to undertake this task. Experienced though they might be, the cost of using them can be high. Also, it must be asked if they will really have access to all the information which is 'stored' in an informal way by managers within the organization. It is a formidable task for an outsider to win the confidence of all the staff and uncover much of the anecdotal evidence well-known to insiders.

Generally speaking, a better solution to the question of who does the audit is to get managers themselves to undertake the analysis within their own areas of responsibility. Where necessary this can be supplemented by the selective use of consultants. This approach has several benefits to commend it:

- The company's own expertise can be tapped and exploited.
- Managers become involved and, therefore, more committed to marketing planning.
- The discipline brought by the analytical process helps to avoid tunnel vision by forcing managers to focus on their total environment on a regular basis.
- Developing a critical appraisal faculty in managers helps them in their personal growth and development.
- Consultants' fees are minimized.

Often, however, the organization's response to the suggestion that their own managers conduct the audit centres around problems of them finding the time and not being sufficiently objective. Naturally, time commitment will always be a critical issue.

> **Nevertheless, managers ought to find time to stop and analyse the broader issues surrounding their sphere of activity.**

Not only does this help the organization, but having this wider vision aids personal performance.

The objection about lack of objectivity can be helped by providing training for the managers, and providing them with easy-to-understand documentation which augments the formal planning approach.

What needs to be covered?

It will be impossible in a book of this length to be able to explain all the possible areas of the marketing audit in specific terms because, undoubtedly, there will be some activities of concern to only a few specialized service companies. However, regardless of their size, or the nature of their business, most companies find that there are certain key determinants to their business. It is on these that we shall focus. (We shall provide some references later in this chapter for those wanting to explore this area in further detail.)

In fact, the services marketing audit can be visualized as a set of five interrelating sub-audits, which focus on different aspects of the business, as shown in Figure 4.1. This figure also shows that the marketing audit draws information from outside the company, via

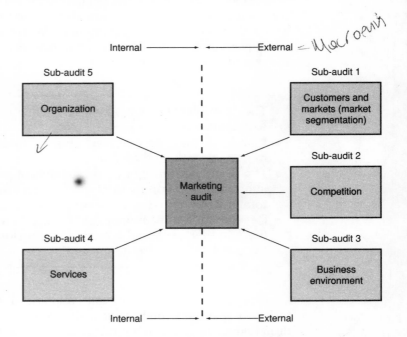

Figure 4.1 The constituent parts of the marketing audit

the customer, competition and environment audits, and from inside the company, by auditing the organization and the services it offers.

Let us now consider each of these sub-audit areas in turn.

Sub-audit 1   Customers and markets

Since the whole purpose of marketing planning is to alert and gear the service organization to market opportunities, the customer and market audit is concerned essentially with analysing trends in these areas, both favourable and unfavourable.

> **By understanding in depth what is happening to its customers and markets, the company can select those opportunities which offer the best prospects for long-term success.**

As the risk of failure is too high to rely on subjective opinion and intuition, the company must be led by accurate, fact-based information.

Market segmentation

In this chapter, a number of diagnostic tools will be introduced. One of the key diagnostic tools of marketing is *market segmentation*; this is a particularly relevant tool to use during the audit process when analysing customers and markets.

The audit process enables the existing methods of segmentation to be reappraised. Sometimes, it can be found that there are more advantageous ways to consider customers when seeking to establish a competitive advantage.

> **The segmentation process is concerned with dividing a heterogeneous market into specific homogeneous groups. The segments thus identified can then be targeted with specific services and a distinctive marketing mix.**

In this way, customer needs can be met more effectively, which in turn opens up the prospect of building customer retention and loyalty. When tackled creatively, market segmentation helps to prevent valuable resources being misdirected into non-productive parts of the business.

There are many ways by which a service company can approach market segmentation (Figure 4.2). These 'segmentation bases' fall under the two broad headings of customer characteristics and cus-

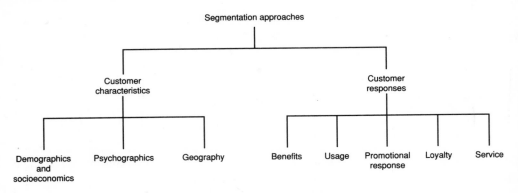

Figure 4.2 Major approaches to services market segmentation

tomer responses. In other words, who are our customers and why do they behave as they do?

Here are brief explanations about the 'segmentation bases' illustrated in Figure 4.2.

Customer characteristics

> **Headings under this category are useful descriptors of the groups buying services. However, on their own, they are rarely sufficient to explain *why* they buy *what* they buy.**

1 *Demographics and socioeconomics*

In consumer service markets, demographics refers to a number of factors including sex, age, family size and so on. In business markets, which are frequently the target of service organizations, demographics refers to company size, Standard Industrial Classification type (SIC), organizational form and so on. Socioeconomic factors can include income levels, educational background, social class, ethnic origins, and the like. By profiling its customers into groups along these lines, the service company can gauge which segment has the greater propensity to spend; the nature of the services with most appeal; the likely sensitivity to price; and so on. Furthermore, by understanding wider trends in demographics and socioeconomics, the company can predict how future demand might be affected.

2 *Psychographics*

This is a more developed form of segmenting customers and is concerned with defining people's behaviour and lifestyles. By understanding more about customers' attitudes, underlying personality types, motivations and aspirations, a company can often develop more meaningful segmentation bases than with demographic or socioeconomic factors alone.

3 *Geography*

Geographical segmentation is relatively simple and is often among the first approaches considered by many services organizations. By dividing customers according to where they live or work, it can be possible to identify local and regional trends. Other issues can involve population density, climate-related factors and the availability of communications media. For the service company operating on a global scale, geographical segmentation might carry with it a whole package of other considerations such as culture, religion and degree of industrialization.

In the UK, geo-demographic information is obtainable from census data and the use of postcodes to locate household types, e.g. ACORN (A Classification Of Residential Neighbourhoods).

Customer responses

Headings under this category are more likely to explain what customers buy and why they buy. Ideally, at least one or more of these categories should be combined with one or more of the customer characteristics categories.

1 *Benefit*

The reason people buy a service is to acquire a benefit. This begins to explain why people buy what they buy.

> **By identifying segments which each seek a common benefit, the service company can tailor its offer in a way that gains high levels of acceptance.**

While on the surface there can be numerous types of benefits sought by customers, in practice they distil down to meeting a few basic needs. For example, in consumer service markets, will the service:

- save money
- make life easier/healthier/safer
- make the customers more attractive in some way
- provide prestige/status/novelty
- enable customers to realize ambitions/dreams?

> **By recognizing the benefits sought, and designing the service to provide these in a quicker or superior way, the company can develop a competitive advantage in each market segment.**

2 *Usage*

Here, customers are often divided into heavy, medium, and occasional users of the service (sometimes it can be useful to analyse non-users as well). Also, it is useful to list details of what is bought and for what purpose it is used. By focusing on the usage patterns of particular services, the company can identify ways to reinforce relationships with existing heavy users and to devise strategies for converting lesser users into bigger ones. Using this type of approach, airlines have competed for the frequent business traveller by providing all sorts of inducements in addition to the basic travel facility. Similarly, hotel chains often reward high-frequency users with special privileges or discounts.

> Usage segmentation, however, might prove to be unreliable in terms of predicting future trends, for there is no reason for past patterns to be repeated.

3 *Promotional response*

This considers how customers respond to various types of promotional activity, such as, for example, advertising, exhibitions, in-store displays, sales promotions, and direct mail.

> By understanding in more detail the relationship between promotional activity and customer preferences and subsequent buying patterns, the service company can become very sophisticated at exploiting its position in each market segment.

4 *Loyalty*

Customers can be characterized by their degree of loyalty: 'hard-core loyals' (who buy from the company all the time); 'soft-core loyals' (who are loyal most of the time); 'shifting loyals' (who will shift between the company and another competitor); and 'switchers' (who show little loyalty towards any supplier or service).

For this type of segmentation to be of use, the company needs to know the reasons for these different behaviour patterns.

> A misconception which can be engendered by this approach is to assume that loyalty equates to customer satisfaction.

This is certainly not always the case. For example, despite numerous criticisms about banks, about 75 per cent of customers remain with the same bank all their adult lives.

5 *Service*

This approach is based on considering the service surround that accompanies the service product. By measuring the importance that particular customer groups attach to various elements of service, it can sometimes become possible to use this as a basis for segmentation. For example, one segment might be attracted by after-sales service, another by the convenience of ordering. Similarly, some customers might prefer to deal with highly technical sales representatives, whereas others are happier faced with far less qualified staff.

Differentiating the service 'package' for each market segment can be more cost effective than offering an 'across the board' level of service for all segments.

In addition, the detailed knowledge about the value of service elements to various customer groups, which is inherent in this approach, can assist the company to achieve a competitive advantage based upon its service provision.

In practice, a sophisticated services company will rarely use one of these methods in isolation, as the end result is one-dimensional and may not to provide any special insights. More creative definitions of market segments can be established by using some of these approaches in combination.

A good example of creative segmentation is that undertaken by SAS (Scandinavian Airline Service). SAS was able to compete successfully with larger competitors by focusing on the market segment of the business traveller. By identifying the specific needs of this group, it was able to provide the services and benefits that business executives sought. This meant tailoring a complex package, which included reservations, ticketing, check-in facilities, choice of aircraft, cabin services, schedules, routes, pricing, and a reputation for punctuality. By specializing in this way, SAS became a highly profitable company, whereas its lack of size and its small domestic population base would have seriously inhibited its chances of success in the airline business in general. Unfortunately for SAS, many of these elements have now been copied by other airlines who are seeking these profitable business travellers.

The importance of getting the segmentation correct cannot be over-emphasized, for it is at the very heart of market success.

The segmentation *process* follows four broad stages:

1 *Define the market to be addressed*

   Market definition involves specifying the customer group (or groups) to which the company is seeking to market its services. Choice of a market to be addressed involves a consideration of the following:

   - Types of customers to be serviced
   - Geographic scope
   - Breadth of services to be provided
   - Decisions regarding single or multisite distribution
   - Areas of the value-added chain in which the service organization decides to be involved.

   A well-formulated mission statement should go some way towards defining the market. If it does not, then the following examples should illustrate what is required: an investment bank decides to focus on individuals with personal assets exceeding one million pounds; a hotel chain focuses on the conference market; a restaurant might concentrate on family customers; etc. Whatever the market definition chosen, it must be realistic and reachable.

2 *Identify alternative bases for segmentation*

   The previous discussion of the segmentation bases in Figure 4.2 covers many of the more common forms of segmentation, but there will be many other valid bases for specific specialized services. The criteria for segmentation might be different if the service company is supplying other companies, or offering a personal service to individuals, since in the former, more people become involved in the buying decision and thus make it susceptible to different pressures and priorities.

3 *Choose the method of segmentation which gives the company a distinctive advantage*

   This stage involves an evaluation and prioritization of the alternative bases of segmentation in order to identify the best approach. This stage is closely linked with the next one, as each segmentation base is broken down into appropriate individual market segments. This categorization of segments may be, in the case of segments based on geography or age, relatively simple and involve an analysis of the service organization's demand patterns. However, in the case of segmentation variables such as psychographics, a major market research study may need to be undertaken.

4 *Identify individual market segments and assess their attractiveness*

   In this stage the individual market segments to be targeted with a distinctive service offered should be identified. The criteria service organizations use to determine these segments need to be defined by themselves but will typically include:

- Size
- Profit potential
- Responsiveness to marketing effort
- Durability
- Competitive threat.

The resulting market segments should be capable of description which clearly separates them from each other. They should also be large enough in size to make it worthwhile for the company to invest its resources.

The company should not attempt to tackle too many segments, because if it tries to be too many things to too many customers, its resources will become stretched and it will also lose the opportunity of becoming recognized for particular distinctive competences.

Having established the best way of segmenting the market (or confirming that the current method is the best), it now becomes necessary to seek answers to the questions shown in Figure 4.3.

The thrust of all of these questions is to get a quantitative and qualitative picture of the position in each market segment regarding its size, future prospects, level of competition and our own company's standing. Taken together, this type of information can help to identify the company's competitive position and what it needs to do to adapt to the changing market.

For readers needing a more in-depth treatment of market segmentation as a process, see McDonald[1] and Weinstein.[2]

- What is the size of the market for each segment we have defined? (Value)
- What share of these do we have? (In volume or value terms)
- What are the growth prospects of each segment?
- How many customers fall within each segment?
- How many of these are current customers?
- With how many of these are we regularly in contact?
- How many customers have we lost, by segment?
- What were the reasons?
- Who are our main domestic competitors?
- Who are our main foreign competitors?
- Do they define their markets in the same way as ourselves?
- What has been happening to their market shares over recent years?
- How have we fared in comparison with these competitors?
- What factors are likely to threaten customers (and therefore these markets)?
- What is the likelihood of these threats materializing?
- Are there cyclical patterns to these markets?
- What might we do to counteract peaks and troughs in service demand?
- How are we perceived in the market?
- What special strengths/expertise do we offer?

Figure 4.3 Key questions to consider in determining market segments

Sub-audit 2   Competitive position

> In any market segment, there are likely to be one or two critical factors which are the key to success, when looked at from the customer's viewpoint.

There is empirical evidence that 20 per cent of any given population can account for 80 per cent of a result (Pareto's Law). In the same way, just as 20 per cent of customers can realize 80 per cent of the sales revenue, or 20 per cent of the possible causes can be responsible for 80 per cent of the total rejects, then just 20 per cent of the possible factors can account for 80 per cent of customer satisfaction.

For example, in the fast food restaurant business, although customers might seek a wide range of things, their overall satisfaction level can be attributed to just a few. These are called the critical success factors. Let us suppose that research showed these to be:

1 Served quickly   (30 per cent)
2 Always a seat   (30 per cent)
3 Clean surroundings   (25 per cent)
4 Reasonable choice   (15 per cent)

Market research should be used to establish customer preferences

It would also be possible to establish by research the relative importance of these factors, as shown by the figures in the brackets above. This means that these customers pay high regard to being served quickly and being able to find a seat. Cleanliness is not quite as important, and having a choice is lower still in their scale of priorities. With this information available, it becomes possible to make a comparison with the main competitors and establish the restaurant's relative strengths and weaknesses, as shown in Table 4.1.

The first column of figures in Table 4.1, represent raw scores out of 100, which reflect the extent to which the various fast food restaurants comply with the listed critical success factors. This shows that, when it comes to speed of service, our company scores 80, which is better than the scores of 70 and 60 of the competitors. However, in terms of seating, our company scores the lowest.

Table 4.1 Example of competitive advantage calculation

	Our company		Competitor A	Competitor B
Served quickly	(.3) × 80 = 24		70 = 21	60 = 18
Always a seat	(.3) × 50 = 15		80 = 24	90 = 27
Cleanliness	(.25) × 90 = 22.5		70 = 17.5	80 = 20
Reasonable choice	(.15) × 90 = 13.5		60 = 9	60 = 9
TOTALS	1.00	75.0	71.5	74.0

The raw scores are multiplied by the weighting factors established earlier. By adding the adjusted scores, it is possible to arrive at a total which reflects the overall competitiveness. In the example, it shows that our company leads the field, with company B second. This type of analysis also discloses other useful information:

- **The seating arrangements must be improved in our company.**
- **The speed of service can also be further improved.**
- **Too much choice is being offered (hence slowing service and perhaps increasing costs).**

This example has obviously been made simple to illustrate the point, yet the principles behind it can be translated into any type of business.

> **As companies find themselves in increasingly fierce trading conditions, it becomes ever more important to be clear about competitive strengths and weaknesses.**

Great attention should be paid to completing SWOT analyses
We should stress here that this process, which effectively constitutes part of the strengths and weaknesses (SW) analysis of the SWOT (discussed later in this chapter), is fundamental to the setting of marketing objectives and strategies, so great attention should be paid to this process.

Competitors will have already featured in analyses of the service's competitive advantage and possible positioning. In fact, like marketing planning itself, all the components considered at the audit stage are interrelated. For example, it is very difficult to consider the service product without connecting it to organizational strengths and weaknesses, competitor activity and the state of the environment at large. Nonetheless it is worthwhile, at least initially, considering the various sub-audits separately in order to bring discipline to the overall marketing audit.

The information which is most valuable in terms of the competitor audit is that which concerns the company's major rivals. To attempt to find out about every competitor would clearly be too costly and time-consuming. What is of particular interest will be knowledge about their:

- Goals and objectives
- Marketplace behaviour
- Market share
- Growth

- Service quality
- Positioning
- Operations and resources
- Marketing mix strategies.

Without being unethical in any way, much of this information can be gathered from competitors' publicity materials and annual reports, from analysing their communications strategy, from talking to their customers, studying their exhibition stands, carrying out specific market research studies, and so on. Indeed, much of the analysis described earlier in the section on the service audit could not be accomplished without access to pertinent information regarding competitor activity.

Each competitor's service offer and organization has to be put under close scrutiny in much the same way, and with equal rigour, as the company examines its own services, strategies and capabilities. To know about one's competitors is to be prepared.

The area of competition analysis, as a formal area of study, has developed greatly in the past decade.[3–5]

By carrying out the competitor audit thoroughly, the company can be proactive about the future, rather than being reactive and running the risk of finding itself beaten by the opposition.

Let us now look at the third aspect of the marketing audit.

Sub-audit 3 The environmental audit

While customers rightly occupy much of the attention of the external audit, there are other external factors which can also impact on the service company and, therefore, need to be taken into account. This is the purpose of the environmental audit.

At first sight, scanning the outside world is a daunting task for the marketer, as there is so much to consider that can have a potential influence on the organization's future success. However, it is essential to approach this audit in a fairly pragmatic way and look at only the most critical factors which can affect the business. There are two frameworks which can help with the task of focusing on these critical factors which we will now examine.

Some of the areas for consideration are highlighted by the work of Porter[6] who has identified five areas which will have significant impact on the company's profitability (see Figure 4.4). These are:

1   The success with which the company is *jockeying for position among current rivals*. This means that not only must the service company be aware of its own position, it must also understand its rivals' ambitions and strategies.

2   The environment must also be viewed from the perspective of *identifying new players*, perhaps foreign companies who are looking to expand, or cash-rich firms who are seeking to diversify into our field.
3   *New technology or substitute services* might also pose a threat or an opportunity to the company and should be reviewed on a regular basis.
4   *The power of buyers* might be increasing or decreasing and it is important for the company to understand what forces are at play for this to be happening.
5   Equally, the *power of suppliers* might be shifting in a way that is increasingly helpful or unhelpful to the company's ambitions. Again, the underlying environmental factors that cause this to be happening must be understood.

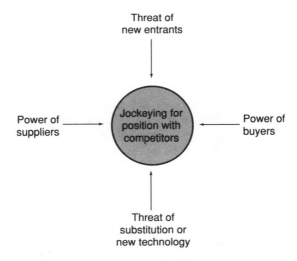

Figure 4.4 Strategic forces impacting on service organizations (*Source*: Based on Porter, M. (1980) *Competitive Strategy*, The Free Press, New York)

A detailed audit of these five forces will help to understand the prospect for future profitability of the service organization.

Another model which provides guidance is one that is discussed in Chapter 1, which described six market domains. These were:

- Customer markets (discussed above in Sub-Audit 1)
- Referral markets
- Influence markets
- Recruitment markets
- Supplier markets
- Internal markets (this will be addressed in the organizational audit).

It clearly makes sense for the service company to appraise its position within these markets, to be aware of trends within them, and to decide whether or not it could benefit from changing the way it relates with them.

Finally, the environmental audit should address some of the political/social/legal/economic factors that will have a significant influence on the business. For example, will government fiscal policy have an undue detrimental effect on the business? Are there legal changes or tax incentives which will make it more attractive for customers to buy? Will currency exchange rates work for or against the company? There are clearly a number of questions of this nature which have to be asked – and answered.

We recommend that the environmental issues that need to be addressed should be specified in sufficient detail by each area to ensure that only relevant data and information are collected.

There is sometimes a blinkered approach adopted by service organizations with respect to the environmental audit. There is a naive belief that external factors will affect all competitors equally and that, somehow, the status quo will be maintained. This is patently not true and companies that adopt such a posture may find themselves overtaken by their smarter and wiser contemporaries.

Environmental audits will be increasingly important in the future. Hamel and Prahalad[7] have argued that future opportunities are to be found in the intersection of changes in technology, logistics, regulation, demographics and geopolitics. They point to the opportunity that TV Channel CNN found for global 24-hour television. This grew out of changes in lifestyle (longer and less predictable working hours), changes in technology (Handicam video cameras and highly portable satellite linkages), and changes in the regulatory environment (licensing and subsequent dramatic growth of cable television companies).

Figure 4.5 suggests that being customer led is necessary but not sufficient in shaping the future plans of service organizations. Service companies in the future will need to look beyond the present articulated needs of current customers and identify services for which there is a future demand but customers cannot yet articulate. Such vision has led to new services such as cellular telephones, 24-hour discount brokerage accounts, hand-held global satellite positioning receivers, automatic telling machines and TV-based home shopping networks.

Sub-audit 4 Auditing the services and products

The services and products currently on offer are generally the things the company knows a lot about. However, sometimes it is possible to

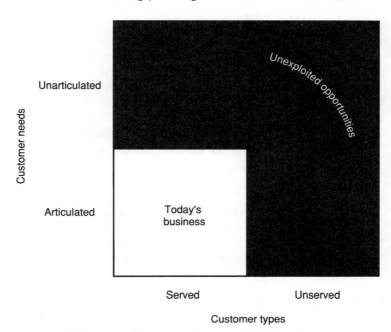

Figure 4.5 Identifying opportunities for service businesses through environmental analysis of the future (*Source:* Based on Hamel, G. and Prahalad, C. K. (1994) *Competing for the Future*, Harvard Business School Press)

be too close to be able to be truly objective about them. Nevertheless, the company must learn to be equally critical about them as it would for all other parts of the marketing audit. In this section we discuss auditing the organization's services and products and look at some tools, including positioning and life cycle analysis, that are useful in undertaking this sub-audit.

Most organizations offer more than one service. Sometimes, these are variations on a theme, as when a restaurant offers a take-away service, outside catering, and special functions, in addition to its normal provision. Equally, the company might offer distinctly different services, as with a leisure group which is involved in hotels, cinemas, golf complexes and airlines. Each service might come under attack from the same competitors, or there might be a range of different competitors who challenge each service. It is increasingly rare for a service organization to be in the position of a monopoly supplier, because services are relatively easy to duplicate, and they cannot be specified and patented in the same way as a product. Many former service monopolies are now subject to competition from new entrants.

How differentiated is the service product?

It has long been recognized that, when selling a service, the notion of a 'unique selling proposition' can give the sales person a compelling advantage over competitors.

> **However, the USP (as it is called in its abbreviated form) can only exist if the service's unique features can translate into unique benefits.**

Therefore, one of the main purposes of the service product audit is to analyse the relative strengths and weaknesses of the company's range of services in comparison with those offered by competitors and help identify points of differential advantage.

Benefits, features and advantages

Sometimes, there is confusion about the difference between features, advantages and benefits, even among sales staff. In order to clarify this, it should be remembered that features are the physical characteristics of the service. For example, in the case of a hotel, these might be:

- High quality accommodation
- French cuisine
- Tennis and golf available
- Trained staff to look after children
- Friendly and informal atmosphere
- Above-average prices.

An advantage is what the service does. For example, high-quality accommodation provides luxuries similar to those in your own home.

A benefit is what the feature provides for the customer *that he or she seeks*. Thus, features and advantages can exist without customers, benefits never can. How a feature translates into an advantage can be illustrated thus:

Feature (what it is)	*Advantages* (what it does)
tennis and golf available	• You can unwind
	• You can keep fit
	• You can improve your game

However, even in this example, there are the seeds of a problem. Suppose some guests arrived at a hotel with the express notion of leaving the children and improving their golf, only to find that the course was filled with amateurs, with little experience, whose objective was to unwind. The former, quite naturally, would be very disappointed. This illustrates that, without knowing a lot about the *benefits* required by customers (from the customer audit), it can be difficult to make a sensible appraisal of the service product.

From what we have said, it is clear that a service organization needs to be able to identify the degree of differentiation of their services when compared with those of their competitors. It is also essential to understand whether these differences match the benefits required by the target segments.

In Figure 4.6 a competitor's service product is shown to be matched by ours in every respect (the shaded areas). Yet, our company offers some added features which differentiate the service and provide unique selling propositions. These, however, are not necessarily benefits unless they appeal specifically to certain groups of customers.

Of course, with such a comparison, one could equally be disadvantaged when a competing service possesses features that ours does not have. In these circumstances, it would make good sense to try to make the lesser service more competitive by developing these added features, or something even better.

Whilst it is a useful starting point to identify the differential features and advantages, we need to adopt a more systematic approach to benchmarking our products and those of our competitors, as shown in Figure 4.7.

Figure 4.7 shows a comparison for a computer software company between their services and those of a competitor scored over a number of features, on a 0–10 scale. We can see that in terms of fees, Competitor B charges more. Both of them provide relatively little disruption to existing work practices, but A provides better training than Competitor B. By contrast, they underperform when it comes to back-up services and reputation for quality.

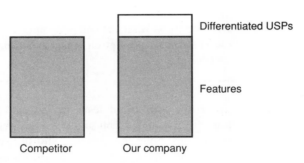

Figure 4.6 Comparison of service features

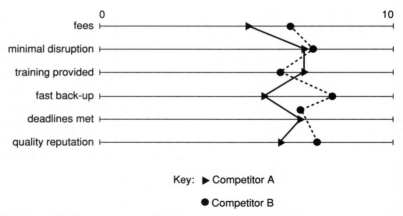

Key: ▶ Competitor A

● Competitor B

Figure 4.7 Example of comparative analysis – a software company

From an analysis like this, it becomes possible to see where a service product performs better or lags behind those against which it is competing. This should be considered not only on aggregate, but also the feature's relative importance within different market segments should be reviewed.

> It is a relatively small step from this type of diagnosis to setting 'benchmarks', or standards, which represent the best practice in each area, thereby measuring the service product against the highest possible relevant standards, not just those of the nearest competitor.

Many service companies are now adopting this type of approach in order to become more competitive.

Service product positioning

> Irrespective of what the company puts into its service product, it is the customer's perception which determines whether or not it is successful.

After all, with 'blind tests' on products, customers often cannot tell the difference between brand X and brand Y. Restore the original brand names, however, and it is another story. Such is the power of branding and the image and expectations it conveys. Because services are intangible, perceptions become ever more important.

Positioning can be based on objective or subjective criteria

It is possible to develop and communicate a differential advantage that makes the organization's service superior and distinctive in the perception of target customers. This is known as positioning. This differentiation can be based on objective criteria (which are fact-based) or subjective criteria (which are more concerned with image and communications).

Every service has the potential for being perceived as different by the customer, because buyers have different needs and are therefore attracted to different offers. The service organization should be keen to discover what differences it can offer which meet the following criteria:[8]

• *Importance*	The difference is highly valued by a sufficiently large or attractive market.
• *Distinctiveness*	The difference is distinctly superior to other services which are available.
• *Communicable*	It is possible to communicate the difference in a simple and strong way.
• *Superiority*	The difference cannot be easily copied by competitors.
• *Affordability*	Target customers will be willing to pay for this difference, i.e. it represents value to them.
• *Profitability*	The service company will achieve additional profits as a result of introducing the difference.

A service company wishing to reappraise its positioning (which already exists in the customers' minds, *even if* it is not the company's intention) should determine which attributes and differences to promote to its target customers. Some marketers advocate promoting a single benefit and striving to gain recognition as leader for that particular attribute. Others recommend that promoting more than one benefit will help to carve out a special niche which can be less easily contested by competitors. Whatever the choice, a successful positioning strategy must take into account existing customers' perceptions of competing market offerings. From this starting point, the company determines the attributes which customers value, but which are not being met by other services. It can then develop and promote these particular aspects of the services it offers. By adopting this approach, it follows that the service organization may have a different positioning strategy for each service and market segment.

While the main emphasis of this chapter is on the positioning of the *goods and services* delivered by the service organization, it must be remembered that positioning can be considered at several levels:

- *Industry positioning,* which seeks to improve customer perception of a service industry as a whole
- *Organizational positioning,* which seeks to position the organization as a whole
- *Product sector positioning,* which seeks to position a range of related products and services being offered by the service company
- *Individual product or service positioning,* which addresses the positioning of specific services.

There should obviously be integration between these levels where companies are positioning at more than one level. Companies need not necessarily be concerned with all of these levels of positioning, just those which hold the prospect of giving it some commercial advantage. It is also advantageous to monitor what major competitors are doing, because shifts in their positioning strategy might require some level of response.

Figure 4.8 illustrates the levels of positioning which might be considered by a bank. In many ways the services and the service sector levels of one bank are very much like those of another, making it important to try and establish superior and differentiated positioning. For this reason, in recent years there have been considerable efforts made at the organizational positioning level, leading to a considerable proportion of total advertising spend being channelled into corporate advertising.

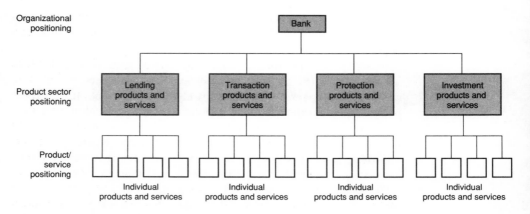

Figure 4.8 Example of levels of positioning for a bank

The process of positioning

Service positioning involves five action steps:

> 1 Determining levels of positioning
> 2 Identifying the key attributes which impact on selected segments
> 3 Locating these attributes on a positioning map
> 4 Evaluating other positioning options
> 5 Implementing the new positioning strategy.

It will be useful to look at each of these steps in more detail.

1 Determining levels of positioning

Often, the level (or levels) of positioning required is fairly self-evident, because it needs to be consistent with the organization's strategy for succeeding in a given market segment. If the service itself has a strong image or brand, it makes good sense to promote this continually. Conversely, the service might be more of a 'me-too' offer. In this latter case, organizational positioning can be a key strategy for success.

Positioning at a product sector level was recently introduced by the Forte Hotel Group. It chose to reposition its Crest Hotels as the 'definitive hotel for business'. To avoid confusion in its customers' minds, its Post House Hotels, for example, were promoted with lower room rates and generally positioned to make them more attractive to the mid-market.

2 Identifying the key attributes

In order to identify the key attributes, it is important to focus on specific market segments and, in particular, on how the purchasing decisions are made. A consideration of the decision-making unit can also help identify key attributes.

Usually, research is carried out to identify the salient attributes and specific benefits required by a target market segment. What must be remembered is that customers make their purchase decision on the basis of *perceived* differences between competing offers. In themselves, what customers look for might not be the most important attributes as perceived by the service company. So, for example, customers' perceptions of a restaurant might rely more on how they are treated by the waiters than on the quality of the meal they are served. Similarly, the decision to invest in a private pension might owe more to the behaviour of the salesperson than to the investment record of the pension fund.

A range of techniques is available to the researcher charged with identifying key attributes. Most of these are computer-based and include perceptual mapping, factor analysis, discriminant function analysis, multiple correlation and regression analysis, and trade-off and conjoint analysis. However, these rather specialized techniques are in the province of the researcher rather than the marketing manager. For that reason, it is not our intention to elaborate on them here.[9]

3 Locating attributes on a positioning map

Usually, two dimensions are used on positioning maps and these are chosen to reflect key customer preferences. Thus, for example, if for a given service these attributes were price and quality, it would be possible to construct a map as shown in Figure 4.9. On such a positioning map, it then becomes possible to plot the various competing services. Of course, in order to plot them accurately, it means that the two axes are graduated in suitable scales. With such data available in this form, it can be seen at a glance how the various services compare. For example, companies E and H offer a service at a similar price, but the latter provides a much higher level of quality. Similarly, companies H and G provide almost identical quality, but G is far more expensive.

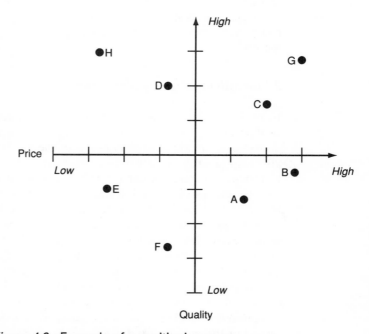

Figure 4.9 Example of a positioning map

Positioning maps can be based on either objective or subjective attributes, or on some combination of the two. For example, a pensions company developed a map which had an objective axis ('proportion of investments used to cover administration'), and a subjective axis ('friendly and courteous service').

In addition to allowing comparisons to be made, such maps can also indicate the area of core demand, which in Figure 4.9 would be the top left-hand quadrant, i.e. high quality/low price – the most attractive combination for customers. Knowing the core demand area enables the company to devise how it can best reposition any of its services which fall outside it. The repositioning task might require a significant communications and advertising campaign being used to alert customers to the changes which are taking place.

Sometimes, the area of core demand is not quite as obvious as in the example above. An example of this might be where there are different subgroups with different preferences. In these circumstances, further analysis is required and a technique known as cluster analysis can be used to identify groups with similar interests. From this, it becomes possible to identify the positioning dimensions which are significant to different market segments.

4 Evaluating positioning options

There are three broad options:

(a) *Strengthening current position against competitors*
Ideally, this is done in a way which avoids a head-on attack. A classic example of this was the campaign of Avis car rental, who created a positive benefit from being number two behind market leaders Hertz. 'Avis is only No. 2, so why go with us? We try harder!' they proclaimed. Not only was this seen as truthful, it also appealed to people's natural sympathy for the underdog.

(b) *Identifying an unoccupied position on the map*
This option seeks to find a gap in the market. Using this approach, Virgin Airlines established a foothold in the business passengers market with its 'upper class' in a UK market dominated by British Airways. By striving to provide better all-round service to customers in this segment, this small airline has developed an intensively loyal and growing group of 'advocates'.

(c) *Repositioning the competition*
In the 1992 General Election in the UK, the Conservative Party was under considerable pressure because it was being seen as the party responsible for creating unemployment and dismantling the National Health Service. For its part, the Labour Party claimed that it would invest in manufacturing, the infrastructure and save the Health Service, all policies with high

voter appeal. However, the Conservatives managed to reposition the Labour Party from being investors to being money raisers, i.e. the 'party which stands for high taxation'. This message was repeated with regularity and in no small way helped to reverse what was, according to opinion polls, a potential lost cause.

Regardless of which positioning option is chosen, in order to enhance or sustain a position the following guidelines[10] should be observed:

- *The positioning should be meaningful* for the target market segment.
- *The positioning must be believable.* Outrageous claims to be the biggest, or the best, which are clearly untrue will prove to be counterproductive.
- *The positioning must be unique.* Companies must find a positioning where they can consistently perform better than their competitors in a given market.

Figure 4.10 illustrates ways in which uniqueness might be converted into positioning.

Market share leader	the biggest
Quality leader	the most reliable products/services
Service leader	the most responsive, e.g. handling problems
Technology leader	the pathfinder/first to break new ground
Innovation leader	the most creative
Flexibility leader	the most adaptable
Relationship leader	the most committed
Prestige leader	the most exclusive
Knowledge leader	the best functional/technical expertise
Global leader	the best positioned for world markets
Bargain leader	the lowest price
Value leader	the best price utility

Figure 4.10 Examples of positioning strategies (*Source*: Based on Kosnik, T. J. (1989) *Corporate Positioning*, Harvard Business School, Note 9-589-087, p. 13)

5 Implementing positioning

The new or reinforced positioning strategy needs to be communicated in all implicit and explicit interactions with target customers. This involves the service company, its staff, its policies and image all conveying a consistent message which reflects the desired positioning.

This has to carry through in all of the tactical marketing and sales activities.

So, for example, for British Airways to truly be 'the world's favourite airline', all of its staff had to refocus on how they viewed the passengers. Staff had to actually care about the customer and, in turn, the airline itself had to demonstrate a caring attitude towards its employees. Its much publicized 'Putting the Customer First' campaign was an integral part of a coordinated internal and external marketing strategy.

> **It must never be forgotten that, like the service itself, a positioning strategy may have a limited life-span. This means that it should be examined from time to time to ensure that it has not become outdated and that it is still relevant to its target markets.**

Because it permits market opportunities to be identified by considering positions which are not met by competitors' services, positioning helps to influence the improvement and redesign of existing offers and the development of new services. It also allows consideration of competitors' possible moves and responses, thereby providing a further input to strategy formulation.

> **Above all, positioning involves giving the target market segment the reason for buying your services, which is clearly the whole purpose of marketing.**

The concept of life cycles

Another key marketing diagnostic tool, which is extremely useful for the purpose of determining appropriate marketing objectives and strategies for the services of an organization, is life cycle analysis. Historians of technology have observed that many technical functions grow exponentially until they come up against some natural limiting factor, which causes growth to slow down and eventually decline, as one technology is replaced by another. There is empirical evidence which shows that this same phenomenon also applies to products and services.

By plotting the sales of a service over time, the life cycle curve, shown in Figure 4.11, can be established.

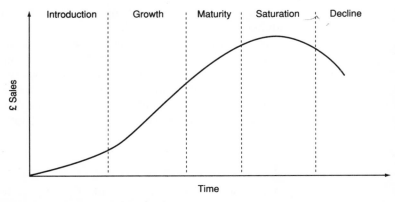

Figure 4.11 The life cycle curve

This curve is characterized by five different phases:

1	*Introduction*	Here, there is a slow growth in sales as the new service struggles to get known and accepted.
2	*Growth*	If the service is successful, its sales take off as repeat purchases are made and customers become aware of it. Not all new services survive long enough to reach this phase. Moreover, the growth potential attracts other companies into this field and so competition also increases.
3	*Maturity*	Since all markets are finite, the rapid growth rate of the earlier phase begins to slow down.
4	*Saturation*	The rate of sales growth eventually levels out. Generally, there are too many firms competing for too little business at this stage. As a result, price wars may break out and there are casualties, or tactical withdrawals, among the competitive companies.
5	*Decline*	Finally, the market itself falls into decline.

These phases in the life cycle concept suggest that if a product or service is introduced to the market successfully, then the momentum of buying will increase over time. Consumers will try the product or service and will then often repeat their purchase decision. They will also pass on information about the product to others who, in turn, will test the product. However, the market will eventually reach its peak. As the market matures, there are many firms in the marketplace and price wars are common as competition develops for market share. Eventually, some firms will be forced out of the market, with the most competitive ones surviving. The market will gradually decline as alternative products are offered and fashions change. The market may be sustained for a small volume, with few producers, though this will often be difficult as economies of scale can be lost.

It is possible to extend the life cycle by taking tactical actions to combat falling sales such as reducing prices, promoting harder, etc., and also by strategic actions which fundamentally reposition the usage of the service. The 'no frills' airline services in the USA, which have become a viable alternative to motor car travel, are a good example of this.

Life cycle analysis can be a useful diagnostic tool
The life cycle has been much written about in marketing literature during the last three decades and, from the management viewpoint, can focus attention on likely future sales patterns if no corrective actions are taken. More importantly, the various life phases carry with them implications for changes in the way the service is promoted and priced. Indeed, all aspects of the marketing mix need to be adapted over the life of a service. We shall examine, in Chapter 5, how the marketing strategy for a service should be largely determined by its position in its life cycle.

An understanding of life cycles of *services businesses* (as well as their services) is also important. The study of life cycles in services, in this regard, has been relatively limited to date. However, one study of multisite service firms' life cycles identified five stages, as follows:[11]

> 1 *Entrepreneurial stage*: where an innovator offers a service at a limited (often one) number of locations.
> 2 *Multisite rationalization*: where successful service entrepreneurs add a limited number of locations.
> 3 *Growth*: where a period of rapid expansion occurs, often through the purchase of competitors or franchising or licensing arrangements.
> 4 *Maturity*: where the rate of growth is reduced through factors such as changing demographics, increased competition, or changing customer tastes.
> 5 *Decline/regeneration*: where either successful extension of the service concept occurs, or the service firm enters a stage of decline and degeneration.

The concept of life cycles is useful, but it should be remembered that products or services do not always follow this idealized pattern. The life cycle concept is helpful as a descriptive model in trying to understand the dynamics of markets. However, it has less value as a predictive model.

In considering life cycles, we also need to differentiate between the service category, the service subcategory and the service brand. For example, if we take the overnight accommodation market (a service category) it may have a considerably different life from that of business hotels, or motels (a service subcategory). Individual brands, e.g. Stakis Country Club Hotels (a service brand), within a category may also exhibit their own individual life cycle behaviour.

The stage where the service firm is at in its life cycle needs to be considered carefully and the firm should be aware of different issues and problems it may encounter during the different life cycle stages. This process can focus attention on future sales patterns and will have a bearing on the key elements to be emphasized within the marketing mix.

Portfolio of services

While it is quite feasible for a company to operate with a single service (in fact, most new firms start in this way), the life cycle concept suggests that in the long term innovation is necessary for services which are in decline. Again, the life cycle curve can provide useful guidance about the best times to introduce (and remove) services from the company's 'portfolio'. If this is done astutely, then the company can meet its objectives by balancing sales growth, cash flow and risk across its range of services (Figure 4.12).

> It is, therefore, essential, that the portfolio of services is reviewed 'regularly' and that the strategic implications of adding, deleting or promoting existing services are considered in their totality.

How this is done will be covered in detail in the next chapter, since it is central to the setting of marketing objectives and formulating the best strategies to meet them.

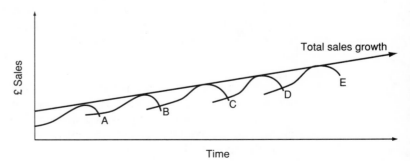

Figure 4.12 How successive services can add to sales growth

Sub-audit 5 The organizational audit

Most organizations are not equally strong in all parts of their business. The sales force might be second-to-none in some areas, yet the company may fall down in others. The company might be great at coming up with new ideas for services, yet be slow to exploit them.

> **The organizational audit sets out to take stock of the company's strengths and weaknesses in terms of how they influence current operations and how they might help or hinder future growth.**

The purpose of an organizational audit is to focus on those aspects of organizational performance that have a positive or a negative effect on business performance. There are several areas that should be considered:

Skills

- What skills does the company have?
- How do these compare with competitors?
- What do they best equip the company for?
- What essential skills are lacking or under-represented?
- What will happen if this skill shortage is not made good?
- If the company heads in a new direction, to what extent will the current skill base be a limiting factor?
- At what organizational level are essential skills in short supply – e.g. strategic, managerial, operational?

There are many questions of this nature which can be asked. In turn, they might focus attention upon the company's recruitment policy and its manpower, training and development.

Resources

In addition to people, how adequate are the resources of the service organization? A number of questions might be asked which, in turn, reflect on past, present and future investment policy. Indeed, resources such as the working conditions could have a direct bearing on the company's capacity to recruit the right kind of people. Equally, the availability of the right data processing systems and equipment can greatly facilitate the availability of data and information into the planning processing.

Systems and procedures

In preparing for marketing planning, the adequacy of their company's management and marketing information systems needs to be evaluated. In addition, there are a number of other procedural issues which could have an impact on business success. For example:

- How are sales leads generated?
- How are they followed up?
- How is the service delivered?
- How are queries and complaints handled?
- How is advertising evaluated?
- How is customer service managed?
- How are new services developed?
- How is lost business analysed and evaluated?

Again, this list will be very much longer for some service organizations. The overriding concern should be to evaluate all such relevant systems and procedures and to identify ways of making them more effective in the context of the company's overall performance.

Roles and relationships

Often organizational problems occur, not because of any of the things listed above, but because people are unclear about the role they are expected to play and how they relate to others. For example, customer contact staff might be unaware of company policy regarding how they should treat customers. Alternatively, interdepartmental rivalry inside the company might get in the way of delivering the best possible service.

> **Equally, an over-reliance on written rules and job descriptions can lead to the organization getting bogged down in bureaucratic 'red tape' and a lack of people empowered to solve customer problems.**

The marketing audit – conclusions

These, then, are some of the issues which have to be addressed in the marketing audit. To find answers to the external factors might result in the company using external market researchers. In some cases, the professionalism and unbiased viewpoint they bring ensures that the information they provide is superior to what might be gathered by the company's own staff.

When a marketing audit is undertaken by internal staff it is useful to have some guidelines, by way of example, to guide the audit process. By way of providing an example, a fairly comprehensive marketing audit checklist is shown in Figure 4.13.

Different service organizations from different service sectors will need to develop different guidelines and checklists appropriate to their own businesses. A list of key audit questions developed by an accounting firm is provided in Figure 4.14, as a contrast to the more general list in Figure 4.13.

Those wishing to review more detailed checklists are referred to Wilson[12]. Those interested in reading further on the marketing audit process should see McDonald and Leppard[13] and Naylor and Wood.[14]

When the marketing audit is completed, it is possible to move on to the next stage of the planning process.

Step 4 The SWOT analysis

The SWOT analysis is one of the most criticial stages in marketing planning

If the previous stage could be likened to providing all the pieces of a jig-saw puzzle, the SWOT analysis takes these and tries to make a picture which makes sense to all those within the company.

It must be stressed here that it is *only* the SWOT analysis that actually appears in the strategic marketing plan itself. This section is, therefore, extremely important and should be read in conjunction with Figure 2.6 in Chapter 2.

This analysis should, if possible, contain not more than four or five pages of commentary focusing on key factors only. It should highlight internal differential strengths and weaknesses *vis-à-vis* competitors, together with key external opportunities and threats. A summary of reasons for good and bad performance should be included. It should be interesting to read, be concise, and include only relevant and important information. The analysis should be highly creative, since a fresh and less obvious approach holds a greater prospect of distancing the company from its competitors.

A well-reasoned SWOT analysis provides the basis for setting objectives and strategies.

A summary of the SWOT analysis can be laid out in the traditional manner shown in Figure 4.15. However, it is our view that SWOT analyses performed in this manner, and only for the organization as a whole, are of relatively limited use. To improve the value of SWOT analysis we make several suggestions.

First, the SWOT analysis should be made more productive by extending it as shown in Figure 4.16. This extended form can be developed like a decision tree where each individual element may have several implications ('which means') and each implication may have several recommended actions. It is important to add

---

EXTERNAL (opportunities and threats)

Business and economic environment

Economic	Inflation, unemployment, energy, price, volatility, materials availability, etc.	as they affect your business
Political/fiscal/legal	Nationalization, union legislation, taxation, duty increases, regulatory constraints (e.g. trade practices, advertising, pricing).	as they affect your business
Social/cultural	Education, immigration, emigration, religion, environment, population distribution and dynamics (e.g. age distribution, regional distribution), changes in consumer lifestyles, etc.	as they affect your business
Technological	Application of technology which could profoundly affect the economics of the industry (e.g. methods and systems, availability of substitutes).	as they affect your business
Intracompany	Capital investment, closures, strikes, etc.	as they affect your business

The market

Total market Size, growth, and trends (value, volume).

Market characteristics Developments and trends.
Services: principal services bought; service characteristics.
Prices: price levels and range; terms and conditions of sale; normal trade practices; official regulations, etc.
Distribution: principal method of distribution.
Channels: principal channels; purchasing patterns (e.g. types of services bought, prices paid); purchasing ability; geographical location; profits; needs; tastes; attitudes; decision-makers; bases of purchasing decision; etc.
Communication: principal methods of communication, e.g. sales force, advertising, direct response, exhibitions, public relations.
Industry practices: e.g. trade associations, government bodies, historical attitudes, interfirm comparisons.

Competition *Industry structure*: make-up of companies in the industry, major market standing/reputation; extent of excess capacity; distribution capability; marketing methods; competitive arrangements; extent of diversification into other areas of major companies in the industry; new entrants; mergers; acquisitions; bankruptcies; significant aspects; international links; key strengths and weaknesses.
Industry profitability: financial and non-financial barriers to entry; industry profitability and the relative performance of individual companies; structure of operating costs; investment; effect on return on investment of changes in price; volume; cost of investment; source of industry profits; etc.

Figure 4.13 Marketing audit checklist for services (expanded)

INTERNAL (strengths and weaknesses)

Own company

Sales (total, by geographical location, by industrial type, by customer, by product/service)
Market shares
Profit margins
Marketing procedures
Marketing organization
Sales/marketing control data
Marketing mix variables as follows:

Market research	Exhibitions
Service development	Selling
Service range	Sales aids
Service quality	Point of sale
Unit of sale	Advertising
Stock levels	Sales promotion
Distribution	Public relations
Dealer support	After sales service
Pricing, discounts, credit	Customer service
People	Training
Processes	

Product

Operations and resources

Marketing objectives
Are the marketing objectives clearly stated and consistent with marketing and corporate objectives?
Marketing strategy
What is the strategy for achieving the stated objectives? Are sufficient resources available to achieve these objectives? Are the available resources sufficient and optimally allocated across elements of the marketing mix?
Structure
Are the marketing responsibilities and authorities clearly structured along functional, product, end-user, and territorial lines?
Information system
Is the marketing intelligence system producing accurate, sufficient and timely information about developments in the marketplace?
Is information gathered being used effectively in making marketing decisions?
Planning system
Is the marketing planning system well conceived and effective?
Control system
Do control mechanisms and procedures exist within the group to ensure planned objectives are achieved, e.g. meeting overall objectives?
Functional efficiency
Are internal communications within the group effective?
Interfunctional efficiency
Are there any problems between marketing and other corporate functions?
Is the question of centralized versus decentralized marketing an issue in the service company?
Profitability analysis
Is the profitability performance monitored by service, served markets, etc., to assess where the best profits and biggest costs of the operation are located?
Cost-effectiveness analysis
Do any current marketing activities seem to have excess costs?
Are these valid or could they be reduced?

Figure 4.13 (continued)

1 **Marketplace understanding**
- Have we identified clearly enough the various groups we are aiming to satisfy (e.g. clients, potential clients, business referrers)?
- Do we understand how the marketplace is evolving?
- Have we checked objectively the satisfactions they require?
- Do we know how well our total offering (i.e. the price/image/service package) is currently satisfying their needs?
- Do we know how well competitive firms are satisfying those needs?

2 **The needs of the company**
- Does the practice have a clear statement of business objectives?
- Is there a clear definition of how the marketing activity should contribute to the business objectives of the firm?
- Are practice development responsibilities and activities firm-wide?

3 **The present and future service offering**
- Do the current services match the current needs of the various clients/potential clients?
- Do we know how the current services compare with those of competitors?
- Have we evaluated the product range vs competition recently?
- Is there a process of developing new products and services and are new services delivered on time?

4 **Pricing approach, policy and structure**
- Do we have a systematic approach to reviewing charge-out rates?
- Are our charge-out rates fully up-to-date in the light of inflation, currency fluctuations, etc.?
- Do we have a logical up-to-date charge-out structure?
- Are appropriate fee strategies being used for different markets and/or products/ services?

5 **Client care**
- Do we clearly understand what our current potential customers mean by 'service'?
- How important is 'service' in choosing between firms of accountants?
- Do we develop competitive advantage through our 'service offering'?

6 **Public relations**
- With which target audiences should we be communicating?
- What are the levels of knowledge, attitude and opinion about the practice?
- What do we want them to think and feel about the practice?
- Do we check to see whether the PR activity has caused the desired changes in knowledge, attitude and opinion?

7 **Advertising**
- Are the target audiences specified clearly?
- Are our messages persuasive?
- Is the agency (if used) properly briefed and controlled?
- Is the advertising measured against the communication objectives set for it?

8 **Sales promotion**
- Have 'pressure points' been identified in the market system where sales promotion can be used effectively?
- Have specific promotion goals been set?
- Do the techniques selected match the goals?
- Are the promotions evaluated in terms of the overall mix of objectives?

9 **Personal selling**
- How is the nature of the sales changing?
- Should other methods of contacting the client be considered?
- Do we have effective strategies for gaining and retaining key clients?
- Do partners and fee earners have the appropriate knowledge and skill?
- Are the partners and fee earners appropariately structured, staffed and motivated?

10 **Checking the marketing plan**
- Are the individual practice development activities congruent, integrated and synchronized?
- Is sufficient time, effort and money being spent on evaluation of the effectiveness of practice development activities?
- Do we have a solid basis for planning future promotional action?

11 **Broader implications of the marketing audit**
- Are we auditing early and regularly enough to allow adequate consideration of the key issues, not simply the current problems?
- Do we know how accurately current management perceptions, attitudes and opinions reflect present realities?
- Is the marketing activity inhibited by or inhibiting the effectiveness of the other functions of the organization?

Figure 4.14 Marketing audit questions for an accounting firm (*Source*: Developed for an accounting firm from a list originally used by Marketing Improvements Ltd)

Strengths	Weaknesses
•	•
•	•
•	•
•	•
Opportunities	Threats
•	•
•	•
•	•
•	•
•	

Figure 4.15 Example of the traditional layout for a SWOT analysis

some explanatory notes, where appropriate, to enable the reader to understand the full portent of the analysis.

Second, the SWOT should be undertaken at several levels:

- For the organization as a whole
- For each major market segment
- For each major service or product
- For the competition.

Finally, the value of SWOT analysis can be improved by quantification.

The broad approach for completing the strengths and weaknesses part of the SWOT analysis was described in detail earlier in this chapter and was illustrated in Table 4.1.

One way of calculating which opportunities and threats should appear in the SWOT analysis is to consider them from the point of view of their impact and their likelihood of occurring. Using these criteria, opportunities and threats can be appraised using a 'risk' matrix as illustrated in Figure 4.17.

Even though there may be an element of subjectivity in positioning either threats or opportunities on this matrix, it is clear that those which appear in the top right-hand boxes (or closely adjacent to them) are emphasized in the SWOT analysis.

Step 5 Key assumptions

The previous discussion has stressed the need for fact finding and data gathering to be the foundations upon which the marketing plan is built. However, it is impossible to start with the facts without also starting out with some assumptions. Assumptions establish the basis for objective and strategy setting. Facts and assumptions can become blurred at times, to the extent that one can be mistaken for the other, and it is important to distinguish between them.

SWOT element	Which means	So actions needed are
Strengths		
• Highly qualified personnel	– Better competence, efficiency and professionalism	1 Promote capability to customers 2 Staff retention programme 3 Incentive package for high achievers
• Larger deposit base	– Better cost base – Higher average deposit	1 Leverage our cost base 2 Automate faster to reduce costs further 3 Emphasize upper and middle tier in bank positioning
Weaknesses		
• Low branch management discretion	– Constant time wasting in referring back to head office	1 Develop improved credit scoring at branches 2 Better training and communications equipment 3 Wider delegation to branch managers 4 Approval 'hot line' at head office
• No overseas representation	– Lost business in key areas	1 Urgent feasibility study for Toronto, New York, Los Angeles and Sydney
Opportunities		
• New industrial development	– Increased bank lending in commercial area	1 Recruit new industrial team 2 Initiate industrial development seminar for branch managers 3 Representation on government and industrial bodies
• Exploit customers' financial needs	– More income from investment and taxation advisory services – Attraction of new customers to bank	1 Initiate study of new business opportunities 2 Survey of banks in four designated countries 3 Market research to confirm initial service concepts 4 Introduce new service
Threats		
• Increased competition	– Loss of market share	1 Strengthen marketing department 2 Develop a marketing plan 3 Improve customer service 4 Emphasize 'no hidden charges' 5 More aggressive advertising
• Key staff loss	– Need to counter aggressive poaching by private sector firms	1 Improve pay/conditions 2 Introduce staff satisfaction survey 3 Lobby to move outside civil service pay structure 4 Internal marketing initiative

Figure 4.16 Partial SWOT analysis for a bank

Chances of occurring

		0–25%	26–56%	57–75%	76–100%
	High				
Impact on company	Med				
	Low				

Figure 4.17 Risk analysis matrix for opportunities and threats

It is important to make assumptions explicit

To avoid unstated assumptions being ignored, it is important to state them explicitly. By making them explicit, it becomes possible to check and monitor assumptions to be certain that they are, and remain, valid, and if not, to develop contingency plans to deal with them.

The purpose of the key assumptions step is to identify explicitly those factors which will be critical to the success or failure of the strategic marketing plan. Key assumptions need to be considered in terms of how they impact on the organization as a whole and on each market segment. Since they are an estimate of the future operating conditions of the marketing plan, they may influence not only its formulation, but also its implementation. Key assumptions might include:

- Inflation rates
- Growth of the economy
- Changes in political/legislative framework
- Interest rates
- Demographic predictions.

In order to be systematic, it can be useful to list key assumptions under a number of general headings such as:

- The general economy
- The service 'industry' sector under consideration
- The company's markets
- Competitors
- Internal organizational factors
- Technological and other developments.

> **Key assumptions should be relatively few in number. The acid test is that if the achievement of the marketing plan is possible, irrespective of a particular assumption, then that assumption is unnecessary.**

When they are identified, it is important to consider their implications for the marketing plan.

A two-column approach can be a useful way of presenting this analysis (Figure 4.18). By using this approach not only are the key assumptions brought into the open, but their impact on the marketing plan is also made explicit. This can remove potential sources of disagreement between managers involved in the planning process and can also indicate where contingency plans might need to be developed, should an assumption prove not to be true. Their usefulness is shown when measuring if a marketing plan is achieving its objectives, and if not why not. The assumptions can then be considered and if they are found to be untrue or inaccurate they can be modified, which in turn will lead to further modification within the plan.

Key assumptions	Implications for market plan
1 Price competition will force prices down by 10 per cent across the board	(i) Need to develop USPs (ii) Focus on less price-sensitive segments (iii) Focus on cost reductions

Figure 4.18 Example of approach for analysing key assumptions

Summary

We saw that Phase Two of the planning process consists of three steps: the marketing audit; the SWOT analysis; and key assumptions. Together, they provide an up-to-date situation review. Of these, the marketing audit is the most far-reaching task and, consequently, most of the chapter was devoted to explaining who should do it and what it involved.

Although outside consultants could tackle the audit, we recommended that the company's own managers should be involved in the auditing process, thereby gaining their interest and commitment. The process itself involves five sub-audits and consists of examining the customers, the services, the business environment, the organization and the competitors in order to identify differential advantages and significant trends. Some tools and frameworks useful in the marketing audit process were also explained.

The mass of auditing information is brought sharply into focus by the SWOT analysis, which identifies all the key factors which will affect the planning period.

Finally, we saw that any plan could only be made in the context of some key assumptions. These need to be put in writing, so that there is no misunderstanding among those who have to contribute to, interpret or implement the plan. They should be few in number and have a direct bearing on the conditions under which the plan is elaborated.

References

1 McDonald, M. (1995) *Market Segmentation: A Step-by-Step Process for Identifying Profitable Market Segments*, Macmillan, Basingstoke.
2 Weinstein, A. (1987) *Marketing Segementation*, Probus Publishing Company, Chicago.
3 Fuld, L. M. (1985) *Competitor Intelligence: How to Get It – How to Use It*, Wiley, Chichester.
4 Sammon, W. L., Kurland, M. A. and Spitalnic, R. (1984) *Business Competitor Intelligence*, Ronald Press, New York.
5 Porter, M. (1980) *Competitive Strategy*, The Free Press, New York.
6 *Ibid.*
7 Hamel, G. and Prahalad, C. K. (1994) *Competing for the Future*, Harvard Business School Press.
8 Based on Kotler, P. (1991) *Marketing Management*, Prentice Hall, Englewood Cliffs, NJ. p. 301.
9 For some examples see: Keon, J. W. (1983) Product Positioning: Trinodal Mappings of Brand Images, and Images and Consumer Preference. *Journal of Marketing Research*, **20**, November, 380–92; and Wind, Y. J. (1982) *Product Policy: Concepts, Methods and Strategy*, Addison Wesley, Reading, MA. Chapter 4.
10 Based on: Kosnik, T. (1989) *Corporate Positioning: How to Assess and Build a Company's Reputation*, Harvard Business School, Note 9-589-087.
11 Sasser, W. E., Olsen, R. P. and Wyckoff, D. D. (1978) *Management of Service Operations: Text, Cases and Readings*, Alleyn and Bacon, London. pp. 534–566.
12 Wilson, A. (1982) *Marketing Audit Check Lists*, McGraw-Hill, Maidenhead.
13 McDonald, M. and Leppard, J. (1991) *The Marketing Audit*, Butterworth-Heinemann, Oxford.
14 Naylor, J. and Wood, A. (1978) *Practical Marketing Audits*, Associated Business Programmes, London.

5 Marketing planning Phase Three – marketing strategy formulation

The strategic marketing planning process for services

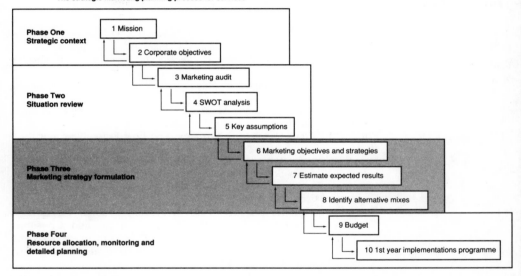

Phase One
Strategic context

1 Mission

2 Corporate objectives

Phase Two
Situation review

3 Marketing audit

4 SWOT analysis

5 Key assumptions

Phase Three
Marketing strategy formulation

6 Marketing objectives and strategies

7 Estimate expected results

8 Identify alternative mixes

Phase Four
Resource allocation, monitoring and detailed planning

9 Budget

10 1st year implementations programme

The situation review should have brought to light most of the key data which enables the marketing strategy formulation phase of the planning process to be undertaken. Even so, it is likely that this next phase will uncover further gaps in the information required if the services organization is to move forward with certainty.

This underlines the point we raised earlier, that the planning process is not as relentlessly linear as the diagram suggests, but is an interactive process, shown by the arrows between the boxes, involving going back to earlier stages from time to time.

The marketing objective and strategy formulation phase of the planning process is, perhaps, the most important of

all. Unless this step is carried out well, everything which
follows will lack focus and cohesion. Not only does it outline
the company's marketing strategy, but it also specifies how
it will be accomplished.

In this chapter, we will look at each of the three planning
steps in Phase Three in more detail, paying particular attention to the area of developing competitive marketing strategies.

Step 6 Marketing objectives and strategies

It is important to be clear from the outset about the difference
between marketing objectives and marketing strategies. Although
these terms are frequently used fairly loosely within companies, we
consider they should be defined more precisely for the purposes of
marketing planning.

- A *marketing objective* is a precise statement which outlines what is
  to be accomplished by the service company's marketing activities.
- A *marketing strategy* is the means by which a marketing objective
  is achieved.

The purpose of setting marketing objectives is to target the profit,
revenue and market share we wish to achieve to satisfy the mission.
In turn, this provides the guidance for marketing strategies to bring
together a marketing mix to achieve the objectives for each segment.

Marketing objectives

With the earlier steps of the planning process behind us, it could
appear that the setting of marketing objectives ought to be com-
paratively straightforward. Unfortunately, this is often not the
case, because companies do not always approach the task in a logical
way. A logical sequence is:

Level 1 *Set broad marketing objectives*
These would be concerned with long-term profitability and be related to the corporate objectives.
By setting broad objectives, communication will be
enhanced and a set of expectations will be engen-
dered among staff.

Level 2 *Set objectives for key result areas*
Here, the objectives are defined more precisely,
especially for those functions with key roles to
play.

Level 3 *Set sub-objectives to support the broad objectives*
The objectives would be based on sales volume,

> geographic expansion and service offering exten-
> sion.

A marketing objective should meet several criteria. It must be:

- *Relevant* – in relation to the corporate mission and objectives
- *Specific* – it should focus on a clear and specific goal
- *Measurable* – it should be in quantifiable terms
- *Time bound* – it should have an achievement date
- *Challenging* – it should be realizable, but at the same time stretching for individuals and the organization as a whole
- *Focused* – it should be concerned only with markets and services which the company plans to address.

This last point is particularly important, for we support the view that it is only by selling a service to someone (a market) that firms remain in business.

> **It is wrong to confuse marketing objectives with elements such as pricing, advertising, sales location, and so on, which are clearly marketing strategies which help to achieve the objective.**

How to set marketing objectives

It is now apparent that when it comes to setting marketing objectives in the way defined above, there are only four possible courses of action:

- Selling existing services to existing markets *cross selling*
- Extending existing services into new markets *market ind*
- Developing new services for existing markets *last s.*
- Developing new services for new markets. *e-business*

The Ansoff matrix is a critical structure for setting marketing objectives

For convenience, we reproduce the Ansoff matrix, which was shown earlier in Chapter 2. The matrix captures these options in organized form (Figure 5.1).

An individual service company's ability to cope with technological newness or developing new markets will clearly be a determining factor regarding which quadrants of this matrix become the most significant.

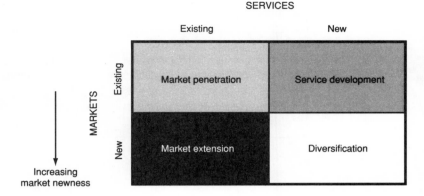

Figure 5.1 Ansoff matrix

Another point to consider is what constitutes 'new' on the Ansoff matrix. When it comes to markets, the answer would concern how long it took for a company's distinctive competence to become known in a specific market. Anything less than this time could be seen as a new market. In a similar way, new services will be those at the early stages of their life cycles, where the company is still 'learning' how to deliver them. For example, it might not yet have solved all the technical problems, or managed to get the quality to the same standard as it has for established services.

Since the marketing audit and SWOT analysis should have provided information about why customers buy the services, what factors are affecting their prospects, which market segments offer the greatest rewards, the anticipated activities of competitors, and so on, creative interpretation of this information should make it possible to set objectives for all service/market combinations. Taken together, these should provide the total sales revenue to enable the corporate objectives to be met. A particularly useful tool, known as 'gap analysis'[1] can also be used in this process of setting marketing objectives.

Gap analysis

This analytical approach is best understood by reference to Figure 5.2. The figure shows that the initial forecast, or trend, of sales revenue only reaches point A, which falls short of the corporate target, point E. The obvious first thing to do in such circumstances will be to consider actions such as increasing productivity, that could close the gap without departing too far from current practices.

Actions to penetrate the current markets further could be:

- Improve the mix of services and markets.
- Generate higher sales via a more effective and better managed sales force.
- Improve customer satisfaction with better service.
- Exploit differential advantages with increased pricing.
- Reduce costs and expenses.
- Change the promotional mix, e.g. level of advertising, service levels.

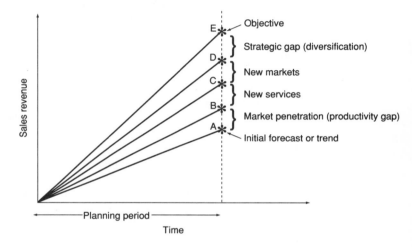

Figure 5.2 Gap analysis

In the example in Figure 5.2, all of these actions have the net effect of pushing the forecast to an improved position, point B. The shortfall between this and the target figure can now only be bridged by having a more radical rethink about the strategies used.

Actions which could be taken to bridge the strategic gap might include:

- Developing new services (taking us to Point C)
- Developing new markets (taking us to Point D)
- Diversifying (the strategic gap). This can be achieved either organically, or by acquisition, joint ventures and the like. Hopefully this or the previous actions take the service organization to Point E.

Each of these possible actions needs to be investigated to determine its potential impact on reducing the identified gap. If the gap still remains even after a creative and rigorous attempt to close it, then top management might need to be informed that the original corporate objectives are not achievable and are unrealistic. However, this should only be done when all other avenues have been explored.

By using the Ansoff matrix and gap analysis, the marketer can begin to focus on marketing objectives and calculate if they will achieve the corporate objectives.

There is, however, another issue to take into consideration and that is whether or not the service portfolio (mentioned in the previous chapter) will be managed effectively. If the company wants to avoid overconcentration of its resources, it will need to invest in those services and markets which will sustain long-term success.

Portfolio management

This issue was first addressed by the Boston Consulting Group[2] in the USA, who identified that the parameters of relative market share and market growth had a critical bearing on the fortunes of any service or product. However, while this consulting firm were extremely successful in applying their concept to a diverse range of businesses, individual organizations (and other consultancies) had problems. They often found it difficult to measure market share with accuracy, or to be confident about market growth rates.

The directional policy matrix is a more useful development of the Boston matrix

As a development from the so-called 'Boston matrix', General Electric, McKinsey & Co and, eventually, Shell evolved a multiple factor portfolio matrix[3] (known as the portfolio matrix or directional policy matrix), shown in Figure 5.3.

Here, the two axes of the matrix are 'market attractiveness' and 'business strengths'. These are more sophisticated proxies for the Boston parameters of 'market growth' and 'market share'. Indeed, the underlying interpretation of information from both the Boston

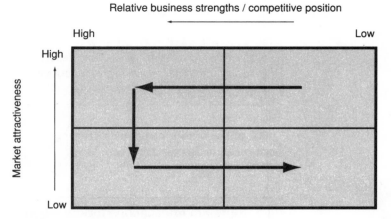

Figure 5.3 The directional policy matrix

matrix and the portfolio matrix is very similar. While both approaches have their proponents, we believe the latter is the more realistic and practical approach, as it involves the use of criteria that are more specific to the service organization using it. It is for this reason that we focus on this technique.

Note that, whilst many texts will show nine boxes, the method described here is a simple and more useful version developed by one of the authors.

The underlying concept of the portfolio matrix is easy to grasp. It is closely related to the life cycle concept. The rationale behind it is this:

> 1 There is little point in introducing a new service unless there is an attractive market for it. (What attractiveness means can vary from company to company, as we shall see.) At the same time, the newness of the service means that the company is at the beginning of a learning curve and, sometimes, does not play to as many strengths as it would for a more established service.
>   Therefore, in portfolio matrix terms, new services often appear in the top right-hand quadrant.
> 2 Assuming the service is well-received, the company builds up strengths in terms of the service getting known and being able to establish differential advantages, while becoming more efficient. The service, therefore, moves into the top left-hand quadrant and becomes better established.
> 3 Eventually, the demand for the service falls, because existing customer needs have been met, a new set of services has greater appeal or the market has matured. Thus, the previously attractive and growing market becomes relatively less attractive than other higher growth markets. The service is now more accurately positioned in the bottom left-hand quadrant.
> 4 Eventually, the less attractive market sometimes encourages the company to switch resources to more promising areas, and the service is denuded of the resources that once led it to success. It now moves into the bottom right-hand quadrant.

All of the service company's offerings should be capable of being positioned on this matrix. There are three very good reasons why this should be done:

> 1 There are implications for the revenue, costs and profit-generating abilities of the overall service portfolio.

> 2 The matrix can be helpful in developing strategic insights regarding how each service should be managed.
> 3 The matrix can provide a forecasting mechanism for revenue generation and can assist strategic thinking.

Revenue generation

Consideration of the four quadrants of the matrix in Figure 5.3 will suggest that, in financial terms, they behave as follows:

- *Upper right-hand box*
  A new service, or one in which the organization has few strengths, will need to be heavily promoted if it is to succeed. At the same time, its sales may be relatively low. It is, therefore, a *net user of funds*. As such, it is more appropriate to use sales and market share goals as a measure of effectiveness than net present value calculations.

  It is also important to have a service champion that has the necessary entrepreneurial skills to lead this type of business.
- *Upper left-hand box*
  Because of the operation's strong competitive position, the service will be achieving high levels of sales, but its success in this attractive market will attract competition. The result of this is that promotional costs may still be high, which might result in modest margins at best, but which on the whole are *neutral in terms of generating funds*. Here, it is probably appropriate to use net present value as a measure of effectiveness, probably using a relatively high percentage discount rate, as an organization needs to be sure that it will eventually recover its investment.

  The type of person who should head up this kind of service needs to be experienced, with a higher risk profile than is necessary for some stable markets.
- *Lower left-hand box*
  With the market becoming less attractive, some competitors withdraw and the company may be able to reduce its promotional efforts and take advantage of its earlier investment in the service. Services in this quadrant are invariably *net generators of funds*. Here, it is probably appropriate to use return on investment as a measure of effectiveness.

  In management terms, it is probably better to have someone in charge of this type of business who is prudent.
- *Lower right-hand box*
  Clearly, sales are at a low level and the company may begin to neglect the service. It might still generate some small amounts of revenue, but questions have to be asked to ascertain whether the resources put into this service would be better invested elsewhere.

Unless, as is sometimes the case, these services are necessary to support other more desirable ones, it is often sensible to *manage these services for cash*. Thus, net free cash flow becomes an appropriate measure of effectiveness.

From the above, it is clear that much of the current revenue and profits come from the services in the bottom left-hand box. It is, essential, therefore, in terms of managing the portfolio of services, that these exist in sufficient quantities, and that, as they diminish in importance, there are successors to take their place. This means that the development of the portfolio cannot be left to chance. Ideally, there should always be one or two developing services in the right-hand box that have the potential to become tomorrow's winners (top left-hand box). Similarly, the cash generators of the future commonly come from today's winners. As a general guideline, there should only be a minimal number of services in the bottom right-hand box.

In our consulting work, we often find that a company's portfolio is badly out of balance and, because the full implications of this are not understood, the 'corrective action' they planned to take would, in most cases, have only exacerbated the situation.

Constructing the portfolio matrix

From the outset, a given service organization must be very rigorous with respect to how it defines the components of the axes for the matrix.

What constitutes *market attractiveness* will obviously vary from company to company. Here are some of the factors which might come into consideration:

> • Overall market size; annual growth rate; profit margins; low level of competition; technical requirements; favourable socioeconomic/political background; environmental conditions; quality requirements.

In terms of *business strengths/competitiveness*, factors like the following determine our competitive positioning:

> • Reputation, e.g. technological; brand/company image; service quality; differential advantages of service; reliability; availability; ability to offer a competitive price.

Since some of these factors will be more important than others, it is usual to weight them, as shown in the example in Table 5.1.

Table 5.1 Ranking market attractiveness and competitive position

	Weight	*Rating (1–5)*	*Value*
Market attractiveness			
Overall market size	0.20	4.00	0.80
Annual market growth rate	0.20	5.00	1.00
Available profit margin	0.15	4.00	0.60
Competitive intensity	0.20	2.00	0.60
Technological requirements	0.15	4.00	0.60
Inflationary vulnerability	0.05	3.00	0.15
Environmental	0.05	3.00	0.15
	1.00		3.90
Competitive position			
Service quality	0.30	4.00	1.20
Brand reputation	0.20	5.00	1.00
Technological reputation	0.15	4.00	0.60
Reliability	0.15	4.00	0.60
Availability	0.10	3.00	0.30
Cost effectiveness	0.10	3.00	0.30
	1.00		4.00

Whilst the criteria for market attractiveness may remain constant, the criteria for the competitive position will be different for each market evaluated. Each market should be evaluated according to its attractiveness and according to the organization's strengths in each market.

If each service is represented on the matrix by a circle whose area is proportional to its sales revenue, then the current balance of the portfolio can be seen at a glance.

The portfolio matrix and the future

Additional value can be gained from the portfolio matrix by projecting the position and sales revenue of each service at the end of the planning period and also plotting these. The end result will look like Figure 5.4, which was produced for a retailer some years ago.

From this example, it can be seen that the pressing need of the company is to improve the competitive position of some of its services in the top right-hand box. Of the three in contention, which would be the best candidate? On balance, perhaps Red Rooster would be the one on which to concentrate if investment funds were limited. The reason for saying this is that it rates the highest in market attractiveness and was on a par with the others regarding competitiveness. However, steps should also be taken to ensure the accuracy of the data collected and to investigate whether it would be possible to expand sales to a higher level than forecast.

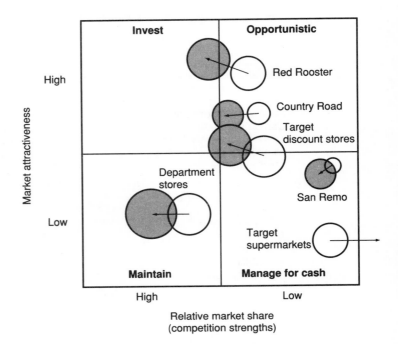

Figure 5.4 Illustrative portfolio matrix for a retailer

The matrix and strategy formulation

From the foregoing discussion of the rationale behind the matrix and its cash-generating implications, it is possible to extract some general 'rules' about marketing strategy. These are illustrated in Figure 5.5. Here, the matrix is shown as a 3 × 3 format so that a finer tuning of strategy can be achieved, depending on where the circles are located.

It is not suggested that the guidelines provided in Figure 5.5 should be followed slavishly. All they do is to provide a general context for the company's marketing deliberations. Similarly, other more specific functional guidelines can be extracted from the matrix, as shown in Figure 5.6. Here, for the sake of simplicity, we have reverted to a four-box matrix format.

Developing competitive strategies

We can consider marketing strategies at two levels. First, we consider marketing strategies at the competitive strategy level. There are two factors which have a crucial effect on the development of competitive strategies for any business:

- How successfully it manages its cost base
- The uniqueness of its service.

Market attractiveness		Strong	Medium	Weak
	High	**Protect position** • invest to grow at maximum rate • Concentrate effort on maintaining strength	**Invest to build** • challenge for leadership • build selectively on strengths • reinforce vulnerable areas	**Build selectively** • specialize around limited strengths • seek ways to overcome weaknesses • withdraw if indications of sustainable growth are lacking
	Medium	**Protect position** • invest heavily in most attractive segments • build up ability to counter competition • emphasize profitability by raising productivity	**Selectivity/manage for earnings** • protect existing programme • concentrate investments on segments where profitability is good and risk is relatively low	**Limited expansion or harvest** • look for ways to expand without high risk; otherwise, minimize investment and rationalize operations
	Low	**Protect and refocus** • manage for current earnings • concentrate on attractive segments • defend strengths	**Manage for earnings** • protect position in most profitable segments • upgrade services • minimize investment	**Divest** • sell at time that will maximize cash value • cut fixed costs and avoid investment meanwhile

Strong *Medium* *Weak*

Business strength

Figure 5.5 Multiple factors matrix – generic strategies

Costs and service differentiation are key determinants of commercial success

Porter[4] has combined these factors in the matrix that is shown in Figure 5.7.

The company with a highly differentiated service (for which it can charge a premium) and a low cost structure is clearly going to be very successful. The company with a run-of-the-mill, 'me-too' service, can only remain competitive if it can keep its costs relatively lower than its rivals (or find a way to achieve differentiation). The company with no means of achieving differentiation and a high cost structure is clearly heading for ruin in the long run. The final case, the highly differentiated offer from a high cost base, does have a prospect of success if it can be focused into niche markets which value the differentiation and are prepared to pay for it.

However, some companies, because of the nature of their business, find their options severely limited. They might, for example, be very labour intensive and, as a result, have inherently high costs which they can do little about. This might suggest that, for them, it will be critical to work at establishing differentiation and to seek niche markets if they are to survive. Of course, they might argue that working on developing a 'special' service would add further to

Main thrust	Invest Invest for growth	Maintain Maintain market position, manage for earnings	Cash Manage for cash	Opportunistic Opportunistic development
Market share	Maintain or increase dominance	Maintain or slightly milk for earnings	Forgo share for profit	Invest selectively in share
Products/services	Differentiation – line expansion	Prune less successful, differentiate for segments	Aggressively prune	Differentiation – line expansion
Price	Lead – aggressive pricing for share	Stabilize prices/raise	Raise	Aggressive – price for share
Promotion	Aggressive marketing	Limit	Minimize	Aggressive marketing
Distribution	Broaden distribution	Hold wide distribution pattern	Gradually withdraw distribution	Limited coverage
Cost control	Tighten control – go for scale economies	Emphasize cost reduction, viz. variable costs	Aggressively reduce fixed and variable	Tight – but not at expense of entrepreneurship
Operations	Expand, invest (organic acquisition, joint venture)	Maximize capacity utilization	Free up capacity	Invest
R & D	Expand – invest	Focus on specific projects	None	Invest
Personnel	Upgrade management in key functional areas	Maintain, reward efficiency, tighten organization	Cut back organization	Invest
Investment	Fund growth	Limit fixed investment	Minimize and divest opportunistically	Fund growth
Working capital	Reduce in process – extend credit	Tighten credit – reduce accounts receivable, increase inventory turn	Aggressively reduce	Invest

Figure 5.6 Other functional guidelines suggested by portfolio matrix analysis

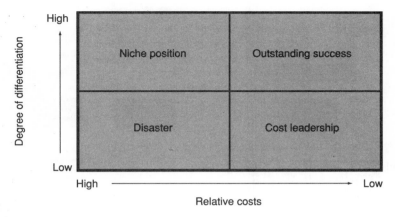

Figure 5.7 The Porter matrix

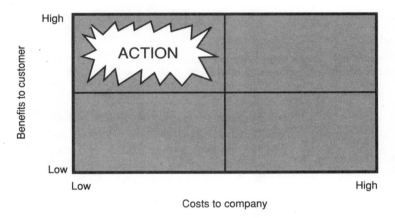

Figure 5.8 Cost-effective service development

their costs. This does not necessarily have to be the case, as Figure 5.8 illustrates.

By considering those benefits the customer seeks and values highly which can be provided relatively cheaply, the company may be able to 'customize' its services at little cost.

A whole range of profit improvement options are shown in Figure 5.9 which summarizes the options to address the gap analysis (described earlier in this chapter).

Marketing strategies

As outlined earlier, what a company wants to accomplish, in terms of such things as market share and volume, are marketing objectives. How the company intends to go about achieving its objectives are marketing strategies. Marketing strategy is the overall route to the

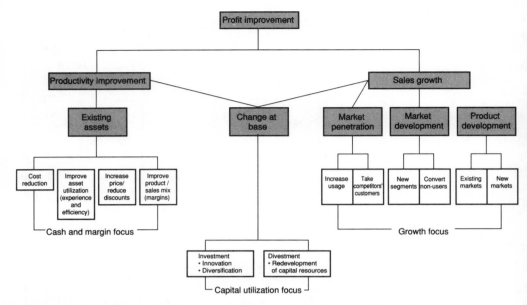

Figure 5.9 Profit improvement options (*Source*: Based on work by J. Saunders, Loughborough University, and used with his kind permission)

achievement of specific objectives and should describe the means by which marketing objectives are to be reached, the time programme and the allocation of resources. It does not delineate the individual courses the resulting activities will follow.

The linkages between marketing objectives and marketing strategies for a service business are shown in Figure 5.10.

There is a clear distinction between strategy and detailed implementation or tactics. Marketing strategy reflects the company's best opinion as to how it can most profitably apply its skills and resources to the marketplace. It is inevitably broad in scope. The first year implementation plan which stems from it (discussed in the next chapter) will spell out specific action and timings and will contain the detailed contribution expected from each department.

Marketing strategies, within Step 6 of the marketing plan, indicate the *general* content of the marketing strategies. They typically include elements such as:

1. Policies and procedures relating to the services to be offered, such as number, quality, design, branding
2. Pricing levels to be adopted, margins and discounts
3. Advertising and sales promotion – the creative approach, type of media, amount of spend, etc.
4. What emphasis will be put on the sales approach, sales training, etc.

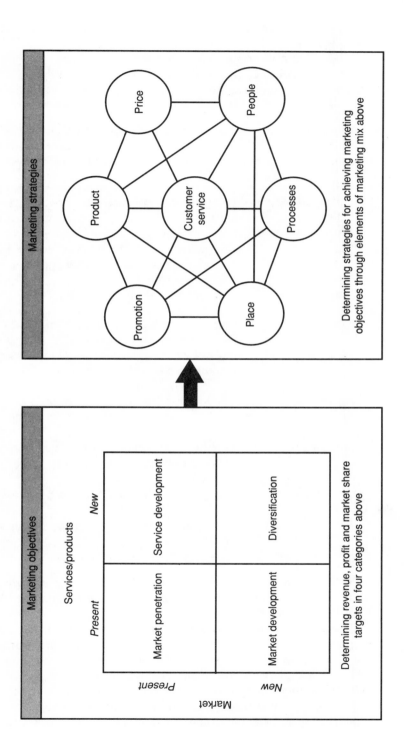

Figure 5.10 Marketing objectives and marketing strategies for a service business

> 5 What intermediaries might be used, i.e. distribution channels
> 6 What customer service levels will be required
> 7 Specification of processes used to deliver services
> 8 Strategic issues relating to staff.

Thus, marketing strategies are the means by which marketing objectives will be achieved and are generally concerned with the seven major elements of the services marketing mix, as follows:

Product/service	The general policies for product and service deletions, modifications, additions, design, packaging, etc.
Price	The general pricing policies to be followed for product/service groups in market segments.
Place	The general policies for channels and intermediaries.
Promotion	The general policies for communicating with customers under the relevant headings, such as: advertising, sales force, sales promotion, public relations, exhibitions, direct mail.
People	The general policies for people management as part of the service delivery process.
Processes	The general policies for processes by which a service is created and delivered to customers.
Customer service	The general policies for customer service management, including service level, which help build long-term customer relationships.

Note that these are *general* policies which lead to much greater amplification later in the first year implementation programme (Step 10 of the marketing plan).

Figure 5.11 provides a list of the marketing strategies (in summary form), which covers the majority of options. The marketing strategies will be made up of three elements: the means; the timetable; and the resources necessary to ensure successful achievement of the objectives. Marketing strategies outline the broad plan of action to achieve marketing objectives through the marketing mix elements.

Marketing strategies are concerned with an overview of the three-year marketing mix strategies which will satisfy customers' needs. The thrust of the marketing mix specification, at this point in the

---

1 **Product**
   - expand the line
   - change performance, quality or features
   - consolidate the line
   - standardize design
   - positioning
   - change the mix
   - branding
2 **Price**
   - change price, terms or conditions
   - skimming policies
   - penetration policies
3 **Promotion**
   - change advertising or promotion
   - change selling
4 **Place**
   - change distribution
   - change service
   - change channels
   - change the degree of forward integration
5 **People**
   - conduct skills analysis and retrain/recruit as appropriate
   - change Account Management structure to Account Relationship Managers
6 **Processes**
   - change service development process
   - change service delivery process
7 **Customer service**
   - change service levels by segment
   - review and improve communications with customers

Figure 5.11 Summary of typical marketing strategies for a service business

marketing plan, involves creating the differential advantage which makes the service firm's offer different (in a way preferred by the segments that are targeted) from its competitors' offers.

Step 10 in the next chapter, the first year implementation plan, is devoted to a much more detailed consideration of the marketing mix for services. This next chapter describes what should appear in advertising, sales, price, distribution, processes, people and customer service plans and is intended for those whose principal concern is the preparation of a detailed one-year operational or tactical plan.

From what we have said about setting marketing objectives and strategies, it should now be clear that the services marketer is faced with a wide range of options, which call for creative, and, at times, inspirational, analysis to address them. This phase of the planning process is closely related to the next two steps.

Step 7   Estimate expected results

The purpose of this step is to determine whether the marketing strategies will actually deliver the desired results.

Once the marketing objectives and strategies have been decided for the various service/segment combinations, the financial implications of introducing them need to be evaluated. This will require a detailed review of:

- Projected sales revenues
- The costs of sales
- The costs of marketing
- Operating expenses
- Overhead expenses.

Such an analysis should show that the chosen approach will indeed deliver the anticipated financial contribution to achieve the required targets. If it does not, then the marketing strategies will need to be examined in more depth in order to discover how they might be redeveloped to achieve the expected results.

It is necessary to estimate a number of possible outcomes

In times of economic uncertainty, it can be useful to calculate three sets of analyses. These would reflect the estimated results based upon the most pessimistic interpretation of all the salient factors, the most likely result, and that based on the most optimistic levels of demands. In this way, it becomes possible to identify the possible spread of expected results and, in that sense, have a feel for the potential 'margin of error' surrounding the most likely result.

Forecasting projected sales levels is never easy, particularly as the service cannot be kept in inventory. Several variables need to be considered at this point. These include the capacity of the service company, costs in extending capacity, moving to multisite locations, changing demand patterns through differential pricing, and so on. Although demand and capacity planning is complicated in manufacturing businesses, the characteristics of services make it much more difficult in the services sector. Therefore, techniques such as extrapolation, regression analysis, delphi forecasting, test marketing and consumer surveys can all make a contribution to identifying demand patterns more accurately.

However, because many of the factors under consideration are interrelated, the task is frequently not simple. Thus, although techniques can help to uncover quantitative data, often this must be augmented with qualitative analysis and market research to promise a better understanding of the service market under consideration.

Step 8   Identifying alternative mixes

Even if the original objectives and strategies do produce the expected results, it is still important to discover if a more effective marketing approach can lead to even better results. Therefore, using techniques such as computer modelling, a number of alternative mixes can be

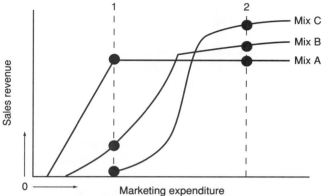

Figure 5.12 Response functions for different marketing mixes

evaluated before deciding on the final marketing mix around which the plan will be based.

It is at this stage that plans should be formulated to cover anticipated lower or higher levels of demand. It is often found that the response curves of different marketing mixes can vary considerably. Figure 5.12 shows a representation of predicted revenue against predicted marketing costs for three alternative marketing mixes. The marketing mix chosen will depend on the budget for marketing effort and its impact on revenues and profit. Marketing mix A will produce better results for low levels of expenditure (Point 1) whilst marketing mix C will provide better results at a higher level of expenditure (Point 2).

Contingency plans[5] should also be considered at this stage of the marketing planning process, in response to the impact of different sets of assumptions which were made earlier. Of course, it will not be possible to develop plans for every eventuality, but it is advisable to have at least:

- A defensive contingency plan which takes into account the possibility that the assumptions surrounding the marketing audit were unduly optimistic and thus responds to threats that might materialize; and
- An offensive contingency plan, which is really the converse of the one above and seeks to take advantage of opportunities, should they occur.

In an ideal world, possible contingencies can be identified well in advance. Unfortunately, in spite of all good intentions, the dynamics of modern markets can trigger unexpected crises. For example, few predicted the rapid demise of communism and the repercussions it would have in the Eastern Bloc countries. Similarly, events such as the Gulf War or natural disasters can suddenly distort existing supply and demand patterns, making it imperative to modify existing marketing plans, through having contingency planning.

In these circumstances, it is particularly important to understand if the event in question is a temporary aberration, or something which will have a fundamental and long-lasting effect on the company's markets.

Figure 5.13 shows the phases of alternative mixes for a large services company operating in consumer markets. It shows the rigorous evaluation of fifteen possible marketing plans, and the resulting process, as these are selected as marketing plans, contingency plans, or are rejected. The figure also shows the linkages with the formulation of the first year implementation and the performance review process.

Paradoxically, it is generally not at times of crisis that danger exists, but when things are going well. It is at times like these that companies become complacent and get lulled into a false sense of security. The idea of developing contingency plans fades from the corporate consciousness and, when something does go wrong, the companies are caught completely unprepared. These contingency plans are an important part of the marketing planning process.

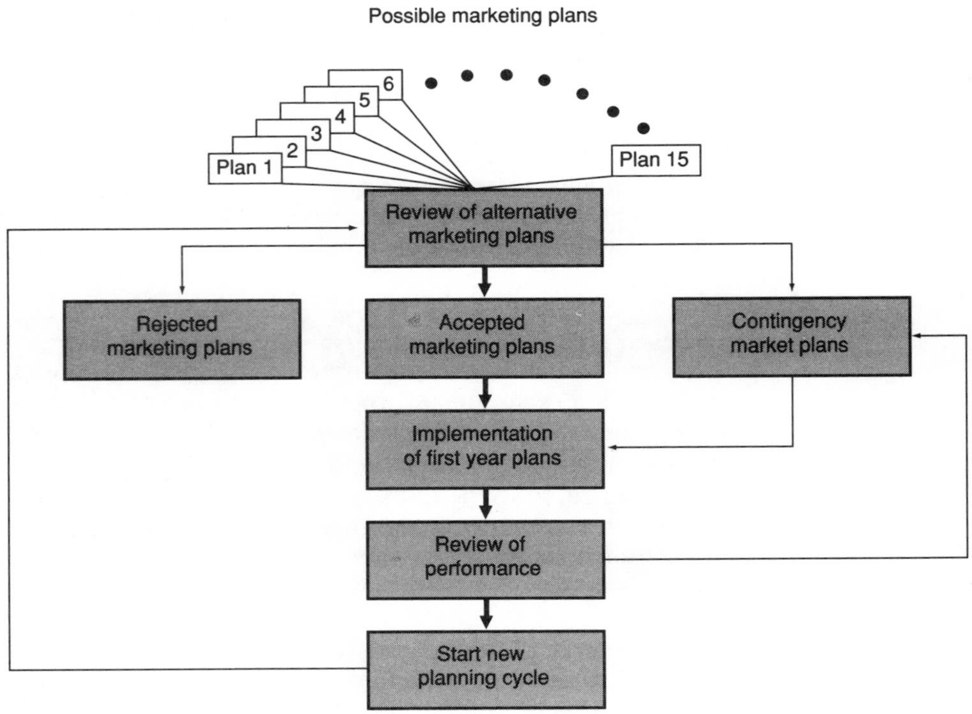

Figure 5.13 The alternative mixes process for a large services company

Summary

In this chapter about the marketing strategy formulation phase of the marketing planning process, we first looked at the differences between objectives and strategies, and at how to set marketing objectives. We saw that, although the marketing audit and SWOT analysis should have provided much of the information required to set marketing objectives, gap analysis might indicate that more needed to be done. Steps might have to be taken to improve productivity and develop new strategies in order to arrive at marketing objectives which met the corporate expectations.

Another consideration was that of managing the service portfolio effectively, bearing in mind that different services have different capacities for either absorbing funds or generating them. By considering the company's output as a 'portfolio', rather than a set of individual services, it was found that underlying strategic issues could influence the way each service was developed and promoted. Indeed, the portfolio matrix provides useful guidelines regarding functional marketing activities.

We saw that developing a competitive marketing strategy is probably the most important phase of the process. Because the planning process is interactive, the steps of setting objectives and strategies, estimating results and considering alternative mixes might have to be reviewed several times before the best formulation emerges.

References

1 For a detailed early treatment of gap analysis, see Ansoff, H. I. (1965) *Corporate Strategy*, McGraw-Hill, Maidenhead. Chapter 8.
2 For a more complete discussion of BCG strategies see Day, G. S. (1975) A Strategic Perspective on Product Planning. *Journal of Contemporary Business*, Spring, 1–34; also Day, G. S. (1977) Diagnosing the Product Portfolio, *Journal of Marketing*, April, 29–38; and Henderson, B. D. (1979) *Henderson on Corporate Strategy*, Abt Books, Cambridge, MA.
3 For the original explanation of the GE and Shell approach see Allen, M. G. Diagramming GE's Planning for What's Watt. In Allio, R. J. and Pennington, M. W. (1979) *Corporate Planning: Techniques and Application*, Amacon, New York, pp. 211–20; and Robinson, S. J. Q., Hichens, R. E. and Wade, D. P. (1978) The Directional Policy Matrix – Tool for Strategic Planning. *Long Range Planning*, June, 8–15.
4 Porter, M. E. (1980) *Competitive Strategy*, The Free Press, New York.
5 For further discussion see Steiner, G. (1979) *Strategic Planning*, The Free Press, New York. Chapter 14: Contingency Planning and Alternative Futures Exploration.

6 Marketing planning Phase Four – resource allocation, monitoring and detailed planning

The strategic marketing planning process for services

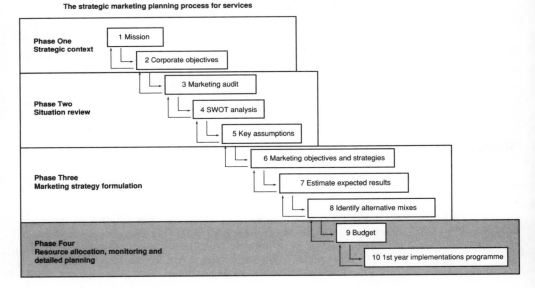

Phase One
Strategic context

1 Mission

2 Corporate objectives

Phase Two
Situation review

3 Marketing audit

4 SWOT analysis

5 Key assumptions

Phase Three
Marketing strategy formulation

6 Marketing objectives and strategies

7 Estimate expected results

8 Identify alternative mixes

Phase Four
Resource allocation, monitoring and
detailed planning

9 Budget

10 1st year implementations programme

Chapter 5, on marketing strategy formulation, showed how the marketing audit information could be distilled and used to determine marketing objectives and strategies. Having these available to guide the thinking process, it was then possible to arrive at the services marketing mix, *at a broad strategic level*, which offered the best prospects for achieving the desired results. This chapter, which examines the final phase of the marketing planning process for services, will look first at the marketing budget and then at how the strategic marketing plan can be made operative through the

> allocation of resources and the formulation of a detailed first year tactical marketing plan involving considerations of the services marketing mix *at a detailed operational level.* It will also address the issues of monitoring and control.

Step 9   The marketing budget

In arriving at the best strategic marketing mix, all of the options under consideration had to be costed out. In that sense the broad strategic marketing budget is known already. However, it should now be developed in a more detailed and careful manner, as it is going to provide the formal expression of the service organization's commitment to its chosen marketing strategy for the coming three years (or whatever the planning period happens to be).

Successful budgeting involves cross-functional co-operation

The responsibility for looking ahead in this way is not solely the prerogative of top management, for many executives will have a part to play in translating forecasts, and what is required to achieve them, into monetary values.

> **Successful budgeting depends upon the thoroughness with which every aspect of future marketing has been considered and how it impacts on other parts of the business.**

The involvement of a wide group of managers in the budgeting process ensures that no important issues are neglected or overlooked. This frequently involves cross-functional cooperation in the planning process, which was discussed in Chapter 2 and illustrated in Figure 2.5. It also serves to remind them that they do have a part to play in working towards a common goal – the future success of the company.

The budget itself can be broken down into a number of component parts.

The revenue budget

As all revenue is ultimately generated by sales, accurate sales forecasts are the critical link in the budgetary process. Not only should they be determined as scientifically as possible, they must also be consistent with the views of field sales staff and others who have an intimate knowledge about customers and the markets for the services under consideration.

The fixing of sales forecasts will include allowances for:

- The sales spread, or 'mix', over the principal service lines
- The volatility of demand for the service(s) both at home and in foreign markets
- The relationship between sales and the capacity to provide the service(s). For example, capacity might be limited by skill shortages, lack of investment in new technology, and so on, some of which may not be capable of swift expansion
- Patterns of seasonal demand
- Special characteristics of the particular service product market.

The 'marketing capacity' budget

This is, in essence, designed to cover marketing staff responsible for providing the services and products over the planning period. It involves a detailed study of what goes into each service, and understanding that labour, material, supplies and equipment need to be available as and when required. Again, no worthwhile conclusions can be reached about the levels of these cost factors without discussion and cooperation between the cross-functional managers involved. From the point of view of maintaining a consistent output as economically as possible, this budget will take into account:

- A consideration of the appropriate levels of service quality to be offered to each major customer segment
- A detailed study of direct labour involved, expressed in man-hours, taking into account different staff grades that might be required
- A study of incentives which may influence sales, hence throughput rates
- The provision of plant, tools and supplies, together with utilities and maintenance facilities
- A study of the most effective material purchasing procedures
- Efficiencies achieved through services re-engineering and redesign
- Other expenses associated with maintaining the marketing output, e.g. use of advertising agency.

The capital expense and finance budget

It will be necessary to draft a long-term capital expense budget for the strategic planning period under consideration. This will address any fixed capital assets which might be required to backup the marketing plans, such as, for example, new service sites, or office expansion.

A cash or finance budget might take into account:

- cash flows, i.e. how revenue will match up with operating expenses and payments to suppliers
- short-term loans
- temporary investment for surplus funds
- a study of money market conditions and interest rates
- the provision for contingent liabilities.

It will be obvious from all of this that the setting of budgets is also more likely to be realistic and related to what the *whole* company wants to achieve when it has this cross-functional emphasis, rather than just having one functional department involved. The problems of designing a dynamic system for budget setting, rather than having poorly thought-through procedures, are a major challenge to marketing and financial directors of all companies.

Annual zero-based budgeting is an excellent discipline

Many managers advocate a zero-based approach to budgeting. With this approach the marketing director justifies all marketing expenditure from a base of zero each year, against the tasks which need to be accomplished.

If this is done, then the marketing plan, which in effect links a hierarchy of objectives cascading down from the corporate objectives, ties every item of expenditure to the corporate objectives. For example, if customer service demanded a higher proportion of the budget, the rationale for this should be directly attributable to a major objective formulated in the marketing planning process.

By proceeding in this way, every item of expenditure is fully accounted for as part of a rational, objective and task approach.

It also ensures that when changes have to be made during the period under consideration, they can be made in such a way that least damage is caused to the organization's financial strengths and long-term objectives.

| Incremental marketing expenses are more difficult to identify in a service organization | In manufacturing, it is easy to see that incremental marketing expenses are all costs incurred after the product leaves the factory, other than costs involved in physical distribution. In a service company, the dividing line is far less obvious, because a 'factory' does not always exist. Those who 'make' the service product might do so partly in the company's offices and partly on the customer's premises. (The types of interaction in service delivery were discussed in Chapter 1 and illustrated in Figure 1.7.) |

> **Furthermore, in some services, such as a small management consultancy, the contact person is in effect the service product, the service surround, the salesperson and the company, all at the same time.**

Just as with the difficult question of whether packaging should be a marketing or production expense, there are some issues where there are no simple answers. Exactly how a service company defines its marketing expenses will need to relate to its circumstances. Common sense will reveal the most useful and workable solutions. The important point is that careful analysis should be made about what is required to take the company towards its goals, and that items of expenditure should be gathered under appropriate headings. A zero-based budgeting approach lends itself to achieving this result. Those wishing to consider further the relationship between marketing planning and budgeting are referred to Abratt, Beffon and Ford.[1]

Step 10 First year implementation programme

Once agreement has been reached regarding budgets, those responsible for the development of the first year implementation programme of the marketing plan can then proceed to develop details of tasks to be completed, together with responsibilities and timings.

> **Such programmes (which in marketing literature are also sometimes called one-year tactical marketing plans, or schedules) constitute detailed guides which ensure that the first year activities direct the service organization on a journey which will achieve its longer-term strategic marketing objectives.**

| The customer judges the organization solely on its output | Before starting to formulate the various marketing programmes, it is important to be clear about the activities upon which they are intended to impact. Guidance for this comes from taking a 'customer's-eye view' of the company. As Figure 6.1 shows, the customer views the service organization through the window of its out- |

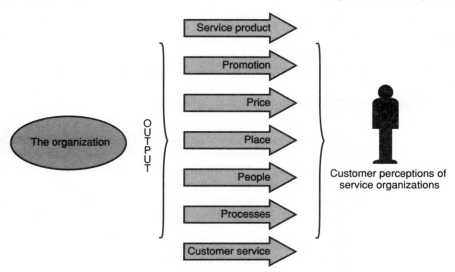

Figure 6.1 The organizational output

put. This, as we saw earlier, is what is termed the marketing mix, which consists of seven key elements – the traditional four Ps (the service product, promotion, price and place) and three additional elements appropriate to services and relationship marketing (people, processes and customer service).

> **By managing the components of the marketing mix effectively, the marketer provides a 'window' which enables the customer to view the service organization offer in an integrated manner.**

We can now see that marketing programmes involve developing plans for managing all seven components of the marketing mix. However, not all marketing plans will have separate plans for all seven elements of the marketing mix. In some cases elements such as the people and processes may be incorporated into the other elements of the plan. Whether or not these are detailed separately or integrated elsewhere in the marketing plan, it is essential that the implication of all the mix elements are considered as part of the planning process.

Thus, we have no wish to be overly dogmatic on the subject of how many elements of the services marketing mix should have detailed plans developed for them. For readers who choose to stay with the 4Ps concept and find that it works for them, then they may wish not to abandon it. There is a danger that extended discussion about what constitutes the marketing mix will reach a sterile level of debate. The pragmatic marketer should make up his or her own mind regarding what constitutes the service company's output. The main point is not to overlook anything.

The marketing mix will now be considered in more detail in terms of what goes into the planning for each of its elements.

Mix element 1   The service product plan

Most of the key elements relating to this element of the marketing mix have already been discussed in Chapter 4 (Sub-audit 4: Auditing the services and products) and in Chapter 5 (Marketing objectives) so will not be repeated here. This earlier discussion covered topics relating to the product plan including the product options (in terms of the Ansoff matrix), differentiation, positioning, life cycles and portfolio analysis.

The formulation of marketing objectives in Step 6 of the marketing plan will have clarified and set targets regarding the quantity and quality of which services go to which markets. What now needs to be done is to schedule the various activities so that they do not compete for scarce resources at the same time, and that they are delivered in sufficient quantity throughout the planning period that the revenue from the total portfolio provides sufficient funds at any one time. The service product plan will also indicate what activities need to go into the development of new services, and over what period of time. It will also show when and how existing services will be withdrawn from the market.

Three further topics, that were not discussed previously, need to be considered within the product plan. These include: branding, physical evidence and new service development strategies.

Branding of services

Branding, formerly the domain of fast-moving consumer goods, is now recognized as being of great importance to services. Branding has an important role in value creation and can help support the positioning strategy that has been determined for the service organization. Establishing a distinctive brand has become a key issue in almost every service sector, as illustrated by Figure 6.2.

Berry and Parasuraman[2] have outlined the key questions that need to be addressed by services marketers when considering their brand:

1   Are we proactive in presenting a strong company brand to our customers (and other stakeholders)?
2   How does our company name rate on the tests of distinctiveness, relevance, memorability and flexibility?
3.   Do we use to full advantage branding elements other than the company name?
4   Is our presented brand cohesive?

Passenger Transport

British Airways: Club World, Super Shuttle
British Midland: Diamond Service
Virgin Atlantic Airways: Upper Class
British Rail: Intercity, Network SouthEast
   Sleeper
Pullman
Avis
Hertz

Freight Transport/Distribution

Royal Mail: Registered, Recorded, Special
   Delivery, Datapost
British Rail: Red Star, Rail Freight
Federal Express
DHL

Travel Trade

British Airways: First, Four Corners
Midland Bank: Thomas Cook
Pickfords
Lunn Poly

Food and Beverage

McDonald's
Grand Metropolitan: Burger King
Trusthouse Forte: Harvester, Happy Eater,
   Welcome Break, Wheelers, Gardner
   Merchant
Whitbread: Pastificio

Hospitality

Trusthouse Forte: Travelodge, Posthouse,
   Exclusive Hotels
Accor: Formula One, Ibis, Novotel, Sofitel
Mount Charlotte: Thistle
Marriott
Ladbroke: Hilton International, Hilton National

Financial Services

Midland Bank: First Direct, Vector, Orchard,
   Meridian
Guardian Royal Exchange: Freedom, Choices

Retail

Next: Next Directory
Burton: Principles, Harvey Nichols
House of Fraser: Harrods
W. H. Smith: Do-It-All, W. H. Smith,
   Paperchase, Our Price, Waterstones
Kingfisher: Woolworths, B&Q, Comet

Leisure

Scottish & Newcastle: Center Parcs
Alton Towers
Disney

Figure 6.2 Examples of well-established brands in various service sectors (*Source*: Based on Dobree, J. and Page, A. S. (1990) Unleashing the power of service brands in the 1990s. *Management Decision*, **28** (6), 21)

5 Do we apply our brand consistently across all media?
6 Do we use all possible media to present our brand?
7 Do we recognize the influence of the service offering on brand meaning?
8 Do we base our branding decisions on research?
9 Are we respectful of what exists when we change our brand or add new brands?
10. Do we internalize our branding?

These questions provide useful guidelines to developing service brands.

Physical evidence

Elements of physical evidence are a means by which, over time, the brand values can be re-informed. Physical evidence is part of the service organization's environment where the services encounter takes place. Physical evidence is a means of providing tangible physical clues for a service which is largely intangible. Physical evidence also helps support the positioning and image of the service firm.

Whilst it has been argued by some writers[3] that physical evidence is of sufficient importance and that it should form a separate element of the marketing mix, our view is that it is a sub-element of the product element of the marketing mix (in the same way that advertising and personal selling are sub-elements of the promotion element of the mix). However, the important issue is that attention is directed at it, regardless of where it is structurally placed in the marketing programme.

Physical evidence can help with the positioning of a service firm and can give tangible support to the outcome of the service experience. For example, banks have traditionally built highly elaborate and decorative facades and banking chambers to give the impression of wealth, substance and solidarity. Currently many service organizations spend large amounts of money to create branding, architecture, layout, furnishings, decor and uniforms that provide physical evidence that reinforces their desired image.

For services which are performed at the location of the service organization, physical evidence has an essential role to play. Familiarity is often a factor used by service franchise operators to provide reassurance. This is achieved by providing systematic physical evidence of what the customer can expect. For example, customers of Ritz Carlton hotels and Oddbins' wine shops have a clear idea of what they can expect when they visit a new outlet.

New product and service development

The option of new product and service development, as part of the product service plan, was mentioned briefly in the earlier discussion of the Ansoff matrix. This is an area of increasing interest to service researchers. Lovelock[4] has provided a framework for considering this option which consists of six categories of service development:

- *Major innovations* These innovations represent major new markets. Examples include Dyno-rod (drain/sewer unblocking services); Federal Express and DHL (overnight distribution); cellular telephones; and Open University (distance education). The risk and reward profile of such major innovations are typically large.
- *Startup businesses* These are new and innovative ways of addressing the current needs of customers and increasing the range of choices available to them. Examples include Prontaprint (stationery and printing through retail outlets); Interflora (florist directory and distribution internationally); and video cassette hire.

- *New products for the market currently served* This allows the service provider to use the customer base to the best advantage and cross-sell other products. The growth in sophistication of database marketing has greatly aided this approach. For example, the Automobile Association established a core range of products related to car breakdown services. The customer base was then offered a range of other car-related services, including car insurance, travel insurance and map books.

- *Product line extensions* These offer customers greater variety of choices within existing service lines. This is typical of a business in maturity, which already has a core market segment which the service provider seeks to maintain. For example, City law firms servicing corporate clients have found increasing demand from clients by offering advice on environmental law. This supplements the commercial legal services already provided, but is in response to both new EC legislation and companies' desire to be perceived as being environmentally conscious.

- *Product improvements* This usually consists of altering or improving the features of existing service products. British Rail's newer faster trains, British Airways/Air France's Concorde, and Fidelity's twenty-four service centres are examples of such improvements.

- *Style changes* These involve cosmetic alterations or enhancement of tangible elements of the service product. The development of a new corporate image and the introduction of uniforms for bank counter staff are examples of style changes.

Managing the service product plan

Grönroos[5] has suggested four key steps that the services marketer needs to manage in providing a service offer:

- *Developing the service concept* – the basic concept or intentions of the service provider.
- *Developing a basic service package* – the core service, facilitating services and goods, and supporting services and goods.
- *Developing an augmented service offering* – the service process and interactions between the service provider and customers, including the service delivery process. It includes a consideration of the accessibility of the service, interaction between the service provider and the customer, and the degree of customer participation.
- *Managing image and communication* – so that they support and enhance the augmented service offer. This is the interface between the promotion and product marketing mix elements.

A consideration of these steps, together with the elements of the product plan addressed in earlier chapters, makes clear some of the linkages with other elements of the marketing mix. When the basic service offer has been decided, attention can then be directed at development of promotion, and the other ingredients of the marketing mix.

> **This particular plan or programme provides the backbone for many of the other organizational activities. For example, recruitment programmes will be based on it. It will also loom large in cash-flow projections.**

Mix element 2 The promotion and communications plan

As we have seen, 'promotions' in marketing mix terminology mean all the activities by which communications are aimed at customers with a view to influencing the buying decision. For planning purposes, it is often convenient to break these communications into two separate groups:

- Impersonal communications
- Face-to-face communications.

Between them, these methods of communication provide the services marketer with a number of options from which to choose, for they can be used either singly or in combination.

A key decision is the split between the personal and impersonal communications mix There is nothing intrinsically better about one means of communication rather than another, for both provide benefits and drawbacks. In essence, personal or face-to-face communications provide a mechanism for a two-way dialogue. However, being 'labour intensive' means that this process is costly to provide. The alternative impersonal methods, such as advertising and promotions, are, in comparison, less expensive (in terms of reaching individuals), yet are limited by the one-way nature of their communication pattern.

Thus, the choice facing the marketer should hinge upon considerations such as:

> - Who is the target audience?
> - What is it they need to know?
> - What is the most cost-effective way of providing this information?
> - Can we afford to do it?

Whenever a wide range of options is counterbalanced by a limited budget, it is inevitable that an element of compromise comes into the solution. Having said this, service marketers should do their utmost to provide the optimum communications mix, because intelligent

1 Unawareness
   ↓
2 Awareness
   ↓
3 Comprehension
   ↓
4 Conviction
   ↓
5 Action

Figure 6.3 Stages of communications

The communication process must follow a logical sequence

planning can ensure that the two different approaches combine in a way which is mutually beneficial and synergistic.

At the heart of any successful promotion programme is a clear understanding of the communication process, seen from the customer's viewpoint. In general terms, this follows the model shown in Figure 6.3. When it comes to winning customers, the first task of communications is to make unaware customers aware of the service on offer. Having brought customers to that stage, it is important that they fully understand what it is the service will do for them. Next, they need to be convinced that what is said is true and that the service will satisfactorily meet their needs. Finally, the customers need to be energized sufficiently to buy, or to sign the order.

It can be seen that this overall process can be accomplished in a number of different ways. For example, the door-to-door salesperson cold-calling will endeavour to cover the whole process in one short visit. Alternatively, somebody opening a new hair salon might resort to using advertisements in the local newspaper, or a leaflet drop, followed by invitations for prospective clients to have an introductory, free, or reduced price appointment. In providing large-scale business-to-business services, the process may be developed over a long period.

The communications process is further complicated in that, in some businesses, it can extend over a long period (e.g. negotiating to supply a service to a government department) or an increasing number of people become involved at the customer end, see Table 6.1. For example, in the supply of international telecommunications to the world-wide operations of a major bank, the communications process might be extended over a period of several years.

As Table 6.1 indicates, if the customer company consisted of 0–200 people, then, on average, three or four people might be involved in the buying decision. As the company size increases, not surprisingly, so does the number influencing the buying decision.

> **The full significance of this information is contained in the third column, which shows that, on average, a sales person only makes contact with about one or two of these people.**

Table 6.1 Buying influences and customer size

Number of employees	Av. no. of buying influences	Av. no. of salesperson contacts
0–200	3.42	1.72
201–400	4.85	1.75
401–1000	5.81	1.90
1000+	6.50	1.65

Source: McGraw-Hill.

Table 6.2 Sources of information

	% small companies	% large companies
Trade and technical press	28	60
Salesperson calls	47	19
Exhibitions	8	12
Direct mail	19	9

Source: MacLean Hunter

The issue of company size can also have a bearing on the likelihood of its staff receiving information, as Table 6.2 shows. In larger companies most information is obtained from the trade and technical press, whereas in smaller companies it is from personal contact.

Even from this brief discussion about the communications mix, it is evident that the make-up of it has to be given careful consideration because:

- More than one person can influence what is bought.
- Salespeople do not see all the influencers.
- Customers get their information from different sources.

Impersonal communications

Generally, the major components of impersonal communications are advertising (in its many different forms), special promotions and public relations (PR) and direct marketing. We will look at these four topics in terms of planning them in a way that maximizes their strategic significance. We will also look briefly at direct marketing, an approach which is gaining much prominence in some types of service businesses.

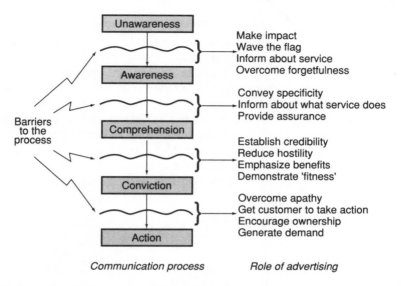

Figure 6.4 Different roles of advertising

Advertising

Based on the communications model (shown in Figure 6.3), Figure 6.4 shows the role of advertising in overcoming the barriers between each step in the communications process.

Thus, for example, for a new service, the role of advertising would be more concerned about establishing a greater level of awareness. In contrast, for a service which is more mature and well-understood, its role could be geared to encouraging ownership and motivating potential customers to take action. It would follow that, since the role is different according to the stage of the communication process, so are the objectives and the measures which would be used to monitor their attainment.

Advertising is
not the only
determinant of
sales

> **There is a popular misconception that advertising success can only be measured in terms of sales increases.**

In most circumstances, advertising is only one of a number of important determinants of sales levels (such as price, quality, customer service levels and so on). Not only this, but there will be times when the role of advertising is to create the basis of future success by getting the service known. In this situation, expecting a relationship between the stimulus of advertising and any immediate response in terms of sales is inappropriate.

Advertising objectives

However, whilst it is often inappropriate to set sales increases as the sole objective for advertising, it is important to set relevant objectives, which will be explicit and measurable. As Figure 6.5 shows, without identifying advertising objectives, any attempt at measuring the performance of a communications programme will be impossible.

In order to address any of the peripheral activities shown in Figure 6.5, the central advertising objectives must be in place. Setting reasonable, achievable objectives is, therefore, the first and most important step in the advertising plan. All the other steps then flow naturally from this and are summarized in Figure 6.6.

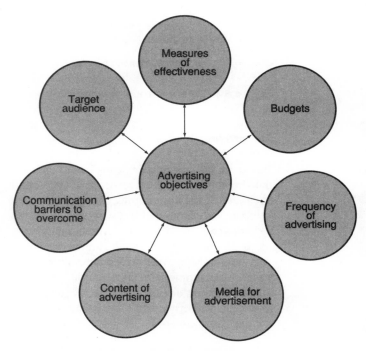

Figure 6.5 The need for advertising objectives

The role of advertising changes over the life cycle of the service

The usual assumption is that advertising is deployed in an aggressive role and that all that changes over time is the creative content. But the role of advertising usually changes during the life cycle of a product.

For example, the process of persuasion itself cannot usually start until there is some level of awareness about a product or service in the marketplace. Creating awareness is, therefore, usually one of the most important objectives early on in the life cycle. If awareness has been created, interest in learning more will usually follow.

Who	. . . are the target audience(s)? What do they already know, feel, believe about us and our product/service? What do they know, feel, believe about the competition? What sort of people are they? How do we describe/identify them?
What	. . . response do we wish to evoke from the target audience(s)? . . . are these specific communications *objectives*? . . . do we want to 'say', make them 'feel', 'believe', 'understand', 'know' about buying/ using our product service? . . . are we offering? . . . do we *not* want to convey? . . . are the priorities of importance of our objectives? . . . are the objectives *written* down and *agreed* by the company and our advertising agency?
How	. . . are our objectives to be embodied in an appealing form? What is our creative strategy/platform? What evidence do we have that this is acceptable and appropriate to our audience(s)?
Where	. . . is the most cost-effective place(s) to expose our communications (in cost terms *vis-à-vis* our audience)? . . . is the most beneficial place(s) for our communications (in expected response terms *vis-à-vis* the 'quality' of the channels available)?
When	. . . are our communications to be displayed/conveyed to our audience? What is the reasoning for our scheduling of advertisements/communications over time? What constraints limit our freedom of choice? Do we have to fit in with other promotional activity on: • our products/services supplied by our company • other products/services supplied by our company • competitors' products • seasonal trends • special events in the market?
Result	What results do we expect? How would we measure results? Do we intend to measure results and, if so, do we need to do anything *beforehand*? If we cannot say how we would measure precise results, then maybe our *objectives* are not sufficiently specific or are not communications objectives? How are we going to judge the relative success of our communications activities (good/bad/indifferent)? Should we have action standards?
Budget	How much money do the intended activities need? How much money is going to be made available? How are we going to control expenditure?
Schedule	Who is to do what and when? What is being spent on what, where and when?

Figure 6.6 Key steps in determining advertising activity (*Source*: Based on a list produced by Professor David Corkindale when at the Cranfield School of Management; used with his kind permission)

Attitude development now begins in earnest. This might also involve reinforcing an existing attitude or even changing previously held attitudes in order to clear the way for the promotion of a new service. This role obviously tends to become more important later in the product life cycle, when competitive services are each trying to establish their own 'niche' in the market.

The diffusion of innovation process

Also relevant to advertising strategy is an understanding of the 'diffusion of innovation' curve (Figure 6.7) which refers to the percentage of potential adopters of a new service over time. Rogers,[6] the originator of this work, found that, for all new products and services, the cumulative demand pattern conformed to a bell-shaped statistical distribution curve. From this, he was able to distinguish certain typological groups as shown in this figure.

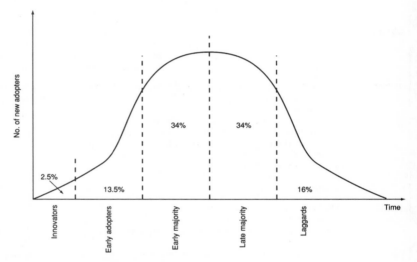

Figure 6.7 Diffusion of innovation curve

Winning over the opinion-leaders is critical in getting a new service accepted in the market

In general, the innovators think for themselves and are active in trying those new services which appeal to them. This 2.5% of the customer population are the fashion leaders, the first to be attracted to the new service offer. The early adopters (13.5%) often have status in society and because they are not seduced merely by novelty, tend to be opinion-leaders.

> **They confer on it acceptability and respectability and are, as such, extremely influential in establishing the success of a new service.**

The early majority (34%) are more conservative, more deliberate, and usually only adopt services that have been given social approbation by the opinion-leaders. When they enter the market, service providers usually enjoy a period of rapid growth in sales. The late majority (34%) are clearly more sceptical. They need to be sure that the service is tried and tested before they risk committing themselves. They also tend to have less money and, often, price becomes more important at this stage. The laggards, are often of lower income and status and are the last to adopt the service.

When all potential users of a service become users, the market can be said to be mature and service providers cannot expect the previous high levels of growth.

> **If, from the outset, the company can identify and target its innovators and opinion-leaders, it increases the chances of creating interest among the early majority and, thereby, initiates the chain reaction which typifies the diffusion process.**

'Other' markets for communication

Finally, it should be remembered that advertising and promotion are not directed only at customer markets. In Chapter 1, we described six key market domains that need to be addressed by marketing. Therefore, supplier markets, shareholders, employees – indeed, anyone who can have an important influence on the firm's commercial success – can be legitimate targets for advertising and promotional activity.

Sales promotion

Sales promotion should not be confused with advertising

There is often an element of confusion regarding what constitutes sales promotion. Part of this stems from the fact that, in North American textbooks, the term is used to describe all forms of communication, including advertising and personal selling. This all-embracing definition is carried over into the marketing mix, where, as we have seen, 'promotion' covers a wide range of activities.

> **It is thus necessary to distinguish between sales promotion as a general expression and 'a sales promotion', which is a specific activity designed to make a featured offer to defined customers within a limited time-span.**

In other words, in a sales promotion, someone must be offered something which is different from the usual terms and conditions surrounding the transaction. Such a special offer must include tangible benefits not inherent in the standard 'customer' package. The

Figure 6.8 Targets of sales promotions

word customer is put in inverted commas because customers are not always the target of a sales promotion.

The reason for having a sales promotion will be to provide a short-term solution to a problem, hence the reason for it operating over a limited period. Typical objectives for sales promotions are: to increase sales; to counteract competitor activity; to encourage repeat purchase; to encourage speedy repayment of bills; to induce a trial purchase; to smooth out peaks and troughs in demand patterns; and so on.

From these examples, it can be seen that, as with advertising, sales promotion is not necessarily concerned with just sales increases. Moreover, since the objective of the sales promotion is to stimulate the recipient's behaviour and bring it more into line with the service organization's economic interests, the promotion can be directed at different groups of people (Figure 6.8). Thus, for instance, intermediaries might be induced to increase their sales effort. Similarly, the company's own sales force might be motivated to sell less popular services, or open up new geographical territories, if motivated by the prospect of something over and above their normal remuneration.

Types of sales promotion

The many and varied types of sales promotion are listed in Figure 6.9. Each one of these is likely to be more appropriate in some situations than others, because all have advantages and disadvantages. For example, cash reductions can often lead to pressure for a permanent price reduction. Then again, coupons, vouchers and gifts might not necessarily motivate their targets sufficiently, yet could involve high administrative costs. Therefore, great care is required in selecting a scheme appropriate to the objective sought.

> **It is essential that, even though sales promotions are short-term tactical weapons, they should still fulfil their role in the overall communications strategy of the company.**

| Target market | **Type of promotion** | | | | | |
| | Money | | Goods | | Services | |
	Direct	*Indirect*	*Direct*	*Indirect*	*Direct*	*Indirect*
Consumer	Price reduction	Coupons Vouchers Money equivalent Competitions	Free goods Premium offers (e.g. 13 for 12) Free gifts Trade-in offers	Stamps Coupons Vouchers Money equivalent Competitions	Guarantees Group participation events Special exhibitions and displays	Cooperative advertising Stamps Coupons Vouchers for services Events admission Competitions
Trade	Dealer loaders Loyalty schemes Incentives Full-range buying	Extended credit Delayed invoicing Sale or return Coupons Vouchers Money equivalent	Free gifts Trial offers Trade-in offers	Coupons Vouchers Money equivalent Competitions	Guarantees Group participation events Free services Risk reduction schemes Training Special exhibitions Displays Demonstrations Reciprocal trading schemes	Stamps Coupons Vouchers for services Competitions
Sales force	Bonus Commission	Coupons Vouchers Points systems Money equivalent Competitions	Free gifts	Coupons Vouchers Points systems Money equivalent	Free services Group participation events	Coupons Vouchers Points systems for services Event admission Competitions

Figure 6.9 Types of sales promotion

Just as advertising has to be utilized to this end, so do sales promotions. There is little point in management subscribing to what is nothing less than a series of unrelated promotional activities with no overall pattern or coherence. Promotions and advertising need to be properly planned and integrated.

Preparing the sales promotion plan

> **There is widespread acknowledgement that sales promotion is one of the most mismanaged of all marketing functions.**

This is partly because of the confusion about what sales promotion is, which often results in expenditures not being properly

159

recorded. Some companies include it with advertising, others as part of sales force expenditure, others as a general marketing expense, others as an operating expense, while the loss of revenue from special price reductions is often not recorded at all.

Sales promotion is an integral part of marketing strategy

Such failures can be extremely damaging because sales promotion can be such an important part of marketing strategy. Also, with increasing global competition, troubled economic conditions, and growing pressures from channels, sales promotion is becoming more widespread and more acceptable. This means that companies can no longer afford not to set objectives, or to evaluate results after the event, or to fail to have some company guidelines. For example, an airline offering £200 allowance on an international airfare with a contribution rate of £600 has to increase sales by 50 per cent just to maintain the same level of contribution. Failure at least to realize this, or to set alternative objectives for the promotion, can easily result in loss of control and a consequent reduction in profits.

In order to manage a service organization's sales promotion expenditure more effectively, careful planning of the process is essential.

> **First, an objective for sales promotion must be established in the same way that an objective is developed for advertising, pricing, or distribution.**

The objectives for each promotion should be clearly stated, such as trial, repeat purchase, distribution, a shift in buying peaks, combating competition, and so on. Thereafter, the following process should apply:

- Select the appropriate technique
- Pretest
- Mount the promotion
- Evaluate in depth.

Spending must be analysed and categorized by type of activity (special demonstrations, special point-of-sale material, loss of revenue through price reductions, and so on).

As for the sales promotional plan itself, the objectives, strategy and brief details of timing and costs should be included. It is important that too much detail should *not* appear in the sales promotional plan. Detailed promotional instructions will follow as the sales promotional plan unwinds. For example, the checklist shown in Figure 6.10 outlines the kind of detail that should eventually be circulated. However, only an outline of this should appear in the marketing plan itself.

	Headings in sales promotion plan	Content
1	Introduction	Briefly summarize content – what? where? when?
2	Objectives	Marketing and promotional objectives for new service launch.
3	Background	Market data. Justification for technique. Other relevant matters.
4	Promotional offer	Detail the offer: special pricing structure; describe premium; etc. Be brief, precise and unambiguous.
5	Eligibility	Who? Where?
6	Timing	When is the offer available? Call, delivery or invoice dates?
7	Date plan	Assign dates and responsibilities for all aspects of plan prior to start date.
8	Support	Special advertising, point of sale, presenters, leaflets, etc.; public relations, samples, etc.
9	Administration	Invoicing activity. Free invoice lines. Premium (re)ordering procedure. Cash drawing procedures.
10	Sales plan	Targets. Incentives. Effect on routing. Briefing meetings. Telephone sales.
11	Sales presentation	Points to be covered in call.
12	Sales reporting	Procedure for collection of required data not otherwise available.
13	Assessment	How will the promotion be evaluated?

Appendices to plan
Usually designed to be carried by sales people as an aid to selling the promotion:

- Summary of presentation points
- Price structures/profit margins
- Summary of offer
- Schedules of qualifying orders
- Order forms
- Copies of leaflets.

Also required by the sales force may be:

- Leaflets explaining the service
- Demonstration specimen of premium item
- Special report forms
- Returns of cash/premiums etc. issued.

Note: It is assumed that the broad principles of the promotion have already been agreed by the Sales Manager.

Figure 6.10 Key elements of a sales promotion plan

Public relations (PR)

This is the planned and sustained effort to establish and maintain goodwill between a service organization and its publics. These 'publics' include the 'six markets' referred to in Chapter 1. These can, however, also be other individuals or bodies who might only have an indirect impact on the business, yet, nevertheless, merit attention. For example, the main publics of a university are shown in Figure 6.11.

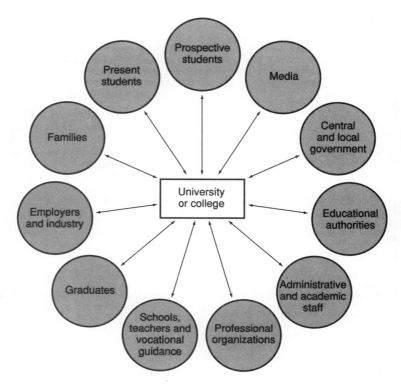

Figure 6.11 Main publics for a university

The tasks most commonly addressed by PR are:

- Building or maintaining an image
- Supporting other communication activities
- Handling specific problems or issues, e.g. a health scare
- Reinforcing positioning
- Assisting in the launch of new services
- Influencing specific publics.

Building a corporate image is of increased importance today.

> **The reason for this is that customers have become more sophisticated and want to know more about the company with whom they will be entering a relationship.**

For their part, companies have used the concept of image development in an attempt to differentiate themselves from competitors.

So, for example, we have 'The Listening Bank', 'The Bank that likes to say yes!', and so on.

As soon as the concept of corporate image is introduced, one is immediately drawn into the concept of customer perceptions, rather than reality. In fact, the whole issue of image is complex, because it is so multifaceted. For example, images can exist at several different levels:

- How a market/public actually sees the company
- How the company sees itself
- How the company would like to see itself
- How the company ought to be seen in order for it to achieve its objectives.

If a company is to tackle this area conscientiously, then it is the first and last of the images listed above that need to be researched and understood. It is these which provide the dimensions of the image gap which can be addressed by public relations activity.

Another issue in the process of image building is to ensure that the perceptions are drawn from appropriate customer groups and segments. For instance, just looking at one market could reveal a different set of images depending upon the type of relationship with the customer:

- Regular customers
- Intermittent customers
- One-off customers
- Potential customers – with whom the company has been in contact
  – to whom the company is largely unknown.

The major PR objectives will be to assess where important image gaps exist and then take actions to close them. A gap can be closed by:

- Changing the company so that it conforms more with the expected image of the market/public
- Changing the market/public's perception so that it moves closer to the company reality
- Some combination of these two broad approaches.

There is no single specific activity that can alter a service organization's image. Everything it does, and every point of contact with a customer, contributes in some way to the end result. The service itself, the quality of dealings with the staff, the nature of its advertising and even the style of the letter headings, all have a part to play.

However, it is in no one's interest to strive for an image which cannot be sustained.

PR 'tools'

A wide range of approaches can be used in the design of a PR programme. These could include:

- Publications, e.g. press releases, annual reports, brochures, posters, articles, videos, and employee reports
- Events, e.g. press conferences, seminars, conferences
- Stories which create media interest, e.g. new contracts, design breakthroughs
- Exhibitions and displays
- Sponsorship, e.g. charitable causes, sports events, theatre and the arts, community projects.

As with the other elements of the communications mix, a PR programme should follow an overall process which consists of specifying the objectives, determining the best PR mix of activities integrating these over the planning period, and evaluating the results.

Direct marketing

Direct marketing is often assumed to be another name for direct mail. This is not correct, because it encompasses a number of media, of which direct mail is just one. There are six main approaches to direct marketing:

- Direct mail
- Mail order
- Direct response advertising
- Telemarketing
- Direct selling
- Digital marketing (using electronic media).

In any direct marketing campaign, these can be used either singly or in combination. The objective is to establish a two-way, personalized relationship between the company and its customers.

When tackled well, that is to say, when well-chosen customers are targeted with personalized communications that are relevant to them, direct marketing is not only very acceptable, but can also deliver spectacular results.

Direct marketing can be very powerful when properly managed	When managed in a poor manner, direct marketing can be seen as an invasion of privacy, a waste of resources (paper, time and money), and a patronizing and inefficient method of communicating.

The initial approach to customers is driven by an identification of prospects which are often obtained through lists which are rented by the company, or built up from its own data banks. Current technology makes it possible for all initial contact with these people to be personalized, not only by use of their name, but also in terms of knowing key aspects about their lifestyle or purchasing intentions. The message will aim to get the recipient to take action of some sort, such as, for example, to attend a demonstration, to call for a free consultation, or to apply for a promotional video or brochure. The purpose is to initiate contact and stimulate the communication process. The service organization can then respond in whatever way is appropriate and move the relationship towards an eventual sale.

As markets become more fragmented, direct sales forces get more expensive to run.

The advances in technology make it easier to personalize communications and so direct marketing becomes a feasible and more attractive proposition.

One of the major reasons for its success is that its cost-effectiveness can be measured, since the results generated by a programme can be compared with its cost. Direct marketing can account for up to 14 per cent of media expenditure in those companies where its value has been recognized. Companies such as British Telecom, American Express, Royal Mail, and most airlines and banks are already using direct marketing extensively to build profitable business.

Since special skills and resources are needed to run direct marketing campaigns, a company may wish to use an outside specialist agency rather than rely on its own staff, in the same way that advertising and sales promotions are typically contracted out. Experimentation with providing incentives for customers to stay in 'dialogue' is helping to improve the success rate of direct marketing still further.

As with all the other aspects of planning, it is essential that the programme for direct marketing starts on the basis of having clear objectives. Once these are in place, it becomes relatively straightforward to schedule the component activities into a coherent plan.

Table 6.3   Personal contact functions in services

Function	Responsibilities	Examples
Selling	To persuade potential customers to purchase services and/or to increase the use of services by existing customers	Insurance agent; stockbroker; bank calling officer; real estate salesperson
Service	To inform, assist and advise customers	Airline flight attendant; insurance claims adjuster; ticket agent; bank branch manager
Monitoring	To learn about customers' needs and concerns and report them to management	Customer service representative; repair person

Source: Based on Johnson, E. M., Scheuing, E. E. and Gaida, K. A. (1986) *Profitable Services Marketing*, Dow Jones-Irwin, Homewood, Illinois. p. 212.

Personal communications

The three main types of customer contact through personal communications are: selling, servicing and monitoring. Table 6.3 provides a framework for considering the personal contact function in services together with responsibilities and some typical examples. This suggests that whilst selling is a pervasive activity in many services organizations, other forms of personal contact including service and monitoring are also important.

The most potent element of face-to-face communications is that provided by the sales force. However, the strategic role of sales has to be assessed in the context of the service organization's overall communications strategy. In order to get things into perspective, top management must be able to answer the following kinds of question:

- How important is personal selling in our business?
- What role does it have in the marketing mix?
- How many salespeople do we need?
- What do we want them to do?
- How should they be managed?

The answers to these questions go a long way towards defining the scope of the sales plan.

The role of personal selling

Personal selling is widely used in many service industries. Financial services, for example, use a high level of media advertising, but still rely heavily on personal selling. Here contact with sales staff is important because with the potential ambiguities surrounding a service, customers need to be able to discuss their needs and the sales-person is needed to explain the choices available.

> Recent surveys have shown that more money is spent by companies on their sales force than on advertising and sales promotion combined. Selling is, therefore, not only a vital element of the marketing mix, but also an expensive one.

Personal selling has a number of advantages over other elements of the marketing mix:

1 It provides two-way communication.
2 The sales message can be more flexible (than with advertising) and can be more closely tailored to the needs of individual customers.
3 The salesperson can use in-depth knowledge of the service to the advantage of the customer, and overcome objections as they arise.
4 Most importantly, the sales person can ask for an order, and, possibly, also negotiate on price and special requirements.

Whilst in front of a customer the salesperson is, to all intents and purposes, not a representative of the company, but the company itself. This means that any personal credibility the salesperson establishes should reflect well on the organization as a whole. Unfortunately, the converse of this is equally true.

What does the company want salespeople to do?

The immediate response to such a question is simple: 'Go out and sell'. However, there are obviously more specific issues to be addressed, including:

- How much should be sold? (Value of unit sales volume)
- What should be sold? (Over the range of services)
- To whom should it be sold? (Which market segments)

In other words, the selling objectives are derived directly from the marketing objectives.

Sales staff undertake a range of activities. The salesperson is not selling all the time, in the sense of being in front of a customer. There are other activities, which combine to make up a typical week's work, and which are shown in Figure 6.12.

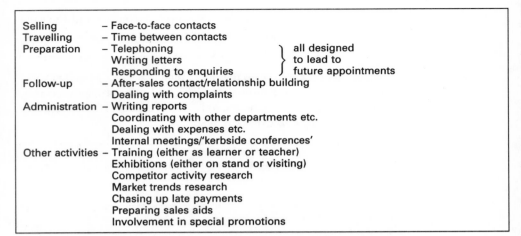

Selling	– Face-to-face contacts
Travelling	– Time between contacts
Preparation	– Telephoning Writing letters Responding to enquiries	} all designed to lead to future appointments
Follow-up	– After-sales contact/relationship building Dealing with complaints
Administration	– Writing reports Coordinating with other departments etc. Dealing with expenses etc. Internal meetings/'kerbside conferences'
Other activities	– Training (either as learner or teacher) Exhibitions (either on stand or visiting) Competitor activity research Market trends research Chasing up late payments Preparing sales aids Involvement in special promotions

Figure 6.12 Typical salesperson activities

From the list in Figure 6.12, it can be seen that some activities are more productive than others. Clearly, it is in the company's interest to structure the sales job so that non-productive activities are kept to a minimum, thus freeing valuable time to be spent where it can make most impact.

Exactly how this is done, and how the sales force is kept motivated and operating at a high level of efficiency, is the task of sales management. Since this topic would merit a book in its own right, we propose to say little more on the subject, except that it is essential that quantitative objectives are set, whatever the sales activity. Whether these are for the number of visits made, sales achieved, letters written, complaints handled, or whatever, without a quantitative target against which to measure achievement, sales management is rendered impotent. The reader wishing to explore this topic further should see Wilson.[7]

How many sales people?

By analysing the current activities of the sales force (using a categorisation like the list in Figure 6.12), and finding out how much time is actually spent on each activity, the company is well on the way to answering this question. When this is undertaken for the first time, it often becomes apparent that the sales force needs to be redirected or that the sales job needs to be redefined.

Nevertheless, it is possible to establish an ideal work pattern which holds a real prospect of generating a particular sales value.

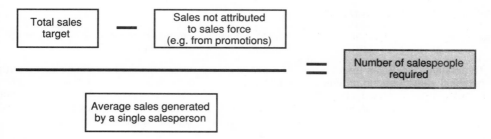

Figure 6.13 Formula for deriving the size of the sales force

The formula in Figure 6.13 can be used to calculate the size of the sales force.

Of course, while the outcome of this calculation is obvious, the end result has to be tempered with common sense. For example, if the coverage of some sales territories incurred a disproportionately high amount of non-productive travel, then there could be a case for employing additional sales staff in some regions. Alternatively, it could act as a stimulus for finding new ways to tackle the problem, perhaps by using telephone sales.

One life insurance company has developed a sophisticated computer model based on the number of enquiries and a probabilistic estimate of the gestation time of direct mail. The purpose of the model is to predict demand and then to recruit and train salespeople well ahead of peak loads.

Preparing a sales plan

No two company sales plans will be the same, because the role of the sales force might well be different.

> **A properly developed sales plan will ensure the sales force does not just go out and sell whatever they can, to whomever they can.**

Thus, the sales plan should indicate *how* the sales force is going to be deployed in pursuit of the company's marketing objectives.

The total sales target should be translated into regional objectives and then into individual goals. Bearing in mind the need for all activities to be quantifiable, and hence measurable, an individual salesperson's plan may look something like the example shown in Table 6.4.

It is at this individual level that the sales plan stands or falls, and it is the role of sales management, supported by top management, to see that it is prepared thoroughly.

Table 6.4 Example of salesperson's plan

Task	The standard	How to set the standard	How to measure performance	What to look for
1 To achieve personal sales target	Sales target per period of time for individual groups and/or products	Analysis of • territory potential • individual customers' potential Discussion and agreement between salesperson and manager	Comparison of individual salesperson's product sales against targets	Significant shortfall between target and achievement over a meaningful period
2 To sell the required range and quantity to individual customers	Achievement of specified range and quantity of sales to a particular customer or group of customers within an agreed time period	Analysis of individual customer records of • potential • present sales Discussion and agreement between manager and salesperson	Scrutiny of • individual customer records • observation of selling in the field	Failure to achieve agreed objectives. Complacency with range of sales made to individual customers
3 To plan journeys and call frequencies to achieve minimum practicable selling cost	To achieve appropriate call frequency on individual customers. Number of live customer calls during a given time period	Analysis of individual customers' potential. Analysis of order/call ratios. Discussion and agreement between manager and salesperson	Scrutiny of individual customer records. Analysis of order/ call ratio. Examination of call reports	High ratio of calls to an individual customer relative to that customer's yield. Shortfall on agreed total number of calls made over an agreed time period
4 To acquire new customers	Number of prospect calls during time period. Selling new products to existing customers	Identify total number of potential and actual customers who could produce results. Identify opportunity areas for prospecting	Examination of • call reports • records of new accounts opened • ratio of existing to potential customers	Shortfall in number of prospect calls from agreed standard. Low ratio of existing to potential customers
5 To make a sales approach of the required quality	To exercise the necessary skills and techniques required to achieve the identified objective of each element of the sales approach. Continuous use of sales material	Standard to be agreed in discussion between manager and salesperson related to company standards laid down	Regular observations of field selling using a systematic analysis of performance in each stage of the sales approach	Failure to • identify objective of each stage of sales approach • specify areas of skill, weakness • use support material

Source: Based on work originally done by F. Norse whilst with Urwick Orr and Partners

Mix element 3   The pricing plan

Pricing is addressed as a separate element of the marketing mix because this provides a sensible way for the complex issues relating to pricing to be considered. In fact, the company may choose not to have a separate plan for pricing, and subsume pricing decisions into the individual service/segment plans. Whether or not the pricing element appears as a separate plan, careful thought will have to be given to the pricing structure.

The pricing decision is important for two main reasons:

> - It affects the margin through its impact on revenue.
> - It affects the quantity sold through its influence on demand.

It must, therefore, be seen as part of a consciously-defined initiative, whose objectives have been clearly defined.

Pricing decisions for services are particularly important, given the intangible nature of the service product. The price charged signals to customers information about the quality that they are likely to receive. Also, because they cannot be stored, services may attract premium prices when demand is high and discounts when demand is low.

Pricing is further complicated in that it is sometimes the subject of conflict between the accounting and marketing departments. On the one hand the traditional accountant's viewpoint is concerned with covering costs and charging prices to get a fixed margin over and above these costs. Sometimes opposing them is the marketer, who recognizes that price is an important determinant of how much will be sold. The marketer may see the need for holding prices, or even reducing them, so as to maintain, or to increase, market share and thereby build the share needed for long-term success.

Prices need to reflect value

> **High-quality services have an intrinsic value for the customer and it is this value, rather than the cost of providing the service, that pricing decisions need to consider.**

Pricing decisions need to reflect the strategic opportunity of the organization. A simple cost-plus approach to pricing disregards the advantages which can be gained by a well-researched and well-managed pricing policy.

Pricing objectives

The different pricing methods or approaches for services are broadly similar to those used for goods. The pricing method to be used should commence with a review of pricing objectives. These might include:

> - *Survival* In adverse market conditions the pricing objective may involve foregoing desired levels of profitability to ensure survival.
> - *Profit maximization* Pricing to ensure maximization of profitability over a given period. The period concerned will be related to the life cycle of the service.
> - *Sales maximization* Pricing to build market share. This may involve selling at a loss initially in an effort to capture a high share of the market.
> - *Prestige* A service company may wish to use pricing to position itself as exclusive. High-priced restaurants and Concorde are examples.
> - *ROI* Pricing objectives may be based on achieving a desired return on investment.

These are some of the most common, but by no means all, pricing objectives. The decision a service organization makes on pricing will be dependent on a range of factors including:

> - Positioning of the service
> - Corporate objectives
> - The nature of competition
> - Life cycle of the service(s)
> - Elasticity of demand
> - Cost structures
> - Shared resources
> - Prevailing economic conditions
> - Service capacity

Three of these elements, the demand, costs and competition, require further discussion.

Demand

It is important to know if demand is elastic or inelastic

Service companies need to understand that there is a relationship between price and demand. Further, demand varies at different pricing levels. It may also vary by market segment. A useful framework to help understand this relationship is the 'elasticity of demand'. This concept helps service managers understand whether demand is elastic (a given percentage change in price produces a greater percentage change in demand) or inelastic (a significant change in price produces relatively little change in levels of demand). These different characteristics of demand are shown in Figure 6.14. Pricing levels are especially important if demand for the service is elastic. Examples where demand for services is elastic include airlines, railways, cinemas and package tours. Other services such as medical care and electricity supply exhibit more inelastic behaviour.

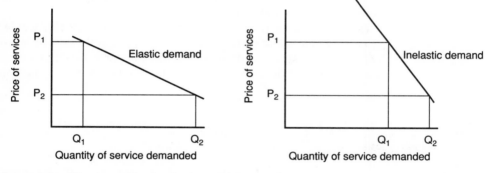

Figure 6.14 Elastic and inelastic demand for services

Costs

Understanding and measuring fixed and variable costs is critical in pricing

The costs of providing services and how these vary over time and with the level of demand also need to be understood. Two major types of costs, fixed costs and variable costs, need to be identified. In addition, some costs may be semi-variable. Fixed costs are those which do not vary with the level of output. They remain fixed over a given period and include buildings, furniture, staff costs, maintenance, etc. Variable costs vary according to the quantity of the service provided or sold. They include part-time employees' wages, expendable supplies, postage, etc. It should be noted that some costs have elements which are partly fixed and partly variable. These include telephone costs and salaried staff used for overtime work.

Many service businesses, such as airlines, have high levels of fixed costs because of the expense of the equipment and staff needed to operate them. For example, in financial services, fixed costs can represent more than 60 per cent of total costs.

> **Total costs represent the sum of the fixed, variable and semi-variable costs at a given level of output. Service managers need to understand how cost behaviour will vary at different levels of service output. This has important implications for decisions to expand capacity, as well as for pricing.**

A useful tool to help managers understand cost behaviour in a service industry is the experience curve. The experience curve is an empirically derived relationship which suggests that as accumulated sales or output doubles, costs per unit (in real terms) typically fall by between 20 and 30 per cent. Many financial service organizations have moved from paper-based processing, which offers no real economies of scale, to mechanization and use of electronic processing, which offers considerable potential for scale economies. Figure 6.15 shows an experience curve for electronic banking compared with paper processing of cheques.

In retail banking, the use of automatic teller machines (ATMs) has had a profound effect on lowering costs. Although the cost of installing an ATM can be high, once installed the per transaction cost is considerably less than using a human bank teller in the transaction.

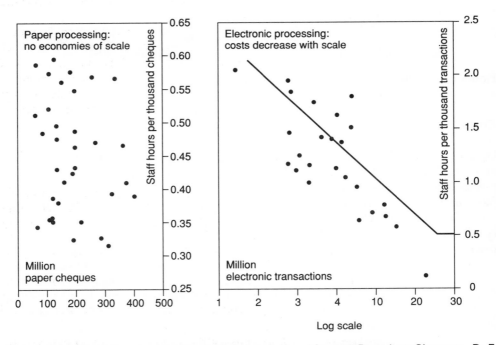

Figure 6.15 Experience curve for electronic banking (*Source*: Based on Channon, D. F. (1988) *Global Banking Strategy*, Wiley, New York, p. 307; material from Boston Consulting Group)

In the USA, volumes of ATM transact[...] age of 4000 transactions per month in 19[...] transactions per month in 1983; and whilst [...] with inflation, the cost of ATMs was falling in re[...] 10 per cent per annum[8].

The experience curve can help service managers [...] potential to use scale and mechanization to improve the[...] position.

Competition

It is also essential to understand the costs and pricing behaviour of competitors. As well as seeking information about the prices of key competitors in each major segment, the cost position of major competitors needs to be considered.

> **An understanding of competitors' costs helps the service marketing manager to make a realistic assessment of competitors' ability to change their pricing structure.**

For example, organizations such as Citibank in its US retail operations have sought to gain competitive advantage by achieving the lowest cost position in clearing transactions.

Benchmarking of competitors should be undertaken to determine their costs, prices and profitability. This can be done by a range of techniques including competitive shopping and market research and should include a price–quality comparison of each major competitor's offer. The competitors' position in terms of profitability, cost position and market share, in each segment, can then be considered when making the pricing decision.

Pricing methods

When the basic pricing objectives have been considered and a review made of demand, costs, competitors' prices and costs, and other relevant factors, the services marketer needs to consider the method by which prices will be set.

Methods for setting prices vary considerably in the services sector and typically include:

> - *Cost plus pricing,* where a given percentage markup is sought.
> - *Rate of return pricing,* where prices are set to achieve a given rate of return on investments or assets. This is sometimes called 'target return' pricing.

...*y pricing*, where prices are set on the
...those set by the market leader.

...*ng*, usually done on a short time basis,
...sition in the market or to provide an
...ss-sell other services.

...*g*, where prices are based on the servi-
...lue to a given customer segment. It
...ket-driven approach which reinforces
...the service and the benefits the custo-
...the service.

...*ng*, where prices are based on consid-
...potential profit streams over the lifetime

Relationship pricing

Cost-plus pricing is rarely appropriate

It is obvious that cost-plus based pricing is often unacceptable, as customers are interested in their own costs, not those of its supplier. Further, costs in many service businesses can be extremely hard to estimate, as companies offer a range of services and typically have a high level of resource sharing.

Relationship pricing can be a major source of competitive advantage

Relationship pricing is the appropriate form of pricing where there is an ongoing contact between the service provider and the customer.

> **Relationship pricing follows closely the market-oriented approach of value-based pricing, but takes the lifetime value of the customer into account.**

It is based on value considerations of all the services provided to the customer and makes an assessment of the potential profit stream over a given period of time – often the lifetime of the customer. Whilst value-based pricing which emphasizes benefits drives this pricing philosophy, it allows the firm to use loss-leader, competitive or marginal costing at appropriate points in time, on relevant services, for both strategic and tactical purposes.

A value-based relationship approach to pricing aims at helping to position the service and reflects the fact that customers are prepared to pay extra for the perceived benefits provided by both the core product and the product surround. This concept is shown in Figure 6.16 and suggests that customers will pay a premium for perceived benefits and especially those supplied by the product surround in terms of brand image, brand values and service quality.

The services marketing mix

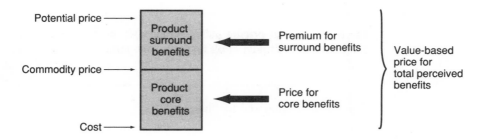

Figure 6.16 Value based pricing

The size of the price premium is not meant to be to scale in Figure 6.16. In fact, the premium provided by the surround could be greater than the price for the core product or service benefit.

An approach increasingly being used by service firms to enhance their product surround and achieve premium prices is the unconditional service guarantee. 'Bugs' Burger Bug Killers (BBBK) are a pest-extermination company based in Miami who charge up to 600 per cent more than some of their competitors and have a high market share with clients who have severe pest problems. Its service guarantee to clients in the hotel and restaurant sectors promises:[9]

---

1 You don't owe one penny until all pests on your premises have been eradicated.
2 If you are ever dissatisfied with BBBK's service, you will receive a refund for up to 12 months of the company's services – plus fees for another exterminator of your choice for the next year.
3 If a guest spots a pest on your premises, BBBK will pay for the guest's meal or room, send a letter of apology, and pay for a future meal or stay.
4 If your facility is closed down due to the presence of roaches or rodents, BBBK will pay any fines, as well as all lost profits, plus $5000.

The significant price premium charged by BBBK for their services and the unconditional service guarantee do not imply staggeringly high costs. In 1986 BBBK paid out only $120 000 in claims on their unconditional service guarantee, on sales of $33 million.

In conclusion, it must be emphasized that the price charged for the service affects, and is affected by, the other elements of the marketing mix. There is no outright guarantee that the lowest price will win the order, nor can it be assumed that a competitive price will, by itself, generate the necessary sales revenue.

> **The reality is that pricing policy should only be determined after account has been taken of all factors which impinge on the pricing decision.**

These are summarized in Figure 6.17.

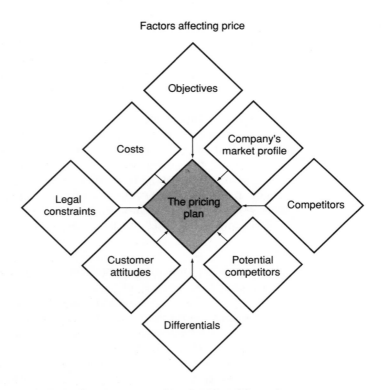

Figure 6.17 Factors to consider in the pricing plan

Mix element 4   The place plan – getting the service to the customers

Deciding on the location and channels for supplying services to target customers determines how the service will be delivered and where this should take place. Between them, these service delivery factors offer the prospect of establishing a competitive advantage, since they influence both the level of service to the customer, and the cost of providing it.

Location decisions

The importance of location will, to a large extent, depend upon the nature of the service provided and the type of interaction it sets up between the suppliers and the customer. (These were discussed earlier in Figure 1.7 in Chapter 1). There are three possibilities:

1 *The customer goes to the service provider*
   In these circumstances, site location is very important. For some service businesses, like a restaurant or holiday centre, location may be the prime reason behind its success. Moreover, there is always a prospect of further growth from offering the service at more than one location, as long as each catchment area is well-chosen. Indeed, some multisite operators have developed sophisticated computer programmes in order to optimize their location strategy.

2 *The service provider goes to the customer*
   Here, site location is a far less critical issue, providing the service company remains sufficiently close to be able to maintain a quality service to its customers. In some cases, the supplier has no discretion in terms of going to the customer. This could be in businesses like plumbing, window cleaning, landscape gardening and so on. In other cases, the service company might have some discretion whether or not they provide the service at the customer's premises or their own. Such business could include personal fitness, hairdressing and TV repair. Some dry cleaning and laundry firms have even found that it is more effective to close down expensive high street outlets and move their operations to a low-cost out-of-town location. They could maintain their business by providing a pick-up and delivery service.

3 *The service provider and customer transact business at arm's length*
   Here, the location is largely irrelevant and so least cost might be the deciding factor on this issue. There will, of course, need to be a suitable communications infrastructure available, depending upon the nature of the service. Thus, a mail-order company will need access to a reliable mail service; likewise an express parcels service will need good access to motorways and airports.
   Many face-to-face services companies have successfully transferred to arm's length transactions. For example, insurance and banking can now be done via the telephone and post.

Channel decisions

These decisions influence who participates in the service delivery, either in terms of organizations or people. A channel will consist of:

- The service provider
- (Possibly) intermediaries, e.g. agents, brokers, franchisees
- Customers.

Whereas, traditionally, services were delivered by direct sales (e.g. professional services), increasingly, intermediaries are now being used. For example, travel agencies act as middlemen for airlines, hotels and leisure services. Similarly, recruitment agencies provide a link between employers and potential employees.

The broad channel options are outlined in Figure 6.18. The ultimate choice of channel will depend upon a number of different factors, which can influence singly or in combination:

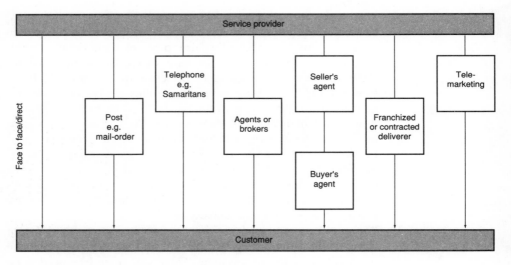

Figure 6.18 Channel options for service companies

- Ease and accessibility for customers
- The added value they provide
- The margins they seek
- The coverage they provide
- Their reputation and reliability
- Their compatibility with the supplier.

In strategic terms, the supplier should be concerned with:

> - Understanding the distribution channels of its competitors
> - Understanding the strengths and weaknesses of these channels
> - Identifying how the company can avoid the problems experienced by competitors in existing channels, or creating alternative channel strategies by changing the type of intermediaries or what they traditionally do.

However, the choice of channel strategy can rarely be made in isolation from the issue of location. So, for example, a decision by a bank to switch to electronic systems, which require fewer face-to-face contacts, reduces the need for high street premises. Instead, customer convenience is enhanced by having cash machines sited in, say, busy out-of-town superstores.

Mix element 5   The people element of the marketing mix

It is the people element, above all, that differentiates services marketing from product marketing

Another issue for the supplier is to ensure that the service received by the customer is of the same high quality, regardless of how it is delivered. This is particularly true where a franchised delivery system is used. Setting rigorous selection standards and providing training are two methods which can help to maintain quality in most situations. The difficult areas are where the service providers are of low education and tend not to remain in one job for very long, such as in the hotel and catering trades. Here, quality control is largely in the hands not of the operatives themselves, but of their supervisors and managers.

People in services

> It is clear that people loom large in the delivery of services. As indicated above, in the final analysis, it is largely a matter of how people are selected, trained, motivated and managed that influences the consistency of its quality. As more companies come to recognize this, so they are paying more attention to the different roles which people might play, both in customer contact and marketing in general.

One way of looking at roles is shown in Figure 6.19. This categorization, developed by Judd,[10] results in four groups:

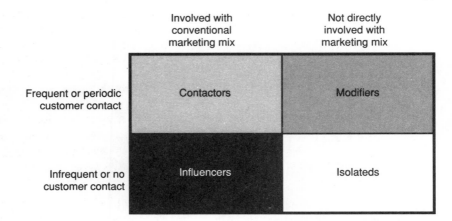

Figure 6.19 Employees and their influence on customers (*Source*: Based on Judd, V. C. (1987) Differentiate with the 5th P. *Industrial Marketing Management*, **16**, 241–7)

- *Contactors* have frequent or regular customer contact and are typically heavily involved with conventional marketing activities. They hold a range of positions in service firms, including selling and customer service roles. Whether they are involved in planning or execution of marketing strategy, they need to be well versed in the marketing strategies of the firm. They should be well trained, prepared and motivated to serve the customers on a day-to-day basis in a responsive manner. They should be recruited based on their potential to be responsive to customer needs and be evaluated and rewarded on this basis.
- *Modifiers* are people such as receptionists, credit department and switchboard personnel, and while they are not directly involved with conventional marketing activities to a great degree, they nevertheless have frequent customer contact. As such, they need to have a clear view of the organization's marketing strategy and the role that they can play in being responsive to customers' needs. They have a vital role to play especially, but not exclusively, in service businesses. Modifiers need to develop high levels of customer relationship skills. Training and monitoring of performance are especially important here.
- *Influencers*, while involved with the traditional elements of the marketing mix, have infrequent or no customer contact. However, they are very much part of the implementation of the organization's marketing strategy. They include roles such as product development and market research. In recruitment of influencers, people with the

> potential to develop a sense of customer responsiveness should be pursued. Influencers should be evaluated and rewarded according to customer-oriented performance standards, and opportunities to enhance the level of customer contact should be programmed into their activities.
>
> • *Isolateds* are the various support functions which neither have frequent customer contact nor a great deal to do with the conventional marketing activities. However, as support people, their activities critically affect performance of the organization's activities. Staff falling within this category include purchase department, personnel and data processing. Such staff need to be sensitive to the fact that internal customers as well as external customers have needs which must be satisfied. They need to understand the company's overall marketing strategy and how their functions contribute to the quality of delivered value to the customer.

This type of analysis illustrates that not only do people play an important part in the transactions between the supplier and the customer, but also that they can be a source of differentiation for the service.

> **By adding value in the way they perform and by maximizing the impact of their activities, people have the capacity to give the company a competitive edge.**

Internal marketing

It is now widely recognized that for services organizations to be successful in their external marketing, they also need to practise internal marketing.

Internal marketing was discussed in Chapter 1 in the context of internal markets. There are at least two key elements to internal marketing:

• Every employee and every department within an organization have roles both as internal customers and internal suppliers. To help ensure high quality external marketing, every individual and department within a service organization must provide and receive excellent service.

• People need to work together in a way that is aligned with the organization's stated mission, strategy and goals. This is obviously a critical element within high-contact service firms where there are high levels of interaction between the service provider and customer.

Leading companies such as British Airways, SAS, and Marks and Spencer have recognized the importance of internal marketing and have developed organizational philosophies along these lines. They subscribe to all members of staff providing the best possible contribution to the marketing activities, and engaging in all telephone, mail, electronic and personal encounters in a manner which adds value to the service. Such internal marketing initiatives are not passing gimmicks, but are backed up with rigorous and frequent training programmes, codes of behaviour, dress standards and awards for outstanding performers. This involvement of staff, in what for many organizations is a new and liberating policy, can set up an irreversible thrust, which only wanes when the organization's culture and climate change in a fundamental way.

A pilot study[11] and ongoing research, conducted since 1991, indicate that relatively few *formal* internal marketing programmes exist in the UK. However, there are many services companies who have adopted elements of internal marketing in a less formal way. The pilot study found that, in companies practising internal marketing:

- Internal marketing is generally not a discrete activity, but is implicit in quality initiatives, customer service programmes and broader business strategies.
- Companies structured activities accompanied by a range of less formal ad hoc initiatives.
- Communication is critical to successful internal marketing.
- Internal marketing performs a critical role in competitive differentiation.
- Internal marketing has an important role to play in reducing conflict between the functional areas of the organization.
- Internal marketing is an experiential process, leading employees to form their own conclusions.
- Internal marketing is evolutionary: it involves the slow erosion of barriers between departments and functions. It has an important role in helping with the balancing of marketing and operations – a problem that is discussed under the processes element of the marketing mix.
- Internal marketing is used to facilitate a spirit of innovation.
- Internal marketing is more successful when there is commitment at the highest level, when all employees cooperate, and an open management style prevails.

The study showed that internal marketing in all its forms was recognized as an important activity in contributing to the people element of the marketing mix and in developing a customer-focused organization (see Chapter 7). In practice, internal marketing is concerned with communications, with developing responsiveness, responsibility and unity of purpose. The fundamental aims of internal marketing are to develop internal and external customer awareness and remove functional barriers to organizational effectiveness.

It is clear that internal marketing is at an early stage of development and is one where practitioners lead academic research. While little has been codified about internal marketing practice, it is clear that a consideration of internal markets is essential. Where internal marketing is concerned with the development of a customer orientation, the alignment of internal and external marketing ensures coherent relationship marketing.[12]

Mix element 6   The processes element of the marketing mix

> **The processes by which services are created and delivered to the customer can be a major factor within the services marketing mix, for customers perceive the delivery system as part of the service itself. This means that operations management decisions can be of great importance regarding the competitive position of the service.**

Process, in the sense it is used here, means work activity. Thus, any procedure, task, schedule, mechanism or routine which helps to deliver the service to the customer will fall under this heading. From this it follows that any policy decisions that are made about customer involvement or employee discretion have a direct impact on the processes element of the marketing mix.

Processes play a crucial role in service delivery

While people play a critical role in the mix, they will be severely handicapped if the process performance is inherently flawed. So, for example, if the processes supporting delivery cannot quickly respond and repair a service fault, or if the hotel kitchen takes too long to prepare a meal, all the initial positive impact of the contact staff is destroyed. This suggests that close cooperation is required between marketing and those who are involved in process management.

> **Furthermore, any improvements in processes will inevitably lead to an improvement in service quality.**

If the service runs efficiently, the service provider will have a clear advantage over less effective competitors.

Decision-making processes are also important in the context of this element of the marketing mix. Some service providers give their service deliverers the autonomy to make decisions up to a certain level. For example, an airline can give its staff powers to upgrade a passenger who is aggrieved about his treatment, thereby enabling them to defuse a situation on the spot in a satisfying way. Similarly Rank Xerox empower quite junior staff to correct service errors on the spot up to a cost of £200.

Not all services can lend themselves to this approach, however. For example, a waiter can only bill for food at the published price. Any discretionary powers are inevitably held by the restaurant manager, which means that customers have to demand to see the manager if their grievance is to be resolved.

It can be seen from these examples that, in general, the more specialized the service, the more decision-making is entrusted to the service provider. This allows for greater customization and personalization of the service. Less specialized services, on the whole, have less scope for doing this.

The 'process plan', therefore, needs to address two main issues:

> ● How can processes be improved in order to help achieve an improved competitive positioning strategy?
> ● How can marketing and operations be managed in a way that is synergistic?

Analysing the processes

Stostack[13] has developed a simple three-step approach for analysing a process:

> 1 Break down the process into logical steps and sequences.
> 2 Identify those steps which introduce the highest prospect of something going wrong because of judgement, choice or chance.
> 3 Set deviation or tolerance standards for these steps, thereby providing a performance band for functioning. (It will be unrealistic to expect process steps to be performed with complete precision every time.)

By adopting this approach, errant processes can be made to fulfil their purpose in a more consistent and service-enhancing way.

Processes can also be considered in terms of their *complexity*, i.e. the number or nature of the steps and sequences, and *divergence*, i.e.

the latitude or variability involved. Thus, for example, a beach ice-cream salesperson has a delivery process which is neither complex nor divergent. In contrast, a book-keeper's job might be quite high in complexity, but relatively modest in divergence. Another example, say a surgeon, would be high on both parameters.

Using this approach for looking at processes, four improvement strategies are possible:[14]

- *Reduce divergence* This option would tend to standardize the service and limit the extent to which it might be customized. While this offers the prospects of reducing costs and improving productivity, it could also alienate those customers for whom customization was a considerable benefit.
- *Increase divergence* This would allow for greater customization and flexibility, for which it might be possible to charge premium prices. This may be a suitable strategy for niche positioning of the service, where high volume sales would not be anticipated.
- *Reduce complexity* Here, steps and activities are omitted from the service process. This has the effect of making distribution and control easier, since some peripheral activities disappear.
- *Increase complexity* With this approach, more services are added to the core service product, usually with the intention of creating a competitive advantage and gaining market penetration. Financial services companies and supermarkets frequently use this approach.

All of these options carry with them advantages and disadvantages. In that sense, no single approach is any better than another. What is significant, however, is that the chosen process strategy will impact on customers' perceptions, in effect causing the service to be repositioned (Figure 6.20).

Assuming that the existing general management consultancy shown in Figure 6.20 could be positioned roughly in the centre of the map, repositioning could be achieved broadly in line with the suggestions in this figure. The alteration in complexity and divergency is analogous to changing elements of design of a product, thus their impact on the marketing mix is both obvious and influential.

Conflict between operations and marketing

While this might not be obvious in most service companies, there may be elements of conflict implicit in the way that operations and

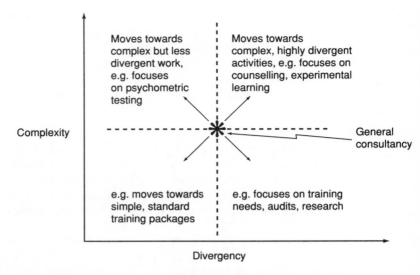

Figure 6.20 Example of service positioning through changing complexity and divergency (a management training consultancy)

marketing people would view the same issue.[15] Table 6.5 illustrates some common areas of contention.

Clearly, all of the issues listed in the table affect both operations and marketing. However, where operations management is a more traditional part of the organizational fabric and marketing less deeply rooted, decision-making may be skewed in favour of operations. This is particularly likely to be the case if the organization tends to operate with a financial 'orientation', where everything is measured in terms of short-term profit or loss.

> **The message for marketers is quite clear. They must take the initiative and make greater impact on operational decisions by providing cost-benefit trade-offs to back up their arguments.**

Mix element 7 The customer service element of the marketing mix

As customers become more sophisticated and demand higher standards, so must companies improve customer service in order to remain competitive.

In most marketing literature, customer service has been subsumed under the broad heading of 'place' in the marketing mix. The reasoning for this was that since reliability and speed of delivery were thought to be the main elements of customer satisfaction, the way

Table 6.5 Potential sources of conflict between operations and marketing on operational issues

Operational issues	Typical operations goals	Common marketing concerns
Productivity improvement	Reduce unit cost of production	Strategies may cause decline in service quality
Standardization versus customization	Keep costs low and quality consistent; simplify operations tasks; recruit low-cost employees	Consumers may seek variety, prefer customization to match segmented needs
Batch versus unit processing	Seek economies of scale, consistency, efficient use of capacity	Customers may be forced to wait, feel one of a crowd, be turned off by other customers
Facilities layout and design	Control costs; improve efficiency by ensuring proximity of operationally related tasks; enhance safety and security	Customers may be confused, shunted around unnecessarily, find facilities unattractive and inconvenient
Job design	Minimize error, waste and fraud; make efficient use of technology; simplify tasks for standardization	Operational oriented employees with narrow roles may be unresponsive to customer needs
Management of capacity	Keep costs down by avoiding wasteful underutilization of resources	Service may be unavailable when needed; quality may be compromised during high-demand periods
Management of queues	Optimize use of available capacity by planning for average throughput; maintain customer order, discipline	Customers may be bored and frustrated during wait, see firm as unresponsive

Source: Lovelock, C. (1992) Seeking synergy in service operations: seven things a marketer needs to know about service operations. *European Management Journal*, **10** (1), 24.

that services were delivered was seen to be a distribution and logistics problem. However, in the light of experience in recent years, companies have developed different perspectives on customer service. Thus, it is possible to identify a range of different views regarding how it may be defined. Here are just some of these:[16]

- All activities required to accept, process, deliver and fulfil customer orders and to follow up any activity that has gone wrong
- Delivering products and services to customers in accordance with their expectations of timeliness and reliability
- A complex of activities involving all areas of the business which combine to deliver the company's products and services in a way that is perceived as satisfactory by the customer and which advances the company's objectives

- Total ordering, all communications, all invoicing and total control of defects, inasmuch as these affect customers
- Timely and accurate delivery of products and services, with accurate follow-up and enquiry response times.

Although it is possible to detect a consistent theme or undercurrent running through all of these definitions, it is clear that the meaning of customer service varies from one company to another.

> **We take the view that customer service is, in fact, broader than any of these definitions, since it is concerned with the building of bonds with customers and other markets or groups to establish long-term, mutually advantageous, relationships which reinforce the other marketing mix elements.**

Customer service takes into account all activities which relate to customers before, during and after the transaction

In this context, and in the pursuance of time and place utilities for customers, customer service must take into account all activities which relate to customers before, during and after the transaction (Figure 6.21). The implication for the company operating in this comprehensive manner is that it must fully understand the reasons why customers buy, and recognize how additional value can be added to the offer.

Many service companies have instinctively recognized this and have focused on their existing client base as never before. By increas-

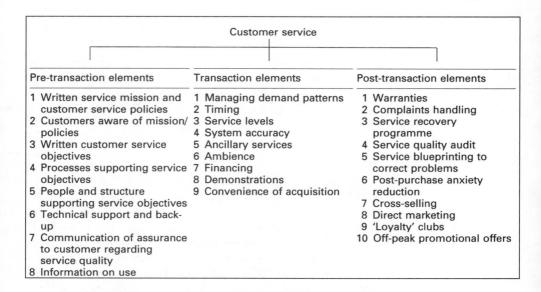

Figure 6.21 Illustration of key elements of customer service

ing their understanding of client needs, they invariably find opportunities for additional cross-selling, thereby tying their customers even more closely to the company. However, because many services require close personal contact between the provider and the customer, improving customer service often hinges on the attitudes and behaviour of the contact staff. It is, therefore, essential that these key people are selected with great care and then given training which reflects the importance of their work.

Creating a customer service strategy

Recognizing the importance of customer service as a weapon, it is incumbent upon the marketer to be clear about how it will be created and used. There are four main steps in creating a customer service strategy:[17]

1 *Identify a service mission* Just as there is a need for a corporate mission statement to clarify the organization's values and general sense of direction, so is there a need for a separate customer service mission. This will distil into a few words the company's philosophy and commitment to customer service.

2 *Setting customer service objectives* This involves asking questions such as:

- How important is customer service compared to other elements of the marketing mix?
- Which are the most important customer service elements?
- How do these vary by market segment?

The answers to these questions will reflect such service quality variables as reliability, responsiveness and assurance. They will also take into account the nature of competitive offers.

The customer service objectives which emerge from this type of analysis need to be considered in the context of pre-transaction, transaction, and post-transaction activities.

3 *Customer service strategy* Not all customers will require the same level of service, therefore appropriate service packages have to be created for different market segments. In order to do this the company must:

- identify the most important services and segments
- prioritize service targets
- develop the service packages.

The most appropriate service packages will be those which offer greater benefits to customers than those of competing services. Such benefits may be real or perceived.

4 *Implementation* The selected service packages are then introduced into the marketing mix. Often, the benefits they provide can be used as part of the promotional campaign.

It is important to remember that, just like the service product itself, customer service strategies have a limited life. With this in mind, the forward-looking service company keeps customer satisfaction levels under constant review and stays in touch with the changing needs of its customers in terms of providing service.

The need for an overall marketing mix strategy

It is clear from the foregoing discussion about the seven elements of the marketing mix that they are closely related to each other. Such is the way they interact that to change one element is to impact on the others. It is essential, therefore, that an overall marketing mix is developed which ensures that all elements are mutually supportive and synergistic. This means that the interaction between the marketing mix elements should be:[18]

- *Integrated*, i.e. there is harmonious interaction
- *Consistent*, i.e. there is a logic behind how the major elements of the mix fit together
- *Leveraged*, i.e. each element is used to best advantage in support of the total marketing mix.

This process can be likened to the way that, in optics, a prism can split white light into its seven constituent colours of the rainbow. However, here it operates in reverse and the seven elements of the mix are focused into a distinctive output which determines the service quality and how the offer is positioned (Figure 6.22).

At this point, some comments should be made on service quality. (Positioning has already been discussed in Chapter 4.)

Service quality is the ability of the service organization to meet or exceed customer expectations. The measure of performance is essentially a measure of *perceived* performance. Thus it is the customers' perceptions of performance which count, rather than the reality of performance. It has been argued that the quality of a service has two important components:

- *Technical quality* – the outcome dimension of the service operations process
- *Functional quality* – the process dimension in terms of the interaction between the customer and the service provider.

These two dimensions of service quality highlight the subjective nature of quality assessments. Generally, clients of professional service firms such as management consultants or insurance brokers have

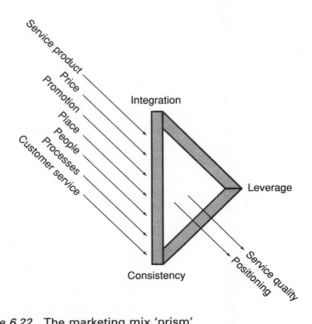

Figure 6.22 The marketing mix 'prism'

difficulty in distinguishing between good and outstanding technical quality of the service; thus judgements are often made on the subjective basis of how the client was treated.

Recently, research has been undertaken in an effort to try and understand the factors which influence service quality. Research by Berry and his colleagues has focused on developing a conceptual model of service quality in which service quality perceptions are influenced by a series of distinct gaps[19] and empirical work which identifies the importance of five key service areas.[20] These five key areas are:

- *Tangibles* – the physical facilities, equipment, appearance of personnel
- *Reliability* – the ability to perform the desired service dependably, accurately and consistently
- *Responsiveness* – willingness to provide prompt service and help customers
- *Assurance* – employees' knowledge, courtesy, and ability to convey trust and confidence
- *Empathy* – caring, individualized attention to customers.

Whilst their empirical research in a number of service industries showed that all the above factors were important, two findings were especially important. Firstly, tangibles have a relatively less important score than other dimensions. Secondly, reliability emerged as by far the most important dimension across all the services studied.

The message for the service marketer seems clear. Above all, be reliable and deliver what is promised to the customer. Further, human performance plays a critical role in the customer's perception of service quality. Three of the five dimensions outlined above – assurance, empathy and response – result directly from human performance; and a fourth factor, reliability, is also largely dependent on human performance.

In developing the marketing mix that delivers service quality, it will be necessary to consider the impact of each marketing mix element on the target market segments. This implies that the marketer must ensure:

- A good fit between the marketing mix and each segment
- A good fit between the marketing mix and the company's strategic capabilities, thus playing to its strengths and reducing the negative influences of its weaknesses
- A recognition of competitors' capabilities, strategically avoiding their strengths and capitalizing on their weaknesses.

The optimum mix strategy, therefore, involves organizing marketing resources, deciding upon levels of marketing expenditure, and being clear about the expected results.

Monitoring, control and review

The marketing programmes which are formulated for each element of the marketing mix should:

- Have an established timetable which indicates what activities have to be achieved at what time
- Indicate the priority tasks and activities
- Identify the resources and people needed to carry them out
- Provide for monitoring and control of performance.

This last point is vital if the marketing plan is to succeed, yet it is often overlooked. Without some means of monitoring, controlling and reviewing the programmes, it will be impossible to ensure that the short-term strategies are working and leading towards the planned long-term objectives.

> **One of the reasons that it is not covered very well in many companies is because they have been weak at setting quantifiable objectives in the first place. Without clearly measurable targets, monitoring progress becomes an extremely difficult, if not impossible, task.**

One study,[21] covering seventy-five organizations in the USA, confirms that inadequate control systems are widespread, particularly in smaller companies. It found that:

- Smaller companies had poorer control procedures than larger ones.
- They made a poorer job of setting objectives and monitoring them.
- Fewer than half of the companies studied knew the profitability of individual products or services.
- One-third had no system to identify weak products or services.
- Almost half failed to analyse costs, evaluate advertising or sales force call reports.
- Many companies had long delays – four to eight weeks – in receiving control reports, and even then many reports were inaccurate.

It is clear that accurate, timely and appropriate control data will not arrive by chance.

> **A conscious effort must be made to set up information and reporting systems so that the right information reaches the right person at the right time.**

The level of detail, the format and the frequency of reporting will, to a large extent, be determined by the nature of the business, and the service markets in which it operates. In some companies, daily feedback will be required; in others, weekly, or even monthly, reporting periods might be perfectly adequate.

In a similar way, the performance criteria against which the market efforts are measured will need to be company-specific, making sense only in the context of its marketing plan and particular business environment. Typical performance measures which might be monitored and controlled could include:

- Revenues
- Market share
- Marketing costs
- Overhead costs
- Profits
- Return on investments
- Consumer attitudes
- New customers
- Sales visits
- Conversion of visits to orders
- Complaints
- Customer retention
- Deliveries
- Bad debts
- Advertising effectiveness
- Sales by service product
- Service quality

The introduction of marketing planning can be a learning process for the whole organization. Its ultimate success comes from the willingness of everyone, from the boardroom down, to learn, to be prepared to experiment, and to adopt the planning system so that it delivers success to the company, regardless of its particular circumstances.

Summary

In this chapter, we have looked at the final phase of the marketing planning process concerned with budget setting, formulating one-year tactical marketing programmes and monitoring, controlling and reviewing their progress. Budgets are a necessary first step to tying the marketing programmes to the economic realities of business life. Although working within a budget might limit the scope of a programme, it should impose no boundaries on its creative and imaginative content.

We saw that the tactical marketing programmes were essentially concerned with translating the marketing objectives and strategies into working one-year plans for each component of the marketing mix. Thus, the programmes would have to address the issues of: service product; promotions; price; place; people; processes; and customer service, making sure that, in each of them, the ultimate choice of actions was designed to provide the company with a competitive advantage.

We also saw that the components of the marketing mix were interrelated in such a way that decisions made in one area could limit options in another. Therefore, it was important that all marketing programmes had an overall coherence which ensured that they were consistent and integrated with each other.

Finally, we saw that, to wait until the end of the plan, and only then discover that it had failed, was no way to run a business. By monitoring progress as the plan unfolds, and taking corrective action whenever it proves necessary, the company not only brings the plan to fruition, but also learns from experience how to improve its planning process.

In the last five chapters we have provided an overview of the marketing planning process and then looked at each of the four phases in detail. In the final two chapters we now examine some key organizational aspects relating to the introduction of marketing planning and provide a step-by-step marketing planning system which shows how the approach outlined in the previous chapters can be successfully implemented through the creation of structured three-year strategic and one-year tactical marketing plans.

References

1 Abratt, R., Beffon, M. and Ford, J. (1994) Relationship Between Marketing Planning and Annual Budget, *Marketing Intelligence and Planning*, **12** (1), 22–28.
2 Berry, L. L. and Parasuraman, A. (1991) *Marketing Services: Competing Through Quality*, The Free Press, New York. p. 131.
3 Booms, B. H. and Bitner, M. J. (1981) Marketing Strategies and Organization Structures for Service Firms. In J. H. Donnelly and W. R. George (eds), *Marketing of Services*, American Marketing Association Proceedings Series, Chicago. p. 48.
4 Lovelock, C. H. (1984) Developing and Implementing New Services. In W. R. George and C. E. Marshall (eds), *Developing New Services*, American Marketing Association, Chicago. p. 45.
5 Grönroos, C. (1990) *Service Management and Marketing*, Lexington Books, Lexington, MA. pp. 73–82.
6 Rogers, E. M. (1962) *Diffusions and Innovations*, The Free Press, New York; Rogers, E. M. (1976) New Product Conception and Diffusion. *Journal of Consumer Research*, **2**, March, 220–230.
7 Wilson, M. (1970) *Managing a Sales Force*, Gower Press, Aldershot.
8 Channon, D. F. (1988) *Global Banking Strategy*, Wiley, New Work. p. 308.
9 Heskett, J. L., Sasser, W. E. and Hart, C. W. L. (1990) *Service Breakthroughs*, The Free Press, New York. p. 89.
10 Judd, V. C. (1987) Differentiate with the 5th P: People. *Industrial Marketing Management*, 16, 241–7. (The descriptions of the four categories are based closely on this work.)
11 Helman, D. and Payne, A. (1992) Internal Marketing: Myth Versus Reality, Cranfield School of Management Working Paper, Cranfield, SWP 5/92.
12 Piercy, N. and Morgan, N. (1990) Internal Marketing: Making Marketing Happen, *Marketing Intelligence and Planning*, **8** (1). Grönroos, C. *op. cit.*, pp. 221–39.
13 This section is based on: Stostack, G. L. (1987) Service Positioning Through Structural Change. *Journal of Marketing*, **51**, January, 34–43.
14 *Ibid.*
15 Lovelock, C. (1992) Seeking Synergy in Service Operations: Seven Things Marketers Need to Know About Service Operations. *European Management Journal*, **10** (1), 22–9.
16 La Londe, B. J. and Zinser, P. H. (1976) *Customer Service: Meaning and Measurement*, NCPDM, Chicago.
17 This section is based on: Christoper, M. (1992) *The Customer Service Planner*, Butterworth-Heinemann, Oxford. Chapter 3.
18 Shapiro, B. (1985) Rejuvenating the Marketing Mix. *Harvard Business Review*, September–October, 28–33.

19 Parasuraman, A., Zeithaml, V. A. and Berry, L. L. (1985) A Conceptual Model of Services Quality and Its Implications for Future Research. *Journal of Marketing*, **49**, Autumn.
20 Berry, L. L., Parasuraman, A. and Zeithaml, V. A. (1988) The Service–Quality Puzzle. *Business Horizons*, September–October.
21 Cited in: Kotler, P. (1991) *Marketing Management*, 7th edn, Prentice Hall, Englewood Cliffs, NJ. p. 709.

7 Organizing for marketing planning

Introduction

Undertaking marketing planning has profound organizational implications

From the foregoing chapters, it should be apparent that the decision to tackle marketing planning is not one that the organization should take lightly. Taking up planning along the lines we have suggested will involve considerable time and effort being expended on a number of aspects of business activity which might earlier have been taken for granted and accepted uncritically. Although well-formulated marketing plans bring with them increased prospects for success, they are not achieved without cost. The forward-looking organization recognizes this and is prepared to invest in the process, ensuring that the organization as a whole is geared up to supporting it. In these circumstances, marketing planning is identified as a critical planning activity and plays a key role in shaping organizational behaviour.

Marketing planning is much more than a mechanical process

Less far-seeing organizations perceive marketing planning as merely the imposition of a series of procedures which, if followed to the letter, deliver a plan at the end. It becomes a sort of 'bolt-on', optional extra. Such an unthinking, mechanical approach completely misses the point of having marketing planning.

> For it is not the marketing procedures that achieve success, but the creative thinking processes that they stimulate.

Planning can never be a neat, remote approach that leaves the company largely untouched. It can be messy and uncomfortable, as attention is directed into organizational activities that have far too long been neglected. It can raise more questions than immediate answers. Above all, it meets reality head on, as facts, rather than opinions, become the focus of organizational initiatives.

In Chapter 2 we looked at some of the organizational barriers which get in the way of marketing planning. We identified these as:

short-termism; lack of support from top management; lack of a plan for planning; lack of line management support; confusion over planning terms; an over-reliance on numbers; too much detail, too far ahead; once-a-year ritual; confusion between operational and strategic planning; failure to integrate marketing planning into the corporate planning system; delegation of planning to a 'planner'; and uncertainty about what should appear in the plan. However, during our explanation of marketing planning, it should be obvious that many of these barriers stem from the lack of understanding of the marketing planning process and how it works.

Avoiding these potential hazards is clearly important, but there is still more that the company must do to organize for effective marketing planning. There are questions to be raised about marketing intelligence systems, the use of marketing research (and how much to spend on it) and database marketing, the impact of marketing planning on the organizational structure, and how to develop a market-focused organization. These are the issues which will be addressed in this chapter.

Marketing intelligence systems

> **Since marketing intelligence is the fuel which powers marketing decision-making, the time and money spent on organizing information flows are inevitably a sound investment.**

As the decision-making arena becomes more uncertain, so there is added pressure for more information. In fact, some managers are prepared to hide behind the lack of information as an excuse for putting off making decisions.

The advent and development of computer technology ought, in theory, to have simplified the gathering and presentation of marketing information. Sadly, this is not the case. Research has shown that it is one of the most badly organized areas of management. By and large, there seems to be a failure to identify both the decisions to be taken and the information essential to make them.

MIS must be based on the information needs of management

Thus, the construction of a successful marketing intelligence system (MIS) has to start with a clear definition of the management information needs. Unfortunately, this seemingly straightforward step is obscured by the fact that many executives fail to isolate the key determinants of success from the many other issues that attract their attention. For example, they misunderstand the meaning and significance of market share, or they over- or under-estimate the strategic impact of service levels, and so on. By not providing a lead, they can be presented with a mass of unfocused data and information in such volume that it becomes virtually impossible for the recipients to isolate what is, or is not, important. Such is the regularity of the arrival of this material that some executives become, quite literally, overwhelmed.

The consequence of such systems is that their output is rarely used. Instead, management regresses to the old ways of relying on intuition and hunch when making marketing decisions.

Too much data and information is counter-productive

In order to construct a productive MIS, there are four steps to be taken:

1 Make a detailed list of all current data and information that are produced.
2 Separately, get each manager to list the important decisions he or she has to make, together with the essential information input required for making those decisions.
3 Compare these two lists and:
   (a) remove all redundant information requirements, i.e. that which is provided but not needed
   (b) rationalize all the remaining manager/information combinations in a way that the managers' needs in total can be met with the fewest pieces of generated information.

   This second category of action is not easy and is likely to involve a rigorous examination of the underlying purpose for all information requirements. While it might be nice for managers to know all sorts of information, much of this can turn out to be peripheral to decision-making.
4 Work towards the 'ideal' MIS.

It is tempting to think that it would be possible to build a new MIS starting from scratch. However, in the real world, this might not be possible for reasons of cost or IT resources. Experience suggests that the way forward is to use a building-block approach. This means that each block, which is a subsystem for meeting a particular group of information needs, is developed one at a time. Eventually an integrated and sophisticated MIS is put together to the benefit of its users.

Internal data sources and MIS*

In theory the internal audit should be relatively straightforward. Analysis and reporting of company results by region, product and segment should merely involve a bit of computer analysis of the sales ledger.

* This section on MIS and database marketing is based on McDonald, M. (1995) *Marketing Plans: How to prepare them; How to use them*, 3rd edn, Butterworth-Heinemann, Oxford.

> In practice there are problems. Sales ledgers are owned by finance and designed to facilitate billings and collections. Their purpose does not include supporting marketing and they rarely do so.

> The information on sales ledgers is incomplete and miscoded from marketing's viewpoint. Ledgers contain accounts and stock-keeping units, which cannot easily be linked to customers, products, regions or segments.

Collecting, consolidating and using sales ledger information may also be difficult. Ledgers are designed to do accounting consolidations and analysis, not market consolidation and analysis.

An MIS (marketing intelligence or marketing information system) is the solution. Building an MIS involves:

- Adding codes to the sales ledger to identify customers and products (in addition to accounts and stock keeping units)
- Summarizing the customer transactions to a level of detail suited to marketing
- Extracting the customer/product data
- Storing it on a database
- Adding extra codes to facilitate segmentation analysis
- Obtaining software tools to analyse and report on the database.

This is easy to describe, but, as those who have tried will know, extremely hard to implement. The main difficulty to overcome is to manage the expectations of computer staff, financial management (who own the sales ledger) and marketing users.

A problem facing anyone contemplating the development of an MIS is whether to hold data at the lowest level of detail or to hold summary statistics. The extra cost of storing and processing detailed data, at customer level, often deters planners. However, only storing summary data is a mistake in most circumstances, for two reasons:

- Flexibility to analyse and segment by different combinations of variables is only possible if the data is held at the lowest possible levels of detail.
- Customer data can subsequently be used for implementing the strategy (i.e. for direct mail, telemarketing and field sales call reporting).

Database marketing – reconciling the tactical with the strategic

Databases have traditionally been too large and expensive, and their performance too slow, for them to be cost-justifiable. Consequently, many of the MIS in use today are summary sales reporting systems. However, with the increased importance attached to direct marketing, telemarketing and sales performance management (using laptop computers), many companies are now more actively engaged in building customer databases.

Databases often represent a compromise between the strategic requirements of the planners and the tactical requirements of direct marketers, telemarketers and sales managers. Another trouble for newcomers to the world of databases is that they fall for many of the pitfalls, and believe many of the myths (Table 7.1).

The consequence of these problems is that databases very often hold data that does not fit the purpose of the tacticians, far less the needs of strategic planners.

Table 7.1 Myths and realities about databases

Myth	Reality
The database collects what we need	We collect what is easily available
The database measures what matters	We measure what is least embarrassing
The database users understand what data they need	We know what we used last, what the textbooks say and what might be interesting on a rainy day
The database needs to hold more and more data	We feel safer with loads of data, even when we haven't a clue how to use it
The database must integrate the data physically	We like neat solutions, whatever the cost
The database will save staff time	We need more and more staff to analyse data
The database will harmonize marketing, finance and sales	We all compete for scarce resources, and this involves fighting
The database is the one source of our market intelligence	We haven't thought through the business problems

> **The attempt to develop databases that serve both strategic and tactical purposes is often referred to as database marketing.**

One of the most acute problems is that of reconciling the internal and external views of the markets. The usual problem is that data retrieved from the sales ledger rarely possesses the details needed to link customer records to market segments. Some of the problems are described in Table 7.2.

Table 7.2 Problems of reconciling internal and external market audits

External audit – variable	Problem with internal
What is bought	Internal systems have rich detail on accounts. However, information about types of products and services can often be missing. Information on the outlets or channels through which they are sold is very often lacking.
Who buys	Internal systems record who paid the invoice and who received delivery of the services. They rarely record who made the buying decision, or who influenced it. Even when the buyer details are on the system, it is rarely easy to determine their characteristics such as age, sex, etc. Information is typically based around quantity of services sold rather than on customers' total usage of various services.
Why	Reconciling external to internal involves: • matching accounts to customers • matching capacity to services required • matching external variables to internal records • collecting data from sources other than the sales ledger (e.g. from surveys of sales representatives) Internal sources of information on why people purchase is scarce. Enquiries can be qualified, using survey techniques, to provide some clues on why people respond, e.g. to an advertising campaign. Customer satisfaction surveys may also yield clues. Call reports from field sales and telesales can also provide valuable clues, especially if survey disciplines can be observed by the sales staff.

Fusing together data from external sources and internal data is becoming increasingly common as a solution to the external–internal problem. This is often referred to as data fusion. Where large volumes of data are involved, computer programs, known as de-duplication routines, are used to automate the matching of the data. However, automation rarely achieves more than 80 per cent accuracy in matching, and manual matching has to be applied to the remaining data.

> **The cost of matching external and internal market-coding schemes is driving a few companies to collect customer profiles at source. This is either when they first enquire, or when their sales ledger records are first created.**

However the cost of the changes to the sales ledger, and the fact that it is owned by finance, are often barriers to success. In the future, marketing will need to work much more closely with finance and the IT Department, if it is to develop databases successfully. To address this problem one major bank has moved its head of marketing into the role of head of the IT department.

The secret of using information successfully

Information, in the minds of most marketing managers, lies in a strange no man's land, part way between the practical focus of marketing management and the abstractions of technologists, cyberneticists and boffins. Widely misunderstood, or equated to 'keyboard literacy', or 'technology awareness', the management of marketing information often ends up neglected.

Information is not the same as technology, nor is it information technology, nor is it necessarily derived from information technology. There are many myths associated with the use of computers to hold marketing data, as Table 7.1 shows.

The information needs of marketing keep changing as a consequence of the evolution of the marketing strategy

Information is not all hard, objective data; we will not necessarily become better informed by collecting more and more raw data, and storing it until we end up knowing 'everything'. Accounting systems are often seen as a source of hard facts, since most accounting transactions have to be audited and therefore must be reasonably accurate. Yet most accounting data has little direct relevance for marketing strategy.

What information is needed to support a marketing strategy? The answer to this question is something of a conundrum, since the information needed depends upon the marketing objectives that form the strategy. If you change the strategic marketing objectives, then you may need different kinds of information to support your strategy.

This observation goes some way towards explaining one of the great puzzles of marketing information:

Why is it so difficult to specify marketing's information needs? The answer is that, unlike accounting or service operations, which have fixed information needs, the information needs of marketing keep changing as a consequence of the evolution of the marketing strategy.

At this point, the sales or marketing director might feel that, because the situation changes so radically every year, there can be no hope for developing an effective system or procedure for obtaining marketing information. Many at this point delegate the need to less experienced junior staff, with the result that they are very ill-informed when they come to develop their marketing strategies.

For all the problems, there are a number of basic underlying marketing issues with which all companies have to contend. Furthermore, the solutions they have adopted can be seen as variations on relatively few themes. The basic model of a marketing system can be visualized as in Figure 7.1.

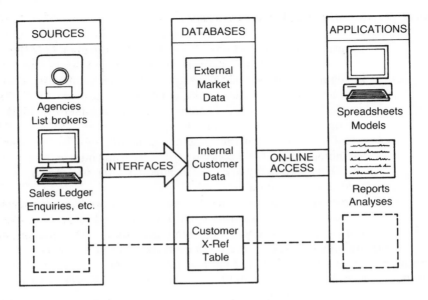

Figure 7.1 Information flows in a marketing system

The main components of the system are as follows:

- *External market data* which is purchased from external agencies. These include governmental agencies, market research firms, list brokers, etc.
- *Internal customer data* which is collected from the sales ledger and other internal sources such as customer service, field sales, telesales, etc. It is coded and segmented in such a way that market-share figures can be created by comparison with external data.
- *Customer reference table* which is needed to make the system work effectively. It identifies customers (as defined by marketing) and provides a cross-reference to sales ledger accounts. Whenever a new sales ledger account is created, the cross-reference table is used to determine the customer associated with that account. This avoids the need for costly manual matching or de-duplication after the account is created. It is also used by marketing applications as a standard reference table for customers.
- *Database* refers to all three of the above data types. It needs to be structured using a technique known as data modelling which organizes the data into the component types that marketing wants, and not the structure that finance or anyone else provides. Usually, the data is held using relational database software, since this provides for maximum flexibility and choice of analysis tools.
- *Interfaces* refers to the computer programs that 'grab' the data from the source systems and restructure it into the components to go onto the marketing database. These programs need to be

written by the in-house IT staff, since they obtain and restructure data from the in-house sales ledger, and other in-house systems.

- *Applications* are the software programs that the planners use to analyse the data and develop their plans. They include data-grabbing tools, that grab the items of data from their storage locations; reporting tools that summarize the data according to categories that marketing defines; spreadsheets that carry out calculations and what-if analyses on the reported summary data. Applications may also include specific marketing planning software such as EXMAR.*

The critical issue when building such a system is that it is not self-contained within marketing. It requires interface programs that will alter the systems used by finance, sales and other internal departments, as well as data-feeds from external sources.

The secrets of success in developing systems for marketing are:

- Understanding what marketing needs and particularly how the internal and external views will be reconciled.
- Developing a strong cost–benefit case for information systems, including financial ones, to be altered to accommodate the needs of marketing.
- Working continuously with internal IT staff until the system is built. They are under pressure from other sources, especially finance, and unless marketing maintains momentum and direction, then other priorities will inevitably win.

Marketing planners need to become far less insular if they are to obtain the information they require to plan effectively. Cross-functional understanding and cooperation must be secured by marketing if they are to develop the systems they need. Building the interdepartmental cross-functional bridges to secure data, information and knowledge is one of the greatest challenges facing marketing today.[1]

Who manages the MIS?

There is no hard and fast rule in answer to this question. It could be argued that, as the MIS is to facilitate decision-making company-wide, it should be managed within a central corporate information office. There are others who advocate that in a marketing-oriented company, it is feedback from the outside world which should drive

---

* **EXMAR** is a major decision-support tool for strategic marketing planning. For further information, contact Professor Malcolm McDonald, Cranfield School of Management, Cranfield, Bedford, MK43 0AL, England.

decision-making. Therefore, it is claimed, the MIS should be managed by the marketing department.

> **At the end of the day, where the system is located is of little consequence. Of far more significance is that the MIS is institutionalized and has procedures which facilitate information flows, both vertically and horizontally and both into and out of the information unit, to assist marketing planning.**

It goes without saying that with an institutionalized system, all who are involved with it are trained to play their role, whether as providers of inputs or users of outputs.

Marketing research

Marketing research is not the same as market research

While the MIS provides the data to make routine decisions and to keep the organization on track, from time to time new and specific pieces of information will be required by management.

> **Providing this is the role of marketing research, which is defined by the American Marketing Association as 'The systematic gathering, recording and analysis of data about problems relating to the marketing of goods and services'.**

Marketing research, therefore, is an approach which can look at the whole marketing process and is not to be confused with 'market research', which as the name implies, is concerned specifically with research about markets. Marketing research can help to resolve problems, be they about distribution channels, competitive advantages of one's services, customer preferences, pricing, or, indeed, anything which is connected with matching the company's capabilities with customer needs. By collecting and analysing the appropriate data, the marketer can proceed to make decisions under conditions of known risk rather than uncertainty.

Information can be elicited in two broad ways:

> - Through non-reactive methods
> - Through reactive methods.

- *Reactive methods* Here, the target audience reacts to test situations, or to questions posed to them by an interviewer, either face-to-face or over the telephone. Equally, they could respond to questionnaires or forms, which they might be handed or which

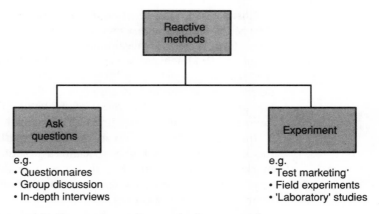

Figure 7.2 Focus of reactive marketing research

are mailed to them. Figure 7.2 summarizes the main forms of reactive marketing research.

● *Non-reactive methods* Here, methods are based on interpretation of observed phenomena, or extant data. They do not rely on data derived directly from respondents. Figure 7.3 summarizes the main forms of non-reactive marketing research.

Cost effectiveness is the ultimate determinant of the marketing research method to be used

All research methods have inherent advantages and disadvantages[2]. For example, structured interviews, controlled by the interviewer against a specific format, might be easy to analyse, but give little scope to explore what could be important departures from the chosen 'script'. In contrast, free-ranging interviews might provide a wealth of anecdotal and qualitative information, but prove to be very difficult to analyse overall.

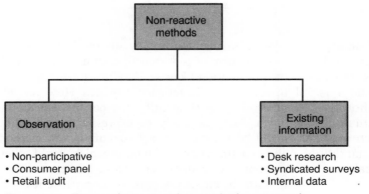

Figure 7.3 Focus of non-reactive marketing research

Cost is also a consideration to take into account. For example, the logistics of sending interviewers door-to-door will clearly cost a lot more than a postal questionnaire. But, then again, whereas the former method achieves a very high 'hit rate' in terms of responses, the latter might yield very little. Cost, therefore, has to be seen as a determinant of the intrinsic quality of the information received. It has to be assessed, not in terms of the value of the research assignment input, but as the usefulness of the actual research output.

Increasing sophistication in the use of marketing research techniques has made it a highly specialized function within the field of marketing management. For this reason, many service companies turn to outside research agencies rather than attempting to develop their own internal resources.

Budgeting for marketing research

As we have seen, marketing information can be costly to obtain. Not surprisingly, how much to spend on marketing research is, therefore, a key question that marketers must address.

> **Information can, in many ways, be seen as a product, for, like a product, it has to be 'made', stored and distributed. Similarly, it has a limited shelf-life, after which it can have a deleterious effect on company health if consumed.**

As with a product, the more use that can be extracted from a piece of information, the greater is its value.

> **The utility value of information is, of course, its ability to reduce the risk attached to making a wrong decision. The greater the risk, the higher the value of the marketing research.**

Probability theory and expected value can be a useful method of calculating how much to spend on marketing research

Since any decision to buy any product or service would be subject to some form of cost–benefit appraisal, it should be possible to handle information likewise. Any investment in research would have to be justified by the return it provided. However, whereas the costs are relatively easy to identify, the benefits can be more elusive to pin down. They can only be expressed as the additional profits that might be achieved through identifying new marketing opportunities, and avoiding the costly failures which would otherwise have resulted without the information. Thus, while the cost–benefit approach looks to be eminently sensible, in practice it is beset with many 'ifs' and 'maybes'.

Another approach which is used with some success is based on the theory of probability and expected value. This operates in the following way. Suppose that the launch of a new service would incur costs of £500,000. The decision to go ahead is hampered by the fact that it is reckoned that there is a 10 per cent chance that the service will fail. In these circumstances, the maximum loss expectation can be calculated as £500,000 × 0.10, i.e. £50,000. This would suggest that it would be worth the company spending up to £50,000 to acquire information which would help to avoid such a loss.

However, the implication of this approach is that perfect information can be put at the company's disposal. Since the cost of gathering perfect information is likely to be prohibitive, the method shown above can only be seen to provide a rough guideline.

> **In truth, budget setting is likely to be based upon a combination of cost/benefit analysis, probability and expected value, and empirical evidence that the service organization has accumulated over the years.**

Marketing planning and company structure

Can marketing planning work in all organizations?

As should be clear by now, marketing planning is not something for the uncommitted manager. In order to get results, companies must undertake the task comprehensively.

> **However, as we have described it, the planning process has a distinctive shape and pattern, whereas service organizations come in all shapes and sizes. It is reasonable to ask, therefore, if such a universal approach can actually be made to fit this wide range of potential customers.**

Can it, for example, fit the large service company and the small one equally well? Will it be appropriate for the bank and the professional service firm? Or does it have to be tailored in order to become suitable? It is equally relevant to ask if the organization should modify its own activities in order to accommodate marketing planning. These questions are asked in order to throw light on often overlooked issues which have a bearing upon the ultimate success of the marketing planning initiative.

In order to address these issues, we need to switch our focus of attention away from the marketing planning process and, for a moment, take a look at service organizations themselves. First of all, let us look at how organizations develop and grow.

The organizational life-line

While in some ways, organizations have an individuality all of their own, in much the same way as people, it can be shown that they also have many similarities when it comes to looking at their overall pattern of development.

> **Just as people go through life-phases of infancy, youth, becoming an adolescent, and so on, so do organizations experience a similar growth pattern.**

Further, just as people experience problems in the transition from one phase of life to another, for example going through puberty or the menopause, so do organizations have equivalent periods of discomfort and crisis.

There are several models upon which to draw to illustrate the organizational life-line, but that of Greiner[3] provides a comprehensive approach which is relevant to service (and most other) organizations. Figure 7.4 outlines the ten phases of evolution and crisis in this model.

Phase 1 The first phase of organizational life is the *creative evolution* phase. Here, the organization is small, very informal and ill-organized, but powered by a sustainable business idea and the energy put in by the founder. This person is

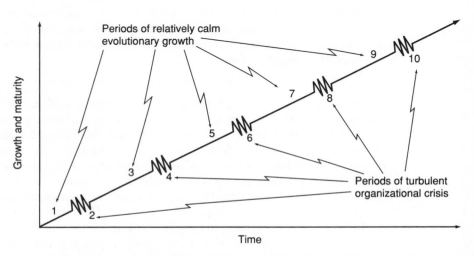

Figure 7.4 The organizational life-line (*Source*: Based on Greiner, L. E. (1967) Patterns of Organization Change. *Harvard Business Review*, May/June)

at the heart of everything – selling, creating, recruiting, rewarding, buying, and so on. The organization's plans are in the founders' heads and the organization itself is used as an extension of the founder. They operate rather like a spider at the centre of a web. No activity in the organization, or indeed among customers, escapes their attention.

Such a company can be very profitable, since the person running it knows the customers personally and can respond to their changing needs immediately. Coupled with this excellent service is an organization low on overhead costs.

Phase 2   The company can grow successfully in a relatively controlled way until, one day, it starts to have problems. Its very success overtaxes the central person, who finds it increasingly difficult to cope. The pressure might originate from extra customers, extra employees, extra machines, or whatever. The net result is that the source of decision-making becomes overcommitted. For example, he or she is with a customer when a problem crops up in the office, or they have to spend so much time negotiating a bank loan that they neglect bringing in new contracts. The organization has, in fact, reached its *leadership crisis* phase.

So serious is this phase that it overwhelms many organizations. This problem can be resolved in one of two ways:

- The entrepreneur/founder sells the business (and then, often, goes off somewhere to start something else).
- The company must manage a transition to its next phase of development.

Phase 3   Here, the principles of textbook management start to be imposed on the organization. If the founder stays, he or she has to learn to devolve some jobs to others, start to employ specialists, define who does what, and introduce systems and procedures that 'run themselves'. From being a reactive type of organization, where planning was largely non-existent, the company starts to enter the world of scientific management, with a defined structure and sets of rules for coping with routines such as costing, payments, and the planning of work. Because it needs firm leadership to draw the company together and give it a new sense of purpose, there needs to be somebody strong at the helm, who knows more about management.

With such a person in position, the company can look forward to another relatively calm period of evolutionary growth. This is the *directed evolution* phase.

Phase 4   This period of growth eventually encounters problems, as the 'director's' expertise about markets, technology, or whatever, is overtaken by subordinates whose day-to-day work ensures that they keep abreast of all the latest developments.

The leader may lose credibility to an extent that his or her judgement and ability to provide direction are no longer trusted by those in the organization. Subordinates who are on top of their jobs feel they could easily make better decisions faster than the out-of-touch boss. The company is now experiencing its *autonomy crisis* phase.

Phase 5   This crisis is only solved by genuine power and authority being pushed down to lower levels in the organization. In this way, all the company's expertise is tapped and a new spirit of enterprise is released. Decisions are made by the people with the best and most current information, not by somebody remote from the situation, who cannot understand all the nuances of what is entailed. Again, if this transition is managed successfully, the company is equipped to benefit from another period of evolutionary growth, its *delegated evolution* phase.

Phase 6   Once more, the seeds of the next crisis start as the company gets larger and more mature. Those at the top of the organization feel that they are losing control. Subordinates are making decisions which, in themselves, might be excellent, but which are essentially parochial and do not take into account the full ramifications for the organization as a whole. There is a *control crisis* as the issue of power and who is actually steering the business is addressed.

Phase 7   As before, a solution is eventually found, whereby the organization is redefined on the basis of greater cooperation between different levels and functions. To facilitate this, roles are carefully defined and attention is paid to information flows. Rules, systems and procedures are developed to ensure that everyone knows their place and what is expected of them. When something slips through the organizational net, a new rule or procedure is established to ensure that it does not happen again. With the crisis of control resolved in this way, the company can enjoy another relatively trouble-free period of growth in its *coordinated evolution* phase.

Phase 8   The next crisis phase occurs because, in its attempts to coordinate its decision-making and optimize the integration of all activities, too many bureaucratic procedures creep in. The company finds that rules, which once helped, now begin to slow down decision-making and blunt personal initiative. The organization becomes impersonal, and ensuring that procedures are completed seems to be the sole reason for its existence. Customers and markets may become distractions to the business of running the enterprise. The company is at its *red-tape crisis* phase and severely restricts itself unless action is taken.

Phase 9   The answer seems to lie in returning to the days before the hand of bureaucracy took the energy out of the organization. What has to happen is for a new approach to management to emerge. Once more, people have to be seen as more important than systems and procedures. Unnecessary routines are dismantled. Impersonal relationships are replaced with face-to-face transactions. Management is by exception, and over-control is replaced by trust. By adapting in this way, the company reaches its *collaborative evolution* phase. It becomes once more flexible and adaptive when it is beset by new challenges.

Phase 10   As we have seen, every evolution phase is born out of a crisis and yet carried with it are the seeds of the next crisis. Since relatively few organizations have genuinely reached their collaborative evolution phase, the exact nature of the next crisis phase is somewhat speculative. There are suggestions that with the collaborative emphasis on teamwork and openness, managers lose the confidence to make decisions on their own. There is also a possibility that 'groupthink' takes over and too much time is spent looking at the functioning of internal teams, at the expense of keeping in touch with events in the outside world. However as the *next crisis* phase materializes, no doubt human ingenuity will eventually find some way out of it.

There are two important points to make about the organizational life-line.

1   A company 'learns' by overcoming new problems and so its level of 'maturity' is not governed simply by its growth and size alone, but also by the complexity of its history. Thus, it is possible to have a very large company, in terms of turnover or number of employees, at an early stage in development terms, for example at its leadership crisis or directed evolution phase. Similarly, a relatively small company might just as easily be enmeshed in its red-tape crisis.

2   There is nothing to suggest that companies are more profitable at any one of the evolution phases than another. However, the

organization can literally die at any of its crisis phases and so does not have a 'right' to experience all of the growth phases.

In his research, which examined marketing planning and corporate culture, Leppard[4] found that:

> • The process of marketing planning is sophisticated and carries with it hidden values regarding organizational openness and access to information. It, therefore, needs an equally sophisticated organization to be able to accept it in its totality. In this sense, the introduction of marketing planning is more than a matter of introducing some systems and procedures, for it can bring with it a challenge to the credibility, authority and style of the management regime.
> • It is difficult to introduce marketing planning at any of the crisis phases, because there are too many other unresolved contextual problems in the organization.
> • The marketing planning process has to be congruent with the corporate culture at each of the evolution phases. Broadly speaking, this suggests the emphasis shown in Table 7.3.

Table 7.3 Approaches to marketing planning for different stages of evolution

Stage of evolution	Marketing planning approach
Creative evolution	No formal marketing planning procedures exist. The owner/manager tends to operate more like a hunter than a farmer. At best, a sales plan might be acceptable, but in general, any kind of formal planning is alien in this culture.
Directed evolution	Here, the marketing planning process has to be imposed from the top, and so an essentially 'top-down' planning system provides the best organizational fit.
Delegated evolution	Here, an essentially 'bottom-up' marketing planning approach works best.
Coordinated evolution	Here, a 'top-down' and 'bottom-up' marketing planning approach can be combined to provide a good organizational fit.
Collaborative evolution	Since few organizations are at this stage of development, no firm conclusions can be drawn. The life-line concept suggests that a radical rethink might be made regarding marketing planning. This might mean the process becomes more non-functional and less mechanical.

> **The conclusion to be reached is that the marketing planning process described in this book is of universal validity. Great care, however, is necessary to ensure that it does not strangle personal initiative and creativity by an overly-bureaucratic implementation of the associated systems and that it is implemented at the appropriate stage of the evolutionary development of the organization.**

Centralized versus decentralized marketing

Regardless of where the service organization is on its life-line, it might at some time or other reach a stage, either from organic growth or by acquisition, where it operates with more than one unit. The question then arises regarding how best to locate the marketing function. The organizational structure might look like either of Figures 7.5 or 7.6.*

Centralized organizations are effective at controlling costs

In Figure 7.5, the centralized head office has taken over the strategic components of the business, including marketing, leaving the operational units A, B and C to produce services as directed. This approach clearly maintains control at the centre and ensures there is no duplication of effort in the operating units. However, unless communications are exceedingly good, it is conceivable that those with responsibility for marketing will lose touch with both the operating unit and its markets. This is particularly true if each unit has a wide range of services and customers. The sheer logistics of managing so many service product/customer combinations is too much to handle.

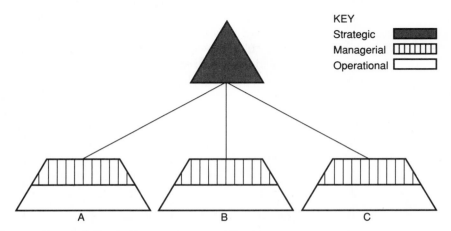

Figure 7.5 Centralized marketing, separate operating units

*This section is based on original work by Visiting Professor Simon Majaro of Cranfield School of Management and is used with his kind permission.

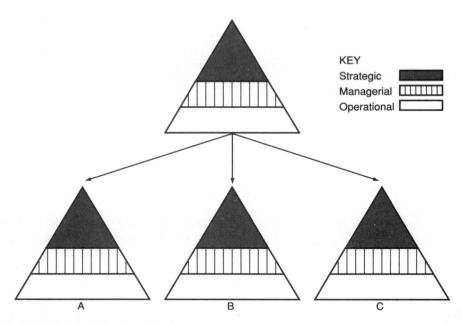

Figure 7.6 Decentralized marketing

Decentralized organizations are effective at responding to market needs

The alternative possibility is shown in Figure 7.6. Here, the Head Office acts as a hub for largely self-autonomous units, which have their own marketing departments. Clearly, in these circumstances, the marketing activities will be highly relevant to the sub-units they are dedicated to serve. They will be well-attuned to the specific needs of each business unit. However, unless all the marketing activities can be coordinated in some way, there could be a considerable duplication of work. For example, each unit might commission marketing research which is virtually identical, therefore spending much more than is necessary. If, however, some way can be found of gaining synergy from all this marketing energy, the rewards could be considerable.

There is no right or wrong answer for this organizational issue

As with so many aspects of marketing, there are no clear answers regarding which structure is the best. Both types have advantages and disadvantages. For this reason, each organization has to find a balance which allows for the right level of marketing specificity, yet imposes a mechanism for avoiding costly duplication (Figure 7.7).

> It is the responsibility of the headquarters to draw up the boundaries regarding how the marketing activities shall be managed and coordinated. Until this is resolved, any attempts to introduce, or improve, marketing planning will be beset with problems.

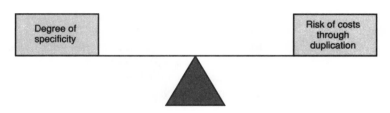

Figure 7.7 The specificity versus duplication balance in marketing planning

The matrix organization

There is another way of considering organization design, which is based on one of the foundations of marketing thinking – that all companies must integrate the management of both their services and their markets. In the so-called 'matrix organization'[5] (Figure 7.8), it is common to find the posts of 'product manager' or 'service manager' and 'market manager', and sometimes all three.

Having an over-emphasis on services or markets can result in problems

In this example, we have a training/consultancy business which does business in three main markets: financial services; distribution; and leisure and travel. It could organize around 'service managers' so that, for example, one manager would be responsible for all training activities in all three markets. The advantage of doing this will be the strong service product orientation which results. While this is an undoubted plus, such a structure can easily lead to superficial market knowledge. Indeed, many companies have suffered from this approach by being slow to recognize changes in their markets.

In contrast to this approach, the 'market manager' orientation can maintain closeness to markets, but lead to unnecessary service dupli-

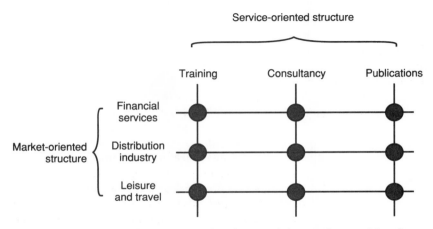

Figure 7.8 A matrix organization for a training and consulting firm

cation, service proliferation and the lack of a coherent policy for developing new services.

Because each approach has its strengths and weaknesses, there can be no simple answer regarding which might be the best. Common sense and experience of the market situation will, in the end, determine which approach is most appropriate.

> **The third option in this range of possibilities is to have both service and market managers. This ought to provide the best of all possible worlds, since close attention is being paid to both services and markets.**

However, for it to work well, there must be close liaison between the two types of manager. Also, it is suggested, in order to avoid deadlock, that one or the other is given the ultimate responsibility to make decisions. It therefore needs a high level of maturity from the staff involved, and a willingness to keep all communication channels open, if it is to work in practice. Too often it is found that vested interests get in the way of genuine service/market issues.

The purpose of this brief discussion into organizational structures was to underline some of the potential drawbacks and advantages which particular structures bring with them. Unfortunately, no single organizational form can be recommended unconditionally, because the final choice must always reflect the particular situation faced by the company.

> **Even so, it is usually sensible to organize around customer groups or markets, rather than services, functions or geographical location.**

By doing this, the whole organization can be mobilized to respond specifically to a unique set of market needs.

There are always a number of factors to take into consideration. We have touched upon these already. There are issues about authority and responsibility, ease of communication, coordination, flexibility, how the cross-functional interfaces are managed (e.g. between internal departments, or the company and its outside world), and, by no means least, human factors.

The way the company organizes for marketing will be one of the major determinants of the effectiveness of any marketing planning.

Plan for marketing planning

Just as important as getting the organization structure to complement the markets it serves, the company must also ensure that there is a plan for marketing planning. That is to say, everyone involved must not only be aware of the marketing planning process (as outlined in this book), but also be very clear about the role they are expected to play in it and the rate at which the planning process unfolds.

The chief executive has to lead marketing planning

Often, when considering the reasons for marketing planning failures, we find that much of the blame can be attributed to chief executives.

> It is their principal role to get the planning process accepted and, by way of their personal commitment and enthusiasm, maintain the energy and momentum of the initiative.

Too often, they have little familiarity with and interest in marketing planning.

In companies where chief executives have been successful in bringing about change, they have actively intervened in:

- Defining the organizational framework
- Ensuring that the strategic analysis covers critical factors
- Maintaining the balance between short and long-term results
- Waging war on unnecessary bureaucracy
- Creating and maintaining the right level of motivation
- Encouraging marketing talent and skills to emerge.

Another area which sometimes causes concern is that of the role of the planning department. As we have seen, it cannot operate successfully if it is trapped inside an ivory-tower mentality. Instead of operating in isolation, it needs to be at the hub of the marketing planning information network. In playing this role it can:

- Advise on improved planning structures and systems
- Facilitate the transmission of relevant data
- Request inputs from managers, departments, or operating divisions
- Act as a catalyst to break down interdepartment/interfunctional rivalry or barriers
- Evaluate marketing plans against the overall corporate strategy

> ● Monitor ongoing plans and keep top management informed
> ● Support and advise line managers and staff
> ● Initiate special research on industries, markets, etc.

Where top management is weak, it might try to avoid its responsibility and ask the planning department to provide not only the plan, but also the objectives and strategies. While this is technically feasible (assuming that the expertise is available), it is not a desirable outcome, for top management input about corporate direction is absolutely necessary.

The marketing planning cycle

The same degree of formality is not required in all cases

The time it takes to produce a strategic marketing plan can be determined by looking at the overall sequence of ten steps and working out what is a reasonable time for completing each one. Of course, for any particular company, the times required will relate to the size of the company (i.e. the number of people likely to get involved) and the complexity of the business (the multiplicity of services and markets). Both of these factors can influence the degree of formality of the final plan as shown in Figure 7.9.

> **Not unexpectedly, this shows that small service organizations with, perhaps, only one or two products or services can get by with much less formal marketing plans than, say, a market leader operating on a global scale.**

Having established the degree of formality that will be appropriate for the company marketing plan, it then becomes possible to 'plan'

Service/market diversity		Small	Medium	Large
	High	Medium formalization	Medium/high formalization	High formalization
	Medium	Low formalization	Medium formalization	Medium/High formalization
	Low	Very low formalization	Low formalization	Medium formalization

Company size

Figure 7.9 Broad guidelines to the degree of marketing plan formality

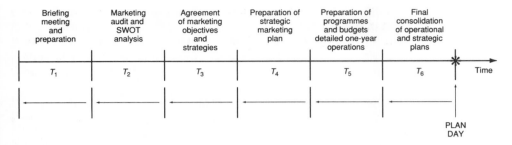

Figure 7.10 The marketing planning time cycle

the planning cycle. It is often easier to consider the time when the plan should be available and then work backwards, as shown in Figure 7.10.

We can now see that the total planning time consists of $T_1 + T_2 + T_3 + T_4 + T_5 + T_6$, where:

T_1 represents the initial preparation time. This is an important, but often overlooked, part of the process. All those who have a part to play in the planning process should be briefed, so that they have a uniform approach to collecting and presenting data. Documentation shall also be explained, so that there are no misunderstandings.

T_2 is the period for carrying out the marketing audit and distilling it into a SWOT analysis. Generally, this represents the largest span of time, because of the work involved. Nevertheless, there must be a deadline for this activity to be completed, otherwise the whole planning schedule will fall behind.

T_3 is the time it takes to formulate marketing objectives and strategies.

T_4 is the period in which the objectives and strategies are converted into a plan which covers the chosen marketing planning time horizon. Again, this will vary from company to company. In the past, the planning horizon was traditionally a five-year period. It is more common now, because of the accelerating rate of environmental change, to use a three-year horizon. To look too far ahead is meaningless, yet not to look sufficiently far ahead robs the company of the discipline to think long-term. Because they can be more flexible and adaptable, small companies generally may not need to look ahead as far as their larger contemporaries.

Most companies will find that there is a natural point in the future beyond which it is meaningless to look. Those with a need to probe further into the future may do this through the use of 'scenario planning'. There are several approaches for doing this, but they all involve getting the most authoritative views about likely shifts such as advances in technology and changes in society and how they are likely to make impact on, and define, future markets. Scenarios are a useful planning tool to enable organizations to consider longer-term opportunities and threats.

T_5 represents the time required to prepare detailed one-year operational programmes and budgets.

T_6 is the time required to consolidate the marketing plan, ensuring that the strategic and operational plans are consistent and represent the best options for the company.

All of these stages could be completed in a matter of weeks in smaller companies selling simple services. In larger, complex service organizations, it is likely to involve many months of work. Having estimated the likely time to complete a plan, it is now possible to look at the planning cycle in its entirety (Figure 7.11).

We can now see that, in order to introduce our first strategic marketing plan on the date T, we must start our preparation in advance. This plan covers the year T to $T + 1$ in detail and that operational plan is derived from the strategic plan, which covers the period T to $T + 3$ (three years being taken as our planning horizon).

In order to produce an updated plan (Plan 2) a year later, preparation must start even before the first operational plan has run its course. The new operational plan will now cover the years $T + 1$ to $T + 2$, while the strategic plan covers $T + 1$ to $T + 4$.

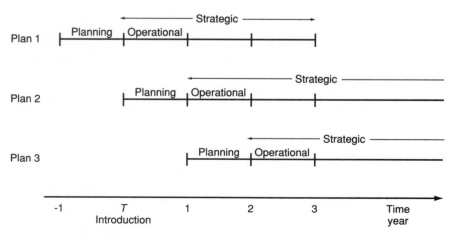

Figure 7.11 The marketing planning cycle – overview

This pattern is then repeated for each succeeding year. It is apparent from Figure 7.11 that the impact of the first strategic marketing plan cannot really be evaluated until it has run its course, i.e. at $T + 3$ years. For that reason, it could take up to three years before a fully refined planning process is developed.

> However, since each marketing audit will take into account how the plan is working out in practice, corrective action and improvements can be introduced into the planning process while the plan is still unfolding.

Finally, whilst Figures 7.10 and 7.11 have been set out as a linear process for the purpose of clarity, it would be more realistic to show it as a *circular* process, which more effectively links operational plans to corporate objectives and shows both the ongoing nature, the process and the interdependence between top-down and bottom-up inputs.

Developing a marketing orientation

Little of what we have outlined in this book will be achieved if the organization does not have a 'marketing orientation'. There are other orientations adopted by service organizations (see Table 7.4). However, it is only the marketing orientation which specifically seeks to create an organization which proactively responds to customers and their needs.

Table 7.4 Some possible types of organizational orientation

Type of orientation	Typical associated attitudes
Marketing orientation	What we do is based on an in-dpeth understanding of the needs and aspirations of our customers and clients.
Product orientation	The technical quality of what we do means that our services sell themselves.
Response orientation	We will respond to any enquiry.
Financial orientation	If we can make money at anything, then we will do it.
Self-orientation	The company exists for the sole benefit of the owner/ partners.
Sheep orientation	We will follow whatever is happening in the marketplace.
Erratic orientation	We run with new ideas only to drop them when a newer 'flavour-of-the-month' appears.

Most organizations consider themselves to be marketing oriented but do not consider other organizations to be marketing-oriented

Within the services sector, we have found that a marketing orientation cannot be taken for granted. Over the past five years we have asked over a thousand senior managers from large and medium-sized service organizations if their chief executive claims their company to be either 'market led', 'customer focused', or 'marketing orientated'. The responses show that over 75 per cent of CEOs claim they are. When these senior managers are asked what percentage of the service companies they know are 'customer focused', here the answer is generally between 10 per cent and 20 per cent!

> There is a considerable difference between how the CEOs of service organizations perceive their marketing orientation and how it appears to outsiders. This suggests to us that most service companies need to do much more in order to improve their market and customer focus.

Kotler[6] has identified five attributes which can be used to audit marketing effectiveness – one of the key elements of customer orientation. Although this audit was developed for companies with products, it can be easily adapted for service companies. These five attributes are:

1 *Customer philosophy* To what extent does top management allow market needs and wants to shape the company's plans and activities?

2 *Integrated marketing organization* To what extent is the company staffed for market analysis, planning, monitoring and control, etc?

3 *Adequate marketing information* Does management receive the information necessary to substantiate an effective marketing programme?

4 *Strategic orientation* Does top management generate innovative marketing strategies and plans for long-term growth and profitability? What is the track-record of success?

5 *Operational efficiency* Does the company have marketing plans which are implemented cost-effectively, with the results monitored to ensure rapid corrective action?

By having several questions under each attribute heading, and scoring them, it becomes possible to arrive at a total points score which reflects marketing effectiveness. We have used such audit questionnaires with a large number of service organizations. The results have shown that, on average, many of these service businesses were operating at less than half their potential in terms of marketing effectiveness. The attributes which tended to be especially low were lack of integrated marketing organization and operational efficiency, but in every service organization surveyed there was scope for improvement in all five areas.

Such an audit can provide useful data regarding how a programme might be designed to improve marketing orientation. It can also provide interesting comparisons between:

- Different operating divisions or subsidiaries
- Different departments or functional areas of the business
- Different companies in the same service industry.

Learning and planning for change

Having identified a need for improvements to be made, it then becomes necessary to formulate a plan for achieving them. Such a plan will involve the steps outlined in Figure 7.12.

Change will not happen without considerable effort

The first stage will be to recognize that a problem exists in the work situation. A problem in this sense is a departure from the expected behaviour, or operational efficiency. Next, the situation has to be analysed so that the various factors that impinge on it can be put into perspective. From this analysis, it becomes possible to specify what learning objectives are required (i.e. who has to learn what and to what standard). Having established what needs to be learned/changed, it is then possible to design a 'learning' programme which, to a large extent, establishes the parameters of the learning situation. Is the learning best carried out on or off the job? Is it for an individual or a group? Does it require special facilities? The

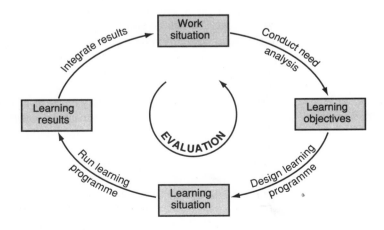

Figure 7.12 The learning/change process

programme is run and achieves results, which are then integrated back into the work situation.

The particular advantage of following this learning 'model' is that it facilitates evaluation. For example, if the change does not bring about the required level of performance in the work situation, is this because the learning results were not properly integrated? The next evaluation question needs to address whether the right learning results were achieved. If they were not, was this to do with the way the programme was run? Was the learning situation the right one? Was the programme correctly designed? Were the learning objectives incorrect? Was the initial analysis at fault? In fact, the evaluation of the required change is achieved by following the model loop in Figure 7.12 in the *reverse* direction.

If the programme is not successful, finding exactly where the attempted improvement programme went wrong enables the organization to learn from its mistakes and do better next time.

The chief executive's role in this process is critical The attitude of chief executives can be a determining factor in whether or not the change to marketing orientation succeeds or fails. Although they can lend weight and show considerable interest in the process, it is unlikely that they will have the time available to become deeply involved.

> **For this reason, it is important that the chief executive nominates and gives full backing to a change agent, whose task is to facilitate the improvements and champion the marketing cause.**

In some organizations this can be a full-time job, at least in the short-term, until momentum gathers pace. It is not always easy to shift deep-rooted attitudes, thus the role of change agent requires a person with experience, imagination, tenacity and belief in what he or she is doing. The whole initiative has to be seen as more than a token management development exercise.

In-company workshops are often necessary to provide appropriate knowledge, skills and attitudes The exact nature of what is to be done must, of course, relate to the individual company analysis. However, it is not unusual for the outcome to involve in-company workshops or programmes involving marketing staff and senior managers from all other functions. In general, the content will cover the skills, knowledge and attitudes necessary to develop and sustain a marketing-oriented service organization. The more that such development programmes can be focused on actual company marketing problems, the more relevant they become, as the development of skills to cope with real situations far outweighs the acquisition of knowledge.

Key support activities

In order to support the drive towards an improved marketing orientation, some additional support activities need to be considered. These are not necessarily relevant to all service companies.

- *Establish a marketing task force* This should comprise of a group of cross-functional senior managers. The group can work with the change agent, not only to provide ideas and suggestions about what might be done, but also to create change within their own parts of the organization.
- *Get rid of the 'wrong culture' carriers* Senior managers convey, by the way they react to situations, especially crises, what they really believe to be important. It is important to change the views or get rid of people who do not fit in with an organization dedicated to building a long-term relationship with its customers.
- *Acquire marketing talent* A programme should be put in place to ensure that suitable marketing talent is hired. This will involve external recruitment and internal development of staff.
- *Use external consultants* Few companies possess the necessary in-house skills to be able to analyse, let alone organize and staff, all marketing activities such as advertising, marketing research, PR, information systems, and even training at senior levels. Therefore, there may be a case for using carefully chosen consultants to help solve problems and develop the company's own staff.
- *Promote market-oriented executives* By making marketing orientation a significant criterion in the company's performance review, promotion and reward systems, the message can be clearly spelt out that it is important and career-enhancing for managers to be market focused.
- *Maximize the impact of management development* Ensuring that management development is endorsed by the chief executive, is well-designed and produces results which can be measured and transferred to the business, is often critical to success.
- *Keep the marketing structure under review* As we have seen earlier, successful companies organize themselves around their markets and deliberately seek to maintain close contact with their customers. There should be a continual search for improving the way that marketing is organized.
- *Develop a marketing information system* Again, as we saw earlier, information is critical to successful marketing

decision-making. Developing an effective MIS can greatly assist the drive to an improved marketing orientation.

- *Recognize the long-term nature of the task* The development of a marketing orientation where it has not previously existed will require a major change in attitudes and a fundamental shift in shared values. One major company set up a marketing orientation programme in which all senior managers were involved. Continuous activity lasting five years was necessary before a marketing orientation was achieved. It can take from three to six years before a real marketing orientation is developed.
- *Publicize successes* Whenever something is achieved which demonstrates that the market orientation has paid off, ensure that it is publicized, either by word of mouth or by more formal channels. Success breeds further success.

From the above list, it is evident that the drive for marketing orientation must have a high profile. It must also operate across a broad front and leave no part of the organization untouched. It has become clear from the studies of excellent companies that their success was no accident. It was won by the total commitment of top management and staff alike to do whatever was necessary to overcome all obstacles in the way of serving customers.

Summary

In this chapter, we looked at some of the issues which, although not directly part of the marketing planning process itself, nonetheless have a direct and profound impact on its ultimate effectiveness.

The first of these was the underlying need for there to be a well-thought-out marketing intelligence system. Without provision of accurate data, marketing planning will not be effective. Not only was attention paid to how a system should be designed, but also to how it might be managed.

Marketing research was also considered in terms of how special information requirements might be identified. In addition to a brief look at research techniques, we addressed the issue of how much to spend on marketing research.

We then looked at marketing planning in terms of how the process might need to be adapted in order to be congruent with the organization's stage of development. We saw that, at some stages of a company's life, it was inappropriate to consider the introduction of marketing planning until more immediate organizational issues had been resolved. There are also other problems facing the marketer, in terms of where to position marketing planning in centralized or decentralized marketing organizations and issues around matrix management in terms of the relative importance placed on product/service management versus market management.

The service organization company still also needs a plan for the introduction of planning. It needs to establish a schedule and a planning cycle in which everyone involved knows when to make their particular contribution.

Finally, we looked at perhaps the most critical issue of all, how the service organization might develop or improve their marketing orientation. We saw that the gap between the degree of marketing orientation that the top management of a services organization believes it has and what actually exists could, in many companies, be vast. Part of the reason for this is a lack of understanding, but often it is because other orientations are too deeply engrained in the organization to allow a marketing orientation to develop. We saw that it was possible to measure marketing effectiveness, an important component of marketing orientation, by analysing the company's approach to customer philosophy, integrating its marketing organization, gathering marketing information, strategy formulation and operational efficiency.

Knowing the extent of a company's marketing orientation is one thing – setting out to improve it is another and far more difficult task. As we saw, it needs a high level of commitment in the company to change and to give marketing initiatives a chance of succeeding. Any change programme has to be underpinned by a number of supporting activities designed to make an impact on the corporate culture. Above all, seeking to raise the level of market orientation is a different task and it requires a carefully formulated approach to achieve success. Such initiatives, whilst difficult and time-consuming, are critical to the success of marketing planning activity.

We have now covered each of the major phases of marketing planning and the related organizational issues in detail. In the final chapter, which follows, we provide an overview and summary of what we have covered and a detailed step-by-step approach for developing a services marketing planning system. This chapter will provide a detailed structure, with accompanying proformas, for creating:

- A three-year strategic marketing plan
- A one-year detailed tactical marketing plan
- A headquarters consolidated plan of several strategic business unit (SBU) strategic marketing plans.

References

1 For a more detailed discussion on database marketing, see: Shaw, R. and Stone, M. (1989) *Data Base Marketing*, Gower Press, Aldershot; Davies, J. M. (1992) *The Essential Guide to Database Marketing*, McGraw-Hill, Maidenhead.
2 Those wishing to examine the topic of marketing research in detail should see a standard text such as:
   Kinnear T. C. and Taylor, J. K. (1991) *Marketing Research: An Applied Approach*, 4th edn, McGraw-Hill, Maidenhead.
   Crimp, M. (1990) *Marketing Research Process*, 3rd edn, Prentice Hall, Englewood Cliffs, NJ.
   Chisnall, P. M. (1991) *The Essence of Marketing Research*, Prentice Hall, Englewood Cliffs, NJ.
3 Greiner, L. E. (1967) Patterns of Organisation Change. *Harvard Business Review*, May/June.
4 Leppard, J. (1989) Marketing Planning and Organisational Culture, M. Phil Thesis, Cranfield University, 1989.
5 Bartlett, C. A. and Ghoshal, S. (1990) Matrix Management: Not a Structure, a Frame of Mind. *Harvard Business Review*, July/August, 138–145. (This articles provides a top management perspective on matrix management.)
6 Kotler, P. (1977) From Sales Obsession to Marketing Effectiveness. *Harvard Business Review*, November/December, 67–75.

8 A step-by-step marketing planning system for services*

> This chapter is in two parts. This first part is a very brief sum-
> mary of the main points relating to marketing planning. The
> second part is an actual marketing planning system which
> operationalizes all the concepts, structures and frameworks
> outlined in this book in the form of a step-by-step approach
> to the preparation, first, of a strategic and, second, of an opera-
> tional marketing plan. Finally, there is a suggested format for
> senior headquarters personnel who may have the task of sum-
> marizing many SBU strategic marketing plans into one conso-
> lidated document.

Part 1 Marketing planning summary

Important

Please use this chapter with some caution. Remember, marketing
planning is about creating better *value* for your customers in order
to give your organization sustainable competitive advantage. So,
please use this chapter for this purpose, rather than as a straitjacket
or as a form-filling exercise. Additionally, please remember to be
creative.

Also, do not do your planning in isolation. Do consult and involve
your colleagues, particularly those in the front line, in the process.

There will be other functional plans, but these will need to be
consistent with your marketing plan.

*This chapter is based on Chapter 13 of McDonald, M. (1995) *Marketing Plans: How
to prepare them; how to use them*, 3rd edn, Butterworth-Heinemann, Oxford, and has
been adapted for service organizations.

Why is marketing planning necessary?

Marketing planning is necessary because of:

- Increasing turbulence, complexity and competitiveness
- The speed of technological change
- The need for *you*
  - to help identify sources of competitive advantage
  - to force an organized approach
  - to develop specificity
  - to ensure consistent relationships
- The need for *superiors*
  - to inform
- The need for *non-marketing functions*
  - to get support
- The need for *subordinates*
  - to get resources
  - to gain commitment
  - to set objectives and strategies

The strategic marketing plan

The strategic marketing plan covers a period of three or more years.

The tactical marketing plan

This is the detailed scheduling and costing out of what needs to be done to achieve the first year of the strategic marketing plan.

Ten barriers to marketing planning

In Chapter 2 and throughout this book, a number of barriers to effective marketing and marketing planning have been described. The ten principal barriers are:

1 Confusion between marketing tactics and strategy.
2 Isolating the marketing function from operations.
3 Confusion between the marketing function and the marketing concept.
4 Organizational barriers – the tribal mentality, for example the failure to define strategic business units (SBUs) correctly.
5 Lack of in-depth analysis.
6 Confusion between process and output.
7 Lack of knowledge and skills.
8 Lack of a systematic approach to marketing planning.
9 Failure to prioritize objectives.
10 Hostile corporate cultures.

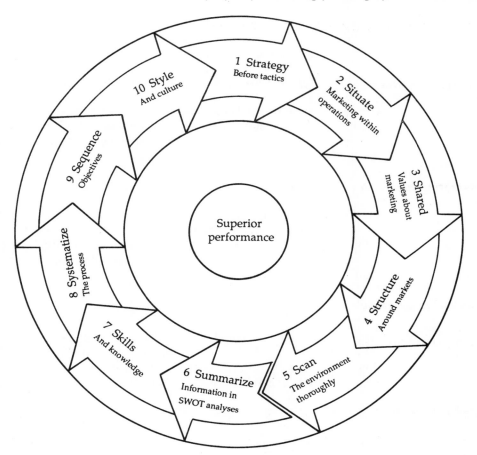

Figure 8.1 Marketing planning for competitive advantage

The 'Ten S' approach to overcoming these barriers

Figure 8.1 summarizes the 'Ten S' approach developed by the author to overcome each of these barriers. The sections which follow elaborate briefly on each of the 'Ten Ss'. Ten fundamental principles of marketing planning are provided.

Marketing planning – Principle 1. Strategy before tactics

Develop the strategic marketing plan first. This entails greater emphasis on scanning the external environment, the early identification of forces emanating from it, and developing appropriate strategic responses, involving all levels of management in the process.

A strategic plan should cover a period of between three and five years, and only when this has been developed and agreed should the one-year operational marketing plan be developed.

Never write the one-year plan first and extrapolate it.

Marketing planning – Principle 2. Situate marketing within operations

For the purpose of marketing planning, put marketing as close as possible to the customer. Where practicable, have both marketing and sales report to the same person, who should not normally be the chief executive officer.

Marketing planning – Principle 3. Shared values about marketing

Marketing is a management process whereby the resources of the whole organization are utilized to satisfy the needs of selected customer groups in order to achieve the objectives of both parties. Marketing, then, is first and foremost an attitude of mind rather than a series of functional activities.

Marketing planning – Principle 4. Structure around markets

Organize company activities around customer groups if possible rather than around functional activities and get marketing planning done in these strategic business units (SBUs). Without excellent marketing planning in SBUs, corporate planning will be of limited value.

Marketing planning – Principle 5. Scan the environment thoroughly

For an effective marketing audit to take place:

- Checklists of questions customized according to level in the organization should be agreed.
- These should form the basis of the organization's MIS.
- The marketing audit should be a *required* activity.
- Managers should not be allowed to hide behind vague terms like 'poor economic conditions'.
- Managers should be encouraged to incorporate the tools of marketing in their audits, e.g. product life cycles, portfolios and so on.

Marketing planning – Principle 6. Summarize information in SWOT analyses

Information is the foundation on which a marketing plan is built. From information (internal and external) comes intelligence.

Intelligence describes *the marketing plan*, which is the intellectualization of how managers perceive their own position in their markets relative to their competitors (with competitive advantage accurately defined – e.g. cost leader, differentiation, niche), what objectives they want to achieve over some designated period of time, how they intend to achieve their objectives (strategies), what resources are required, and with what results (budget).

A SWOT should:

- Be focused on each specific segment of crucial importance to the organization's future.
- Be a summary emanating from the marketing audit.
- Be brief, interesting and concise.
- Focus on *key* factors only.
- List *differential* strengths and weaknesses *vis-à-vis* competitors, focusing on competitive advantage.
- List *key* external opportunities and threats only.
- Identify and pin down the *real* issues. It should not be a list of unrelated points.
- The reader should be able to grasp instantly the main thrust of the business, even to the point of being able to write marketing objectives.
- Follow the implied question 'which means that . . . ?' to get the real implications.
- Not over-abbreviate.

Marketing planning – Principle 7. Skills and knowledge

Ensure that all those responsible for marketing in SBUs have the necessary marketing knowledge and skills for the job. In particular, ensure that they understand and know how to use the more important tools of marketing, such as:

- Information
  - How to get it
  - How to use it
- Positioning
  - Market segmentation
  - Ansoff
  - Porter
- Product life cycle analysis
  - Gap analysis
- Portfolio management
  - BCG matrix
  - Directional policy matrix
- Marketing mix management
  - Product
  - Price
  - Place
  - Promotion
  - People
  - Processes
  - Proactive customer service

Additionally, marketing personnel require communications and interpersonal skills.

Marketing planning – Principle 8. Systematize the process

It is essential to have a set of written procedures and a well-argued common format for marketing planning. The purposes of such a system are:

1 To ensure that all key issues are systematically considered.
2 To pull together the essential elements of the strategic planning of each SBU in a consistent manner.
3 To help corporate management to compare diverse businesses and to understand the overall condition of, and prospects for, the organization.

Marketing planning – Principle 9. Sequence objectives

Ensure that all objectives are prioritized according to their impact on the organization and their urgency and that resources are allocated accordingly.

A suggested method for prioritization is given in Figure 8.2.

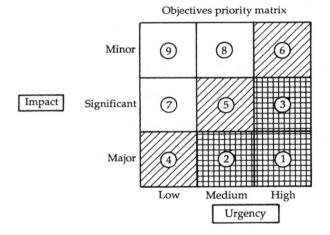

Figure 8.2 Prioritization of objectives

Marketing planning – Principle 10. Style and culture

Marketing planning will not be effective without the active support and participation of the culture leaders. But, even with their support, the type of marketing planning has to be appropriate for the phase of the organizational life-line described in Chapter 7. This phase should be measured before attempting to introduce marketing planning.

Conclusion to Part 1

Contents of a marketing plan

Your marketing plan should answer the following questions:

- What is your purpose?
- What is your market?
- Has it declined or grown?
- How does it break down into segments?
- What are the trends in each?
- Who are your customers?
- What are your services?
- What does the customer need?
- How well do your services satisfy these needs?
- What are your objectives?
- What are your strategies?
    - What new services should be developed?
    - How should you price your services?
    - What service levels should you provide?
    - What should your channel strategies be?
    - How should you communicate with your target markets?
    - How should people and processes strategies be developed?
- How can you allocate your resources optimally?

What should appear in the strategic marketing plan

A summary of what appears in a strategic marketing plan and a list of the principal marketing tools/techniques/structures/frameworks which apply to each step are given in Figure 8.3.

It will be understood from the foregoing that marketing planning never has been just the simple step-by-step approach described so enthusiastically in most prescriptive texts and courses. The moment an organization embarks on the marketing planning path, it can expect to encounter a number of complex organizational, attitudinal, process and cognitive problems, which are likely to block progress. By being forewarned about these barriers, there is a good chance of successfully using the step-by-step marketing planning system which follows in Part 2 of this chapter and of doing excellent marketing planning that will bring all the claimed benefits, including a signifi-

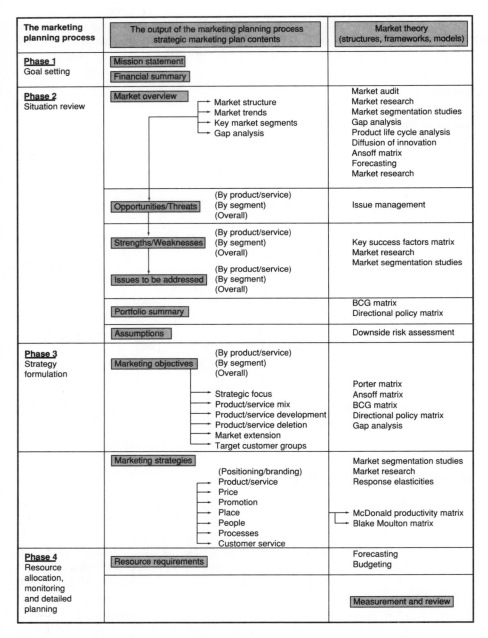

The marketing planning process	The output of the marketing planning process strategic marketing plan contents		Market theory (structures, frameworks, models)
Phase 1 Goal setting	Mission statement Financial summary		
Phase 2 Situation review	Market overview	Market structure Market trends Key market segments Gap analysis	Market audit Market research Market segmentation studies Gap analysis Product life cycle analysis Diffusion of innovation Ansoff matrix Forecasting Market research
	Opportunities/Threats	(By product/service) (By segment) (Overall)	Issue management
	Strengths/Weaknesses	(By product/service) (By segment) (Overall)	Key success factors matrix Market research Market segmentation studies
	Issues to be addressed	(By product/service) (By segment) (Overall)	
	Portfolio summary		BCG matrix Directional policy matrix
	Assumptions		Downside risk assessment
Phase 3 Strategy formulation	Marketing objectives	(By product/service) (By segment) (Overall) Strategic focus Product/service mix Product/service development Product/service deletion Market extension Target customer groups	Porter matrix Ansoff matrix BCG matrix Directional policy matrix Gap analysis
	Marketing strategies	(Positioning/branding) Product/service Price Promotion Place People Processes Customer service	Market segmentation studies Market research Response elasticities McDonald productivity matrix Blake Moulton matrix
Phase 4 Resource allocation, monitoring and detailed planning	Resource requirements		Forecasting Budgeting
			Measurement and review

Figure 8.3 Principal marketing tools which can be utilized at different phases of the marketing planning process

cant impact on the bottom line, through the creation of competitive advantage. If they are ignored, however, marketing planning will not be successful.

Part 2   A marketing planning system

Introduction

This marketing planning system is in three sections. Section A takes you through a step-by-step approach to the preparation of a strategic marketing plan. What actually appears in the strategic marketing plan is given under the head 'Strategic marketing plan documentation'.

Section B takes you through the preparation of a one-year marketing plan. What actually appears in a one-year marketing plan is given under the heading 'The one-year marketing plan documentation'. Finally, section C refers to the need for a headquarters consolidated plan of several SBU strategic marketing plans. A suggested format is given under the heading 'Example of a format for a headquarters consolidated strategic plan.'

Section A   Step-by-step approach to the preparation of a strategic marketing plan

There are four main steps in the planning process (presented in diagrammatic form in Figure 8.4), which any strategic business unit* interested in protecting and developing its business must carry out:

1 *Analysis* – it must analyse both its marketplace and its own position within it, relative to the competition.
2 *Objectives* – it must construct from this analysis a realistic set of quantitative marketing and financial objectives, consistent with those set by the organization.
3 *Strategy* – it must determine the broad strategy which will accomplish these objectives, conforming with the organization's corporate strategy.
4 *Tactics* – it must draw together the analysis, the objectives and the strategy, using them as the foundation for detailed tactical

*A strategic business unit:
● Will have common segments and competitors for most of its products.
● Will be a competitor in an external market.
● Will be a discrete and identifiable unit.
● Will have a manager who has control over most of the areas critical to success.
SBUs are not necessarily the same as operating units and the definition can, and should if necessary, be applied all the way down to a particular product or customer or group of products and customers.

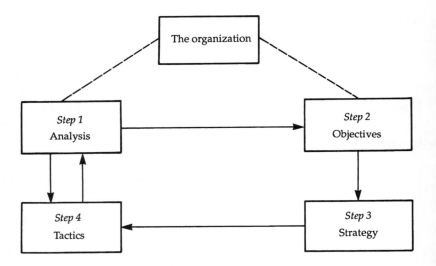

Figure 8.4 Main steps in the planning process

action plans, capable of implementing the strategy and achieving the agreed objectives.

This process is formally expressed in two marketing plans, the strategic marketing plan and the tactical marketing plan, which should be written in accordance with the format provided in this system. It is designed for strategic business units (SBUs) to be able to take a logical and constructive approach to planning for success.

Two very important introductory points should be made about the marketing plan:

1 *The importance of different sections* – in the final analysis, the strategic marketing plan is a plan for action, and this should be reflected in the finished document. The implementation part of the strategic plan is represented by the subsequent one-year marketing plan.
2 *The length of the analytical section* – to be able to produce an action-focused strategic marketing plan, a considerable amount of background information and statistics needs to be collected, collated and analysed. An analytical framework has been provided in the forms, included in the database section of the 'Strategic marketing plan documentation', which each SBU should complete. However, the commentary given in the strategic marketing plan should provide the main findings of the analysis rather than a mass of raw data. It should compel concentration upon only that which is essential. The analysis section should, therefore, provide only a short background.

Basis of the system

Each business unit in the organization will have different levels of opportunity depending on the prevailing business climate. Each business unit, therefore, needs to be managed in a way that is appropriate to its own unique circumstances. At the same time, however, the chief executive officer of the SBU must have every opportunity to see that the ways in which these business units are managed are consistent with the overall strategic aims of the organization.

This system sets out the procedures which, if adhered to, will assist in achieving these aims.

Sections A, B and C set out the three basic marketing planning formats and explain how each of the planning steps should be carried

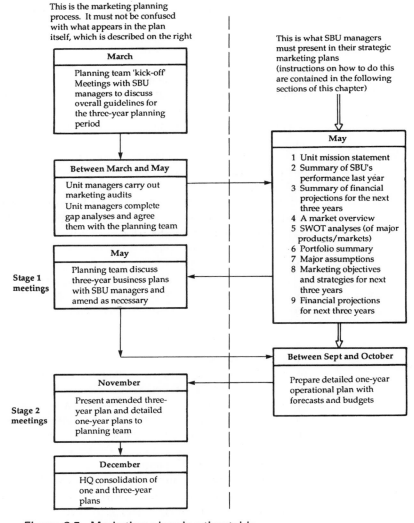

Figure 8.5 Marketing planning timetable

out. They explain simply and clearly what should be presented, and when, in the three-year marketing plan, in the more detailed one-year operational plan and in the headquarters consolidated marketing plan.

A glossary of planning terms is included at the end of the book. The overall marketing planning format is described in Figure 8.5. (Note that, for the sake of simplicity, it has been assumed that the organization's year runs from January to December.) The following sections explain how each of the steps in the planning process should be completed.

The marketing audit

(for completion between February and May each year)
(Note: not for inclusion in the plan or its presentation)

Every market includes a wide variety of customer groups, not all of which will necessarily provide SBUs with opportunities for servicing profitably.

In order to study those areas of the market which are potentially most favourable to the SBU's operations, it is necessary to divide the market into different *market segments* (hereafter just referred to as 'segments') and to analyse sales potential by type of service within each segment.

All SBUs must, therefore, analyse and evaluate the key segments in their market, plus any other segments which have been identified and selected as being of lesser importance to them.

It is appreciated that all the basic information required for this marketing audit may not be readily available. Nevertheless, an analysis and evaluation of the SBU's situation in each of the selected segments, i.e. a marketing audit, will provide the basis from which objectives can be set and plans prepared.

For the purpose of a marketing planning system, it is usual to provide users with an agreed list so that all SBUs using the system use similar nomenclature for services and markets.

All managers carrying out their audit should use internal sales data and the SBU marketing information system to complete their audit. It is helpful at this stage if the various SBU managers can issue to any subordinates involved in the audit a market overview covering major industry and market trends. The audit will inevitably require considerably more data preparation than is required to be reproduced in the marketing plan itself. Therefore, all managers should start a *running reference file* for their area of responsibility during the year, which can also be used as a continual reference source and for verbal presentation of proposals.

It is essential to stress that the audit, which will be based on the running reference file, *is not a marketing plan and under no circumstances should voluminous documents relating to the audit appear in any business plans.*

The contents of a strategic marketing plan

The following sections (1–9) describe what should be presented in strategic marketing plans. These should be completed by the end of May each year.

These sections contain instructions. The actual documentation for the strategic marketing plan is also provided in this section.

1 SBU mission statement

This is the first item to appear in the marketing plan. The purpose of the mission statement is to ensure that the raison d'être of the SBU is clearly stated. Brief statements should be made which cover the following points:

1 *Role or contribution of the unit* – for example, profit generator, service department, opportunity seeker.
2 *Definition of business* – for example, the needs you satisfy or the benefits you provide. Do not be too specific (e.g. 'we sell insurance') or too general (e.g. 'we are in the communication business').
3 *Distinctive competence* – this should be a brief statement that applies only to your specific SBU. A statement that could equally apply to any competitor is unsatisfactory.
4 *Indications for future direction* – a brief statement of the principal things you would give serious consideration to (e.g. move into a new segment.) A statement about what you *will* consider, *might* consider and *will never* consider can be quite useful.

Note: This is Form 1 in the strategic marketing plan documentation.

2 Summary of SBU's performance

This opening section is designed to give a bird's eye view of the SBU's total marketing activities.

In addition to a quantitative summary of performance, as shown in Table 8.1, SBU managers should give a summary of reasons for good or bad performance.

Use *constant revenue* (t–1) in order that the comparisons are meaningful. Make sure you use the same base year values for any projections provided in later sections in your plan.

Note: This is Form 2 in the strategic marketing plan documentation.

Table 8.1 Summary of SBU performance

	Three years ago	Two years ago	Last year
Volume/turnover			
Gross profit (%)			
Gross margin (000 ecu)			

3 Summary of financial projections

This is the third item to appear in the marketing plan. Its purpose is to summarize, for the person reading the plan, the financial implications over the full three-year planning period. It should be presented as a simple diagram along the lines shown in Figure 8.6.

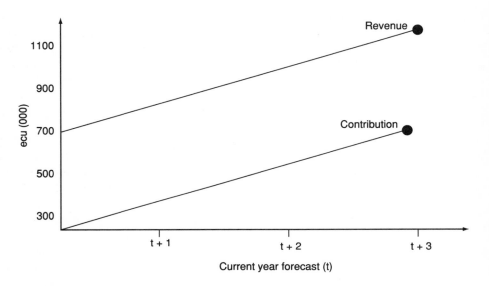

Figure 8.6 Summary of financial projections

This should be accompanied by a brief commentary. For example:

'This three-year business plan shows an increase in revenue from 700,000 to 1,100,000 ecu and an increase in contribution from 200,000 ecu to 680,000 ecu. The purpose of this marketing plan is to show how these increases will be achieved.'

Note: Please refer to Form 3 in the strategic marketing plan documentation.

In order to comply with this form, it is strongly recommended that the strategic planning (gap analysis) forms (which follow as Forms 4 and 5 in the strategic marketing plan documentation) are completed first. Note that the 'objective' point should be (as a minimum) that point which will enable you to achieve the corporate objectives set for the SBU. *Ideally, however, it should be set at a point which will make this SBU the best of its kind amongst comparable competitive SBUs.* Note that the sales revenue form must be completed first, followed by the profit form.

4 Market overview

This section is intended to provide a brief picture of the market before descending to the particular details of individual market segments, which form the heart of the marketing plan.

This system is based upon the *segmentation* of markets, dividing these into homogeneous groups of customers, each having characteristics which can be exploited in marketing terms. *This approach is taken because it is the one which is often the most useful for SBU managers to be able to develop their markets.* The alternative, service-orientated, approach is rarely appropriate, given the variation between different customer groups in the markets in which most organizations compete.

The market segmentation approach is more useful in revealing both the weaknesses and the development opportunities than is an exclusively service orientation.

While it is difficult to give precise instructions on how to present this section of the marketing plan, it should be possible (following completion of the marketing audit) to present a market overview which summarizes what managers consider to be the key characteristics of their markets.

In completing this section, SBU managers should consider the following:

1 What are the major services, markets (or segments) which are likely to be able to provide the kind of business opportunities suitable for the organization?
2 How are these changing? That is, which are growing and which are declining?

This section should be brief and there should be some commentary by the SBU manager about what seems to be happening in their market.

It is very helpful if SBU managers can present as much of this information as possible visually (i.e. bar charts or pie charts, service life cycles, etc.). A market 'map' can be extremely useful for clarifying how the market works.

Note: Please refer to Form 6, in the strategic marketing plan documentation.

5 SWOT analyses of major services/markets

Compiling the SWOT analyses

To decide on marketing objectives and future strategy, it is first necessary to summarize the SBU's *present* position in its market(s). This was done in the previous section.

In respect of the major products and services/markets (segments) highlighted in the previous section, the marketing audit must now be summarized in the form of a number of *SWOT analyses*. The word *SWOT* derives from the initial letters of the words *strengths, weaknesses, opportunities* and *threats*. In simple terms:

- What are the unit's differential strengths and weaknesses *vis-à-vis* competitors? In other words, why should potential customers in the target markets prefer to deal with your organization rather than with your competitors?
- What are the opportunities?
- What are the present and future threats to the SBU's business in each of the segments which have been identified as being of importance?

Guidelines for completing the SWOT analysis

The market overview in Section 4 will have identified what you consider to be the key service/market (segments) on which you intend to focus. For presentation purposes, it is helpful if you can present a brief SWOT for each of these key service/market segments. Each of these SWOTs should be brief and interesting to read. Complete SWOTs only for the key segments.

Section I concerns *strengths* and *weaknesses*. Section II which follows is intended to indicate how the *opportunities* and *threats* section of the SWOT should be completed. Section III summarizes *key issues to be addressed*. Section IV describes the setting of assumptions, marketing objectives and strategies for each service/market segment. Section V summarizes the position of competitors.

I Some important factors for success in this business (critical success factors)

How does a competitor wishing to provide services in this segment succeed? There are always relatively few factors that determine success. Factors such as service performance, breadth of services, speed of service, low costs, and so on, are often the most important factors for success.

You should now make a brief statement about your organization's *strengths and weaknesses* in relation to these most important factors for success that you have identified. To do this, you will probably wish to consider other suppliers to the same segment in order to identify why you believe your organization can succeed and what weaknesses must be addressed in the three-year planning period.

These factors are called critical success factors. A layout such as that shown in Figure 8.7 is useful. You should then weight each factor out of 100 (e.g. CSF 1 = 60; CSF 2 = 25; CSF 3 = 10; CSF 4 = 5). It is suggested that you score yourself and each competitor out of ten on each of the CSFs. Then, multiply each score by the weight. This will give you an accurate reading of your position in each segment *vis-à-vis* your competitors. It will also highlight which

Critical success factors \ Competitors	Weighting factor	Your organization	Competitor A	Competitor B	Competitor C
CSF 1					
CSF 2					
CSF 3					
CSF 4					
Total weighted score	100				

Figure 8.7 Ranking approach to critical success factors (CSFs)

are *the key issues that should be addressed* in the three-year planning period.

Great caution is necessary to ensure that you are not guilty of self-delusion. Obviously, it is desirable to have independent evidence from market research in order to be able to complete this section accurately. If you do not have independent evidence, it is still worth doing a SWOT, because it will at least indicate what you need to know. Also, it is quite useful if you can get a number of managers to complete this independently, as, sometimes, it reveals a lot about what they believe to be the factors for success.

II   Summary of outside influences and their implications (opportunities and threats)

This should include a brief statement about how important environmental influences such as technology, government policies and regulations, the economy, and so on, have affected this segment. There will obviously be some opportunities and some threats.

III   Key issues to be addressed

From I and II above will emerge a number of key issues to be addressed.

IV Assumptions, marketing objectives, marketing strategies

Assumptions can now be made and objectives and strategies set. It should be stressed at this point that such assumptions, objectives and strategies relate only to each particular service/market segment under consideration. These will guide your thinking when setting overall assumptions, marketing objectives and strategies later on (see section below).

Note: Please refer to Form 7 in the strategic marketing plan documentation. This form incorporates all the points made in I, II, III and IV above and should be completed for all service/market segments under consideration.

V Competitor analysis

Here you should summarize the findings of the audit in respect of *major competitors* only. For each competitor, you should indicate their sales within the particular service/market segment under consideration, their share now, *and their expected share three years from now*. The greater a competitor's influence over others, the greater their ability to implement their own independent strategies, hence the more successful they are. It is suggested that you should also classify each of your main competitors according to one of the classifications in the guide to competitive position classifications, below, i.e. leadership, strong, favourable, tenable, weak.

Also list their principal services. Next, list each major competitor's business direction and current strategies. There follows a list of business directions and business strategies as guidelines. *These should not be quoted verbatim*, as they are only given as guidelines. Next, list their major strengths and weaknesses.

The format shown in Figure 8.8 is useful.

Note: Please refer to Form 8 in the strategic marketing plan documentation.

Guide to competitive position classifications

Leadership	• Has a major influence on the performance or behaviour of others
Strong	• Has a wide choice of strategies
	• Is able to adopt an independent strategy without endangering their short-term position
	• Has low vulnerability to competitors' actions
Favourable	• Exploits specific competitive strengths, often in a service-market niche
	• Has more than average opportunity to improve their position; has several strategies available
Tenable	• Their performance justifies continuation in business
Weak	• Currently has an unsatisfactory performance and significant competitive weaknesses
	• They must improve or withdraw

The following list includes five business directions/strategies that are appropriate for almost any business. Select those that best summarize the competitors' strategies.

Competitor analysis					
Main competitor	Services and products/ markets	Business direction and current objectives and strategies	Strengths	Weaknesses	Competitive position

Figure 8.8 Competitor analysis audit

Business directions/strategies

1 *Enter* – to allocate resources to a new business area. Consideration should include building from prevailing company or division strengths, exploiting related opportunities and defending against perceived threats. This may involve creating a new industry.
2 *Improve* – to apply strategies that will significantly improve the competitive position of the business. Often, this requires thoughtful service/market segmentation.
3 *Maintain* – to maintain one's competitive position. Aggressive strategies may be required, although a defensive posture may also be assumed. Service/market position is maintained, often in a niche.
4 *Harvest* – to relinquish intentionally competitive position, emphasizing short-term profit and cash flow, but not necessarily at the risk of losing the business in the short term. Often, this entails consolidating or reducing various aspects of the business to create higher performance for that which remains.

5   *Exit* – to divest a business because of its weak competitive position, or because the cost of staying in it is prohibitive and the risk associated with improving its position is too high.

6 Portfolio summary (summary of SWOTs)

All that remains is to summarize each of these SWOTs in a format which makes it easy to see at a glance the overall position and relative importance of each of these segments to the organization. This can be done by drawing a diagram in the form of a four-box *matrix* which will show each of the important service/market segments described earlier. A matrix is shown as Figure 8.9. Some easy-to-follow instructions follow on how to complete such a matrix.

The *portfolio matrix* (referred to as the directional policy matrix in Chapter 5) enables you to assess which services, or which groups of customers/segments, will offer the best chance of commercial success. It will also aid decision-making about which services (or market segments) merit investment, both in terms of finance and managerial effort.

In this example, market segments are used, although it is possible to use services. We recommend that you follow the instructions given below.

This is how you arrive at a portfolio matrix for your SBU.

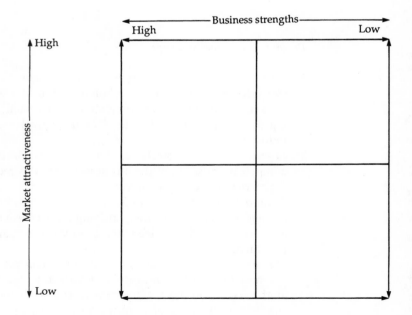

Figure 8.9   Portfolio summary matrix

1 List your market segments on a separate piece of paper and decide which ones are the most attractive. (Note that these 'segments' can be countries, divisions, markets, distributors, customers, etc.) To arrive at these decisions, you will no doubt take several factors into account:

- The size of the markets
- Their actual or prospective growth
- The prices you can charge
- Profitability
- The diversity of needs (which you can meet)
- The amount of competition in terms of quality and quantity
- The supportiveness of the business environment
- Technical developments, etc.

Imagine that you have a measuring instrument, something like a thermometer, but which measures not temperature, but market attractiveness. The higher the reading, the more attractive the market. The instrument is shown in Figure 8.10. Estimate the position on the scale *each* of your markets would record (should such an instrument exist) and make a note of it as

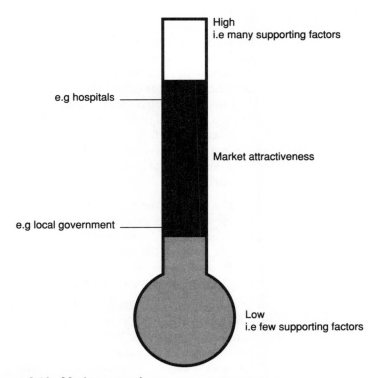

Figure 8.10 Market attractiveness measurement

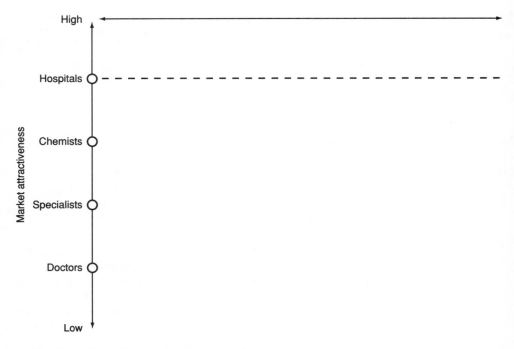

Figure 8.11 Step 1: Rank market attractiveness

shown by the example above. You should use the methodology outlined in Chapter 5.

2 Transpose this information on to the matrix in Figure 8.9 writing the markets on the left of the matrix.

3 Still using the matrix, draw a dotted line horizontally across from the top left-hand market as shown in Figure 8.11.

4 Now ask yourself how well your SBU is equipped to deal with this most attractive market. A whole series of questions needs to be asked to establish the company's business strengths, for example:

- Do we have the right services?
- How well are we known in this market?
- What image do we have?
- Do we have the right technical skills?
- How close are we to this market?
- How do we compare with competitors?

The outcome of such an analysis will enable you to arrive at a conclusion about the 'fitness' of your unit and you will be able to choose a point on the horizontal scale of the matrix to represent this. The left of the scale represents many unit strengths, the right few unit strengths. The analysis completed in the previous section (Section 5 on SWOT analyses) should be used, since you have

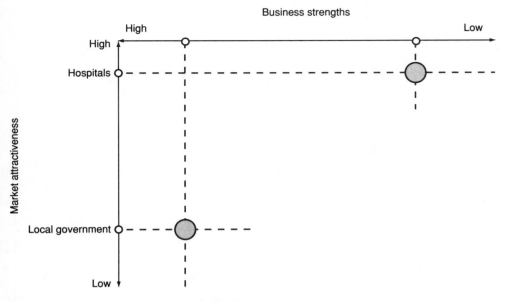

Figure 8.12 Step 2: Rank business strengths

already completed the necessary quantification. Draw a vertical line from this point on the scale as shown in Figure 8.12 so that it intersects with the horizontal line.

5 Now *redraw* the circles, this time making the diameter of each circle proportional to that segment's share of your total sales turnover. (Please note that to be technically correct you should take the square root of the volume, or value.)

6 Now indicate where these circles will be in three years' time and their estimated size. The matrix may, therefore, have to show segments not currently served. There are two ways of doing this. First, in deciding on market or segment attractiveness you can assume that you are at t0 (i.e. today) and that your forecast of attractiveness covers the next three years (i.e. t + 3). If this is your chosen method, then it will be clear that *the circle can only move horizontally along the axis*, as all that will change is your business strength. The second way of doing it shows the current attractiveness position on the vertical axis, based on the past three years (i.e. t–3 to t0) and then forecasts how that attractiveness position will change during the next three years (i.e. t0 to t + 3). In such a case, the circles can move both vertically and horizontally. This is the method used in the example provided (Figure 8.13), but it is entirely up to you which method you use. It is essential to be creative in your use of the matrix. Be prepared to change the name on the axes and to experiment with both products and markets.

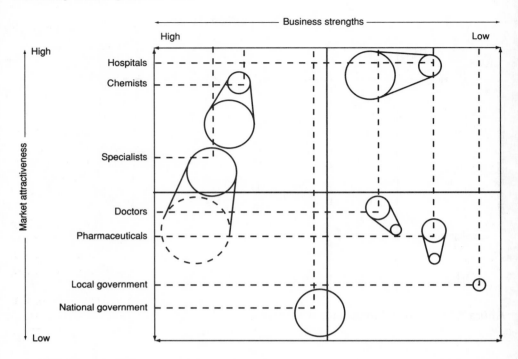

Figure 8.13 Step 3: Identify present and future sales turnover and position on matrix

Note: Please refer to Form 9, in the strategic marketing plan documentation.

7 Overall assumptions

Each SBU must highlight the assumptions which are critical to the fulfilment of the planned marketing objectives and strategies.

Key planning assumptions deal, in the main, with outside features and anticipated changes which would have a significant influence on the achievement of marketing objectives. These might include such things as market growth rate, your organization's costs, capital investment and so on.

Assumptions should be few in number and relate only to key issues such as those identified in the SWOT analyses. If it is possible for a plan to be implemented irrespective of the assumptions made, then those assumptions are not necessary and should be removed.

You should find that the more detailed lists of assumptions made for each of the principal service/market segments analysed in the SWOT stage (Section 5) will be helpful in deciding what the macro assumptions should be.

Note: Please refer to Form 10, in the strategic marketing plan documentation.

8 Overall marketing objectives and strategies

Marketing objectives

Following identification and statement of key strengths, weaknesses, opportunities and threats, and the explicit statement of assumptions about conditions affecting the business, the process of setting marketing objectives is made easier, since they will be a realistic statement of what the SBU desires to achieve as a result of market-centred analysis.

As in the case of objective setting for other functional areas of the business, this is the most important step in the whole process, as it is a commitment on an SBU-wide basis to a particular course of action which will determine the scheduling and costing out of subsequent actions.

An *objective* is what the unit wants to achieve. A *strategy* is how it plans to achieve it. Thus, there are objectives and strategies at all levels in marketing. For example, there can be advertising objectives and strategies, pricing objectives and strategies, and so on.

However, the important point about marketing objectives is that they should be about services and markets only, since it is only by selling something to someone that the SBU's financial goals can be achieved. Advertising, pricing and other elements of the marketing mix are the means (the strategies) by which the SBU can succeed in doing this. Thus, pricing objectives, sales promotion objectives, advertising objectives and so on should *not* be confused with marketing objectives.

If profits and cash flows are to be maximized, each SBU must consider carefully how its current customer needs are changing and how its products offered need to change accordingly. Since change is inevitable, it is necessary for SBUs to consider the two main dimensions of commercial growth, i.e. service development and market development.

Marketing objectives are concerned with the following:

- Selling existing services to existing segments
- Developing new services for existing segments
- Extending existing services to new segments
- Developing new services for new segments.

Marketing objectives should be *quantitative*, and should be expressed where possible in terms of *values*, *volumes*, and *market* shares. General directional terms such as 'maximize', 'minimize', 'penetrate' should be avoided unless quantification is included.

The marketing objectives should cover the full three-year planning horizon and should be accompanied by broad strategies (discussed in the following section) and broad revenue and cost projections for the full three-year period.

The one-year marketing plan should contain specific objectives for the first year of the three-year planning cycle and the corresponding strategies which will be used to achieve these objectives. *The one-year and the three-year plans should be separate documents. At this stage, a detailed one-year plan is not required.*

At this point it is worth stressing that the key document in the annual planning round is the three-year strategic marketing plan. The one-year plan represents the specific actions that should be undertaken in the first year of the strategic plan.

Marketing strategies

Marketing strategies should state in broad terms *how* the marketing objectives are to be achieved, as follows:

- The specific service policies (the range, technical specifications, additions, deletions, etc.).
- The pricing policies to be followed for service groups in particular market segments.
- The customer service levels to be provided for specific market segments (such as maintenance support).
- The policies for communicating with customers under each of the main headings, such as sales force, advertising, sales promotion, etc., as appropriate.

Guidelines for setting marketing objectives and strategies are given in Chapter 5. However, the following summarizes some of the marketing objectives and strategies that are available to SBU managers.

Objectives

1 Market penetration.
2 Introduce new services to existing markets.
3 Introduce existing services to new markets (domestic).
4 Introduce existing services to new markets (international).
5 Introduce new services to new markets.

Strategies

1 Change service design, performance, quality or features.
2 Change advertising or promotion.
3 Change unit price.
4 Change delivery or distribution.
5 Change service levels.
6 Improve marketing productivity (e.g. improve the sales mix).
7 Improve administrative productivity.
8 Consolidate service line.

9 Withdraw from markets.
10 Consolidate distribution.
11 Standardize design.
12 Acquire markets, services, facilities.
13 Improve processes.
14 Upgrade people.

Guidelines for setting marketing objectives and strategies

Completing a portfolio matrix (which you have done in Section 6) for each major service/market segment within each unit translates the characteristics of the business into visible and easily understood positions *vis-à-vis* each other.

Additionally, each service/market segment's position on the matrix suggests broad goals which are usually appropriate for businesses in that position, although unit managers should also consider alternative goals in the light of the special circumstances prevailing at the time.

The four categories on the matrix are:

- Invest
- Maintain
- Profit
- Selective

You may prefer to use your own terms, although it should be stressed that it isn't necessary to attach any particular names to each of the quadrants. Each of these is considered in turn.

Invest

Services in this category enjoy competitive positions in markets/segments characterized by high growth rates and are good for continuing attractiveness. The obvious objective for such services is to maintain growth rates at least at the market growth rate, thus maintaining market share and market leadership, or to grow faster than the market, thus increasing market share.

Three principal factors should be considered:

1 Possible geographical expansion.
2 Possible service line expansion.
3 Possible service line differentiation.

These could be achieved by means of internal development, acquisition, or joint ventures.

The main point is that, in attractive marketing situations like this, *an aggressive marketing posture is required*, together with a very tight budgeting and control process to ensure that capital resources are efficiently utilized.

Maintain

Services in this category enjoy competitive positions in markets/segments which are not considered attractive in the longer term. Here, the thrust should be towards maintaining a profitable position, with greater emphasis on present earnings rather than on aggressive growth.

The most successful service lines should be maintained, while less successful ones should be considered for pruning. Marketing effort should be focused on differentiating services to maintain share of key segments of the market. Discretionary marketing expenditure should be limited, especially when unchallenged by competitors or when services have matured. Comparative prices should be stabilized, except when a temporary aggressive stance is necessary to maintain market share.

Profit

Services in this category have a poor position in unattractive markets. These services are 'bad' only if objectives are not appropriate to the company's position in the market segment. Generally, where immediate divestment is not warranted, these services should be managed for cash.

Service lines should be aggressively pruned, while all marketing expenditure should be minimized, with prices maintained or where possible raised.

However, a distinction needs to be made between different types of services. The two principal categories are:

- Those which are clearly uncompetitive in unattractive markets.
- Those which are quite near to the dividing line.

Services in the first of these categories should generally be managed as outlined above. The others should generally be managed differently. For example, the reality of low growth should be acknowledged and the temptation should be resisted to grow the service at its previous high rates of growth. It should not be viewed as a 'marketing' problem, which will be likely to lead to high advertising, promotion, inventory costs and lower profitability. Growth segments should be identified and exploited where possible. Service quality should be emphasized to avoid 'commodity' competition. Productivity should be systematically improved. Finally, the attention of talented managers should be focused on such services.

Selective

Here, it is necessary to decide whether to invest for future market leadership in these attractive markets/segments or whether to manage for present earnings. Both objectives are feasible, but it must be remembered that managing these services for cash today is usually inconsistent with market share growth and it is usually necessary to select the most promising markets and invest in them only.

Further marketing and other functional guidelines

Further marketing and other functional guidelines which operating unit managers should consider when setting marketing objectives and corresponding strategies are given in Chapter 5.

It should be stressed, however, that there can be no *automatic* policy for a particular service or market, and SBU managers should consider three or more options before deciding on 'the best' for recommendation. Above all, SBU managers must evaluate the most attractive opportunities and assess the chances for success in the most realistic manner possible. This applies particularly to new business opportunities. New business opportunities would normally be expected to build on existing strengths, particularly in marketing, which can be subsequently expanded or supplemented.

Database and summary of marketing objectives

The forms included in the database provide both an analytical framework and a summary of marketing objectives which are relevant to all strategic business unit managers. This summary is essential information which underpins the marketing plan.

Forms included in database

Form 11: *Market segment sales values*, showing, across a five-year period, total market demand, the business unit's own sales and the market share these represent for the various market segments.

Form 12: *Market segment gross profits*, showing, across a five-year period, the business unit's sales value, gross profit, and gross margin for the various market segments.

Form 13: *Service group analysis*, showing, across a five-year period, the business unit's sales value, gross profit, and gross margin for different service groups.

Form 14: Summary (in words) of main marketing objectives and strategies.

9 Financial projections for three years

Finally, SBU managers should provide financial projections for the full three-year planning period under all the principal standard revenue and cost headings as specified by your organization.

Note: Please refer to Form 15, in the strategic marketing plan documentation.

Strategic marketing plan documentation

Form 1: Unit mission statement

Unit mission statement
This is the first item to appear in the marketing plan.
The purpose of the mission statement is to ensure that the raison d'être of the unit is clearly stated. Brief statements should be made which cover the following points:
1 *Role or contribution of the unit*
e.g. profit generator
service department
opportunity seeker
2 *Definition of the business*
e.g. the needs you satisfy or the benefits you provide. Don't be too specific (e.g. 'we sell insurance') or too general (e.g. 'we're in the communication business').
3 *Distinctive competence*
This should be a brief statement that applies only to your specific unit. A statement that could equally apply to any competitor is unsatisfactory.
4 *Indications for future direction*
A brief statement of the principal things you would give serious consideration to (e.g. move into a new segment).

Form 2: Summary of SBU's performance

Summary of SBU's performance

This opening section is designed to give a bird's eye view of the SBU's total marketing activities.

In addition to a quantitative summary of performance, as follows, SBU managers should give a summary of reasons for good or bad performance.

Use *constant revenue* in order that comparisons are meaningful. Make sure you use the same base year values for any projections provided in later sections of this system.

	3 years ago	2 years ago	Last year
Volume/turnover			
Gross profit (%)			
Gross margin (000 ecu)			

Summary of reasons for good or bad performance

Form 3: Summary of financial projections

Summary of financial projections
This is the third item to appear in the marketing plan
Its purpose is to summarize for the person reading the plan the financial results over the full three-year planning period.
It should be presented as a simple diagram along the following lines:

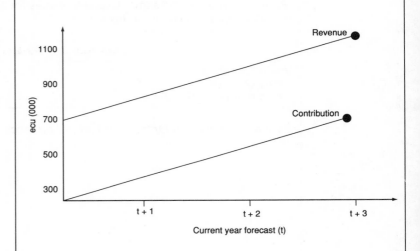

This should be accompanied by a brief commentary
For example:
'This three-year business plan shows an increase in revenue from 700,000 ecu to 1,100,000 ecu and an increase in contribution from 200,000 ecu to 680,000 ecu. The purpose of this business plan is to show how these increases will be achieved.'

Form 4: Strategic planning exercise (gap analysis) 1 Revenue

1 Objective

(a) Start by plotting the sales position you wish to achieve at the end of the planning period, point E

(b) Next plot the forecast position, Point A

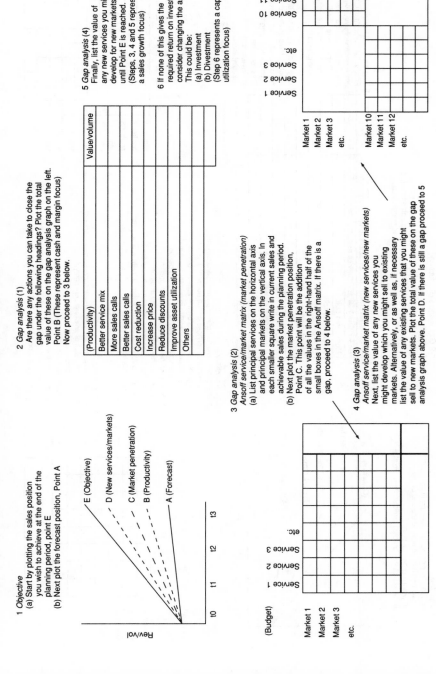

E (Objective)

D (New services/markets)

C (Market penetration)

B (Productivity)

A (Forecast)

Rev/vol

t0   t1   t2   t3

2 Gap analysis (1)

Are there any actions you can take to close the gap under the following headings? Plot the total value of these on the gap analysis graph on the left. Point B (These represent cash and margin focus) Now proceed to 3 below.

(Productivity)	Value/volume
Better service mix	
More sales calls	
Better sales calls	
Cost reduction	
Increase price	
Reduce discounts	
Improve asset utilization	
Others	

3 Gap analysis (2)

Ansoff service/market matrix (market penetration)

(a) List principal services on the horizontal axis and principal markets on the vertical axis. In each smaller square write in current sales and achievable sales during the planning period.

(b) Next plot the market penetration position, Point C. This point will be the addition of all the values in the right-hand half of the small boxes in the Ansoff matrix. If there is a gap, proceed to 4 below.

(Budget)   Service 1   Service 2   Service 3   etc.

Market 1

Market 2

Market 3

etc.

4 Gap analysis (3)

Ansoff service/market matrix (new services/new markets)

Next, list the value of any new services you might develop which you might sell to existing markets. Alternatively, or as well as, if necessary list the value of any existing services that you might sell to new markets. Plot the total value of these on the gap analysis graph above. Point D. If there is still a gap proceed to 5

5 Gap analysis (4)

Finally, list the value of any new services you might develop for new markets until Point E is reached. (Steps, 3, 4 and 5 represent a sales growth focus)

6 If none of this gives the

required return on investment consider changing the asset base. This could be:

(a) Investment

(b) Divestment

(Step 6 represents a capital utilization focus)

Service 1   Service 2   Service 3   etc.   Service 10   Service 11   Service 12   etc.

Market 1

Market 2

Market 3

etc.

Market 10

Market 11

Market 12

etc.

Form 5: Strategic planning exercise (gap analysis) 2 Profit

1 Objective
(a) Start by plotting the sales profit position you wish to achieve at the end of the planning period, point E
(b) Next plot the forecast profit position, Point A

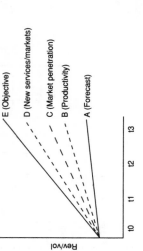

(Budget)

	Service 1	Service 2	Service 3	etc.
Market 1				
Market 2				
Market 3				
etc.				

Graph:
Rev/vol (vertical axis)
t0 t1 t2 t3 (horizontal axis)

E (Objective)
D (New services/markets)
C (Market penetration)
B (Productivity)
A (Forecast)

2 Gap analysis (Productivity)
Are there any actions you can take to close the gap under the following headings? Plot the total value of these on the gap analysis graph on the left. Point B (These represent cash and margin focus) Now proceed to 3 below.

(Productivity) (Note: not all factors are mutually exclusive)	Profit
Better customer mix. Service mix	
More sales calls	
Better sales calls	
Cost reduction	
Increase price	
Reduce discounts	
Charge for deliveries	
Reduce debtor days	
Cost reduction	
Others (specify)	

3 Gap analysis (2)
Ansoff service/market matrix (market penetration)
(a) List principal services on the horizontal axis and principal markets on the vertical axis. In each smaller square write in current sales and achievable sales during the planning period.
(b) Next plot the market penetration position, Point C. This point will be the addition of all the values in the right-hand half of the small boxes in the Ansoff matrix. If there is a gap, proceed to 4 below.

4 Gap analysis (3)
Ansoff service/market matrix (new services/new markets)
Next, list the value of any new services you might develop which you might sell to existing markets. Alternatively, or as well as, if necessary list the value of any existing services that you might sell to new markets. Plot the total value of these on the gap analysis graph above. Point D. If there is still a gap proceed to 5

5 Gap analysis (Diversification)
Finally, list the profit value of any new services you might develop for new markets until Point E is reached. (Steps, 3, 4 and 5 represent a sales growth focus)

6 Gap analysis (Capital utilization)
If none of this gives the required return on investment consider changing the asset base. This could be:
(a) Investment
(b) Joint venture
(Step 6 represents a capital utilization focus)

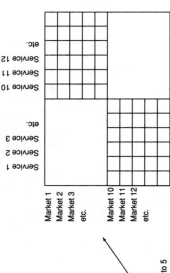

	Service 1	Service 2	Service 3	etc.		Service 10	Service 11	Service 12	etc.
Market 1									
Market 2									
Market 3									
etc.									
Market 10									
Market 11									
Market 12									
etc.									

Form 6: Market overview

Market overview

Form 7: Strategic planning exercise (SWOT analysis)

(Note: This form should be completed for each service/market segment under consideration)

1 SBU description

Here, describe the market for which the SWOT is being done

2 Critical success factors

What are the few key things from the customer's point of view, that any competitor has, to do right to succeed?

1
2
3
4
5

3 Weighting

How important is each of these CSFs?
Score out of 100

Total 100

4 Strengths/weaknesses analysis

Score yourself and each of your main competitors out of 10 on each of the CSFs. Then multiply the score by the weight

CSF \ Comp	You	Comp A	Comp B	Comp C	Comp D
1					
2					
3					
4					
5					
Total (score x weight)					

5 Opportunities/threats

What are the few key things outside your direct control that have had, and will continue to have an impact on your business?

Opportunities

1
2
3
4
5

Threats

6 Key issues that need to be addressed

7 Key assumptions for the planning period

1
2
3
4
5
6
7

8 Key objectives

8 Key strategies

Financial consequences

Form 8: Competitor analysis

Note: This form should be completed for each service market segment under consideration)

Main competitor	Serviced products/ markets	Business direction and current objectives and strategies	Strengths	Weaknesses	Competitive position

Form 9: Portfolio summary

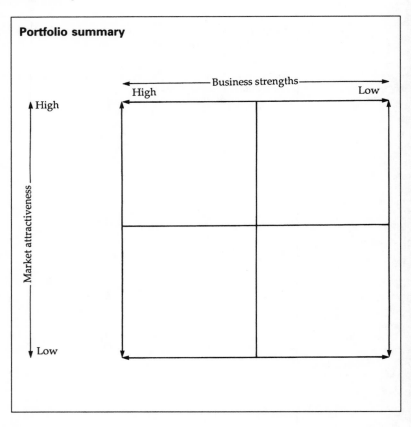

Form 10: Assumptions

Assumptions

Form 11: Database and summary of marketing objectives – sales

Database and summary of marketing objectives
Market segment sales values

Sales values	*Last year (t–1)*	*Current year (t0)*	*Next year (t+1)*	*(t+2)*	*(t+3)*
Key market segments (list)	Total company market segment sales share	Total company market segment sales share	Total company market segment sales share	Total company market segment sales share	Total company market segment sales share
Total					

Form 12: Database and summary of marketing objectives – profits

Database and summary of marketing objectives
Market segment gross profits

Sales values	*Last year (t-1)*	*Current year (t0)*	*Next year (t+1)*	*(t+2)*	*(t+3)*	
Key market segments (list)	Total company market segment sales share	Total company market segment sales share	Total company market segment sales share	Total company market segment sales share	Total company market segment sales share	
Total						

Form 13: Services analysis

Service group analysis												
Service Groups	Last year (t–1)			Current year (t0)			Next year (t+1)			(t+2)			(t+3)		
	Sales value	Gross profit	Gross margin (%)	Sales value	Gross profit	Gross margin (%)	Sales value	Gross profit	Gross margin (%)	Sales value	Gross profit	Gross margin (%)	Sales value	Gross profit	Gross margin (%)
Total															

Form 14: Marketing objectives and statement

Summary (in words) of main marketing objectives and strategies

Form 15: Financial projections

Financial projections for three years

Section B   The one-year marketing plan

(This should be kept separate from the three-year strategic marketing plan and should not be completed until the planning team has approved the strategic plan in May each year.)

Specific sub-objectives for services and segments, supported by more detailed strategy and action statements, should now be developed. Here, include *budgets* and *forecasts* and a *consolidated budget*. These must reflect the marketing objectives and strategies, and in turn the objectives, strategies and programmes *must* reflect the agreed budgets and sales forecasts. Their main purpose is to delineate the major steps required in implementation, to assign accountability, to focus on the major decision points, and to specify the required allocation of resources and their timing.

If the procedures in this system are followed, a hierachy of *objectives* will be built up in such a way that every item of budgeted expenditure can be related directly back to the initial financial objectives (this is known as task-related budgeting).

Thus when, say, advertising has been identified as a means of achieving an objective in a particular market (i.e. advertising is a strategy to be used), all advertising expenditure against items appearing in the budget can be related back specifically to a major objective. The essential feature of this is that budgets are set against both the overall marketing objectives and the sub-objectives for each element of the marketing mix.

The principal advantage is that this method allows operating units to build up and demonstrate an increasingly clear picture of their markets. This method of budgeting also allows every item of expenditure to be fully accounted for as part of an objective approach. It also ensures that when changes have to be made during the period to which the plan relates, such changes can be made in a way that causes the least damage to the SBU's long-term objectives.

Contingency plan

It is important to include a *contingency plan* in the one-year marketing plan. Notes on this are included below.

Guidelines for completion of a one-year marketing plan

Because of the varying nature of strategic business units, it is impossible to provide a standard format for all SBUs. There is, however, a minimum amount of information which should be provided to accompany the financial documentation between September and October. There is no need to supply market background information, as this should have been completed in the three-year strategic marketing plan.

Suggested format for a one-year marketing plan

1 (a) *Overall objectives (see Forms 1 and 2 in the one-year marketing plan documentation)* – these should cover the following:

Volume or value	Value last year	Current year estimate	Budget next year
Gross margin	Last year	Current year estimate	Budget next year

Against each there should be a few words of commentary/explanation

(b) *Overall strategies* – e.g. new customers, new services, advertising, sales promotion, selling, customer service, pricing.

2 (a) *Sub-objectives (see Form 3 in one-year marketing plan documentation)* – more detailed objectives should be provided for services, or markets, or segments, or major customers, as appropriate.

(b) *Strategies* – the means by which sub-objectives will be achieved should be stated.

(c) *Action/tactics* – the details, timing, responsibility and cost should also be stated.

3 *Summary of marketing activities and costs (see Form 4 in the one-year marketing plan documentation).*

4 *Contingency plan (see Form 5 in the one-year marketing plan documentation)* – it is important to include a contingency plan, which should address the following questions:

(a) What are the critical assumptions on which the one-year plan is based?

(b) What would the financial consequences be (i.e. the effect on the operating income) if these assumptions did not come true? For example, if a forecast of revenue is based on the assumption that a decision will be made to buy a new plant by a major customer, what would the effect be if that customer did not go ahead?

(c) How will these assumptions be measured?

(d) What action will you take to ensure that the adverse financial effects of an unfulfilled assumption are mitigated, so that you end up with the same forecast profit at the end of the year?

To measure the risk, assess the negative or downside, asking what can go wrong with each assumption that would change the outcome. For example, if a market growth rate of 5 per cent is a key assumption, what lower growth rate would have to occur before a substantially different management decision would be taken? For a capital project, this would be the point at which the project would cease to be economical.

5 *Operating result and financial ratios (see Form 6 in the one-year marketing plan documentation)*
   Note: This form is provided only as an example, for, clearly, all organizations will have their own formats – this should include:
   - Net revenue
   - Gross margin
   - Adjustments
   - Marketing costs
   - Administration costs
   - Interest
   - Operating result
   - ROS
   - ROI

6 *Key activity planner (see Form 7 in the one-year marketing plan documentation)* – finally, you should summarize the key activities and indicate the start and finish. This should help you considerably with monitoring the progress of your annual plan.

7 *Other* – there may be other information you wish to provide, such as sales call plans.

Form 1

One-year marketing plan documentation

Overall objectives

Service/ market/ segment/ application customer	Volume			Value			Gross margin			Commentary
	t–1	t0	t+1	t–1	t0	t+1	t–1	t0	t+1	

Form 2

Overall strategies

	Strategies	Cost
1		
2		
3		
4		
5		
6		
7		
8		
9		
10		

Comments

Form 3

Sub-objectives, strategies, actions, responsibilities, timing, cost					
Service/ market/ segment/ application/ customer	Objective	Strategies	Action	Responsibility	Timing	Cost

Total _____

Form 4

	t–1	*t0*	*t+1*	*Comments*
Depreciation Salaries Postage/telephone/stationery Legal and professional Training Data processing Advertising Sales promotion Travelling and entertainment Exhibitions Printing Meetings/conferences Market research Internal costs Other (specify)				
Total				

Form 5

Suggested downside risk assessment format

Key assumption	Basis of assumption	What event would have to happen to make this strategy unattractive?	Risk of such an event occurring (%) High P(7–10)	Medium P(4–6)	Low P(0–3)	Impact if event occurs	Trigger point for action	Actual contingency action proposed

Form 6

	t–1	t0	t+1
Net revenue Gross margin Adjustments Marketing costs Administration costs Interest			
Operating result			
Other interest and financial costs			
Result after financial costs			
Net result			

Form 7

Key activity planner

Date/activity	Jan				Feb				March				April				May				June				July				Aug				Sept				Oct				Nov				Dec			
	1	2	3	4	1	2	3	4	1	2	3	4	1	2	3	4	1	2	3	4	1	2	3	4	1	2	3	4	1	2	3	4	1	2	3	4	1	2	3	4	1	2	3	4	1	2	3	4

Section C   Headquarters consolidation of several SBU strategic marketing plans

The authors are frequently asked how several SBU strategic marketing plans should be consolidated by senior headquarters marketing personnel. A suggested format for this task is provided below.

Directional statement

1   *Role/contribution* – this should be a brief statement about the company's role or contribution. Usually, it will specify a minimum growth rate in turnover and profit, but it could also encapsulate roles such as opportunity seeking service and so on.

2   *Definition of the business* – this statement should describe the needs that the company is fulfilling, or the benefits that it is providing for its markets. For example, 'the provision of information to business to facilitate credit decision making'. Usually, at the corporate level, there will be a number of definitions for its strategic business units. It is important that these statements are not too broad so as to be meaningless (e.g. 'communications' – which could mean satellites or pens) or too narrow (e.g. credit cards – which could become obsolete if a better method of fulfilling the need for credit is found).

3   *Distinctive competence* – all companies should have a distinctive competence. It does not have to be unique, but it must be substantial and sustainable. Distinctive competence can reside in integrity, specialist skills, technology, distribution strength, international coverage, reputation and so on.

4   *Indications for future direction* – this section should indicate guidelines for future growth. For example, does the company wish to expand internationally, or to acquire new skills and resources? The purpose of this section is to indicate the boundaries of future business activities.

Summary of the main features of the plan

1   Here draw a portfolio matrix indicating the current and proposed relative position of each of the strategic business units. Alternatively, this can appear later in the plan.

2   Include a few words summarizing growth in turnover, profit, margins, etc.

3   Draw a graph indicating simply the total long-term plan. At least two lines are necessary – turnover and profit.

Financial history (past five years)

Include a bar chart showing the relevant financial history, but, at the very least, include turnover and profit for the past five years.

Major changes and events since the previous plan

Here, describe briefly major changes and events (such as divesting a subsidiary) which occurred during the previous year.

Major issues by strategic business unit

Market characteristics

Here, it might be considered useful to provide a table listing strategic business units, alongside relevant market characteristics. For example:

	SBU1	SBU2	SBU3	SBU4
Market size				
Market growth				
Competitive intensity				
Relative market share				
etc.				

Competitive characteristics

Here, it might be considered useful to list the critical success factors by strategic business unit and rate each unit against major competitors. For example:

Critical success factors/competitors	Our company	Competitor 1	Competitor 2
CSF 1 CSF 2 CSF 3 CSF 4 CSF 5			

Key strategic issues

This is an extremely important section, as its purpose is to list (possibly by strategic business unit) what the key issues are that face the company. In essence, this really consists of stating the major strengths, weaknesses, opportunities and threats and indicating how they will be either built on, or dealt with.

Key strategic issues might consist of technology, regulation, competitive moves, institutional changes, and so on.

Strategic objectives by strategic business unit and key statistics

This is a summary of the objectives of each strategic business unit. It should obviously be tailored to the specific circumstances of each company. However, an example of what might be appropriate follows:

Objectives / Strategic business unit	Market Share		Relative market share		Real growth		Key statistics				
							Sales per employee		Contribution per employee		etc.
	Now	+5 years	Now	+5 years	+5 years	p.a.	Now	+5 years	Now	+5 years	
SBU1											
SBU2											
SBU3											
SBU4											
SBU5											

Alternatively, or additionally, put a portfolio matrix indicating the current and proposed relative position of each of the strategic business units.

Financial goals (next five years)

Here, draw a bar chart (or a number of bar charts) showing the relevant financial goals. At the very least, show turnover and profit by strategic business unit for the next five years.

Appendices

Include whatever detailed appendices are appropriate. Try not to rob the total plan of focus by including too much detail.

Timetable

The major steps and timing for the annual round of strategic and operational planning are described in the following pages. The planning process is in two separate stages, which are interrelated to provide a review point prior to the detailed quantification of plans. 'Stage One' involves the statement of key and critical objectives for the full three-year planning period, to be reviewed prior to the more detailed quantification of the tactical one-year plan in 'Stage Two' by 30 November, for subsequent consolidation into the company plans.

Planning team's 'kick-off' meetings (to be completed by 31 March)

At this meeting, the planning team will outline their expectations for the following planning cycle. The purpose of the meeting is to give the planning team the opportunity to explain corporate policy, report progress during the previous planning cycle, and to give a broad indication of what is expected from each SBU during the forthcoming cycle. The planning team's review will include an overall appraisal of performance against plan, as well as a variance analysis. The briefing will give guidance under some of the following headings (as appropriate).

1 *Financial*
   - Gross margins
   - Operating profits
   - Debtors
   - Creditors
   - Cash flow
2 *Manpower and organization*
   - Organization
   - Succession
   - Training
   - Remuneration
3 *Export strategy*
4 *Marketing*
   - Service development
   - Target markets
   - Market segments
   - Volumes
   - Market shares
   - Pricing
   - Promotion
   - Marketing research
   - Quality control
   - Customer service

This is an essential meeting prior to the mainstream planning activity which SBUs will subsequently engage in. It is the principal means by which it can be ensured that plans do not become stale and repetitive due to over-bureaucratization. Marketing creativity will be the keynote of this meeting.

Top-down and bottom-up planning

A cornerstone of the marketing planning philosophy is that there should be widespread understanding at all levels in the organization of the key objectives that have to be achieved, and of the key means of achieving them. This way, the actions and decisions that are taken by managers will be disciplined by clear objectives that hang logically together as part of a rational, overall purpose. The only way this will happen is if the planning system is firmly based on market-centred analysis which emanates from the SBUs themselves. Therefore, after the planning team's 'kick-off' meetings, audits should be carried out by all managers in the SBUs down to a level which will be determined by SBU managers. Each manager will also do SWOT analyses and set tentative three-year objectives and strategies, together with proposed budgets for initial consideration by their superior manager. In this way, each superior will be responsible for synthesizing the work of those managers reporting to them.

The major steps in the annual planning cycle are listed below and depicted schematically in Figure 8.14.

Activity	Deadline
• Planning team's 'kick-off' meetings with SBU managers to discuss overall guidelines for the three-year planning period	31 March
• Prepare marketing audits, SWOT analyses,	31 May

Figure 8.14 Strategic and operational planning cycle

proposed marketing objectives, strategies and
budgets (cover the full three-year planning
horizon)

- *'Stage One'* meetings: presentation to the   31 May
  planning team for review
- Prepare short-term (one-year) operational   31 October
  plans and budgets, and final three-year SBU
  managers' consolidated marketing plans
- *'Stage Two'* meetings: presentation to the   30 November
  planning team
- Final consolidation of the marketing plans   31 December

Examples of marketing plans

Introduction

The marketing plans produced here are intended solely to provide readers with a variety of ideas about the process and content of a strategic marketing plan. They are not intended to be perfect examples. Rather, they are real plans produced by real organizations struggling to produce their first serious effort to move from turgid long range forecasts and budgets to something more sophisticated. The names and data, of course, have been changed to protect confidentiality.

We recommend that you read through all of them, as each one has its own merits (and faults). All, however, exemplify many of the processes and ideas contained in this book.

Contents

Alison, Hazlewood and Partners*

Introduction

Alison, Hazlewood and Partners are solicitors based in the Home Counties to the west of London. The firm was started in the 1930s by the original Mr Alison, who later took on Hazlewood as a partner. It continued to be run as a family business until the 1960s, when the sons of the original partners retired. Thus, despite the name, there is no longer an Alison nor a Hazlewood featured among the partners.

The firm is situated in an imposing listed building, just off the High Street of a thriving town, and has experienced steady, if unspectacular, growth over the years. At present there are six partners and fourteen fee earners, together with the necessary back-up secretarial staff.

Like many of its contemporaries, the firm has tended to be reactive in its approach to business. Local reputation and word-of-mouth seemed to ensure that enough clients crossed the threshold and generated fees.

However, the turbulent times in which we live have caused the partners to reappraise whether or not the firm would remain viable by retaining such a traditional stance. The outcome of their deliberations was that the firm should have a marketing plan, something entirely new for them.

Lacking the expertise to do this themsleves, they approached a consultant. What follow are, in essence, the key components that went into their strategic marketing plan.

Three-year strategic marketing plan

1 Mission statement

(a) *Definition of the business* The firm's aim is to ensure that clients are treated in an attentive and personal manner, and that their legal problems are handled speedily and accurately.

Internally, the firm aims to provide satisfying and fulfilling work for all who work here, directed to a profitable business.

---

* Alison, Hazlewood and Partners will not be found in any directory, because the name is fictitious. The real company preferred to remain anonymous, and even then in order to safeguard its identity, some of the business information has been changed from the original.

For similar purposes, fee incomes for various parts of the business are expressed as percentages rather than actual figures.

Having said this, the marketing plan which follows is an accurate representation of the diagnostic process which was used.

(b) *Distinctive competence* We believe our ability to produce good quality work for our clients, at a reasonable price, in a friendly manner is something that sets us apart from our competitors. As firms become larger and more impersonal, our approach will become even more important.

(c) *Indications for the future* A more business-like approach must be taken to finding new clients and winning new business. However, growth will always go hand-in-hand with our developing capabilities, not pursued as an end in itself.

We will invest in the development of our staff and attempt to recruit people of high calibre and potential. In doing this we will develop new competencies and thereby broaden the range of services we can offer, and boost productivity and profitability.

2 Summary of performance

(a) *Fee income* In the last year this was generated as follows:

Trusts, wills and probate	30%
Family	40%
Conveyancing	22%
Commercial	8%

More significantly, in terms of growth or decline, three years ago these business areas looked like this:

Trusts, wills and probate	36%
Family	30%
Conveyancing	30%
Commercial	4%

This shows that Trusts, wills and probate work is slightly reducing. Family is exhibiting quite substantial growth, as is Commercial. In contrast to this, Conveyancing is reflecting the downturn of the housing market.

(b) *Profitability* It is not possible to calculate the profitability of the different types of work, because systems do not exist to allocate costs with any degree of accuracy. This is something which will be addressed in the next financial year.

3 Financial projections

Average growth in recent years has been in the order of 10 per cent. However, this was achieved by passive, evolutionary growth and is, therefore, far less than might be expected with a more focused, business-like approach.

Accordingly, financial projections over the next three years aim for a 15 per cent growth in fee income each year.

This marketing plan will indicate how this level of growth will be achieved.

4 Market overview

(a) *Segmentation of customers and markets*
Clients for the products offered by the firm could be described thus:

Wills, trusts and probate	Private clients, mainly socio-economic classes A and B
Family	Private clients, mainly A, B, C1 and C2 classes, mainly divorce related.
Conveyancing	Private clients, mainly domestic, but some retail. Some local property developers.
Commercial	Local firms and some private clients.

From this information, clients of the firm as a whole could be summarized as follows:-

1 Private clients (generally wealthy)
2 Private clients (with domestic problems)
3 Property developers
4 Local companies.

The potential for growth in fee income between these four categories varies quite significantly, and goes some way towards explaining the relative growth and decline of some parts of the business.

1&2 *Private clients* On the whole this group is reluctant to meet large legal bills unless their particular circumstances merit it. However, a large number of people, by dint of owning property, have a sufficiently sized estate to make it worth their while making a will. This market is unknown in size locally, but must be considerable, especially in high-value neighbourhoods.

At another level, divorce and other family matters show no signs of being on the decrease. Indeed, more legislation, such as the Children's Bill, can provide new areas of work.

3 *Property developers* At present this group is not very productive, but if the housing market is experiencing a cyclical downturn, they could feature prominently again.

4 *Local companies* These fall into two categories:
  (i) *Successful ones* Here the work is concerned with contracts, intellectual property, and the like.
  (ii) *Unsuccessful ones* Here the work is involved in failure to meet contracts, insolvency, etc.

While short-term growth can be expected from the latter category, the firm's long-term interests are best met by cultivating relationships with successful local companies.

5 Changes in the market

A   *General*

(a)   *The Courts and Legal Services Bill* will have an impact on the market in four ways:

   (i)   Banks and building societies will be able to do conveyancing work.
   (ii)   Trust corporations will be allowed to do probate work.
   (iii) Barristers will be able to operate from firms of solicitors.
   (iv)   Lawyers can defer their fees in certain cases and take an increase at the end of the case, if they are successful. (A form of payment by results.)

Of these, only item (i) is likely to impact on us. Even so, banks and building societies have yet to establish credibility in this area.

(b)   *European developments*   This can affect us in two main areas:

   (i)   Giving general advice on European law.
   (ii)   Legal work arising from cross-border commercial business.

This will require us to develop new expertise.

(c)   *The legal industry*   There is a growing tendency for large city firms to expand by acquisition or planned growth, and set up offices in strategically situated localities. Such firms can offer a wide range of services to their clients, by having specialists in all fields.

B   *Local*

(a)   It is rumoured that a small local firm is going to close on the imminent retirement of the senior partner. The only other partner is in ill-health.

We can expect to pick up a proportion of the business which at present goes to this practice.

6 SWOT Analysis on key business areas

Wills, trusts and probate

(a) *Critical Success Factors*
These are as follows:

Personal service and aftercare	(40%)
Quality of advice	(40%)
Promptness of service	(15%)
Standard of presentation of documents	(5%)

The relative importance of these factors is shown in brackets. Comparing us with our three main competitors in our catchment area, we come out as shown. (Raw scores are given out of 10 and multiplied by the above weighting.)

	AH & P	COMP A	COMP B	COMP C
Personal service	3.6	3.6	2.0	3.2
Quality	2.8	3.6	3.2	2.8
Promptness	1.2	0.75	1.2	1.2
Presentation	0.4	0.4	0.4	0.4
	8.0	**8.35**	**6.8**	**7.6**

Using this comparison, in absolute terms we come second best to Competitor A. However, closer analysis shows that it is only on quality of advice where we fall down, something which can be remedied.

(b) *Opportunities and threats*
Apart from the obvious threat posed by needing to match Competitor A on quality of advice, other authorized practitioners will be allowed to work in this area. Opportunities centre on making other clients aware of our service and reputation. This can be achieved by cross-referral.

There is an untapped potential among those in high property value households and the elderly without wills.

(c) *Key issues to be addressed*
(i) What action is required to improve quality of advice? For example, shall we 'buy in' expertise or develop it ourselves?
(ii) What is the realistic level at which to target this sector of business so that it doesn't compete for resources from other parts of the firm?

Family

(a) *Critical success factors*

Most of this work centres on divorce. There are two critical factors:

  (i) The client must have absolute confidence in the firm's representative. (60%)
  (ii) The firm must have experience and a good reputation. (40%)

Again, the relative weighting of these factors is shown in brackets. In comparison with our main competitors, we emerge as shown.

	A H & P	COMP A	COMP B	COMP C
Confidence	4.8	4.2	4.8	4.2
Experience and reputation	3.2	2.8	2.8	3.2
	8.0	**7.0**	**7.6**	**7.4**

In overall terms we rate the best and are not surpassed on these two factors by any competitor, although some are equally as good as us on one or the other.

(b) *Opportunities and threats*

Opportunities stem from new legislation, mainly associated with the Children's Bill. Issues concerned with international marriages could also be a growth area.

The main threat is the unwillingness of private clients to meet the ever-increasing fee levels this sort of work generates.

(c) *Key issues to be addressed*

We need to take measures to increase the amount of work referred from other departments.

We need to look for means of reducing costs.

Conveyancing

(a) *Critical success factors*

By far the most important factor is speed, for time equals money. However, there are other factors, as shown here. Again, weightings are in brackets.

Speed	(80%)
Quality of service	(15%)
Personalized service	(5%)

	A H & P	COMP A	COMP B	COMP C
Speed	7.2	7.2	5.6	5.6
Quality	0.9	1.2	1.35	1.2
Personalization	0.4	0.3	0.35	0.35
	8.5	**8.7**	**7.30**	**7.15**

In overall terms, we come second to Competitor A, against whom we fall down on quality. In fact, our quality score is the lowest of all the competing firms.

In contrast to this, our personalization score is the highest, and nobody actually beats us on speed.

We must improve quality.

(b) *Opportunities and threats*

The downturn of the property market is the most obvious threat, although there are some signals that an upturn might be expected.

Banks, building societies and 'other authorized practitioners' can now do conveyancing work. We will have to monitor to what extent their entry affects the market, especially in terms of the prices they charge for the service.

Opportunities exist for providing more 'insolvency advice' for hard-pressed mortgage payers. Also, cross-referencing from family clients could provide new prospects, e.g. when one partner of divorce seeks to move to a new property.

(c) *Key issues to be addressed*

We must monitor the effect of new 'players' in this sector.

We must cross-reference prospective clients.

We must get a more accurate assessment of how many conveyances can be expected in the local market, thereby gaining insights about our market share.

Commercial

(a) *Critical success factors*

The overriding priority in this sector is high quality service and having equally high quality staff. However, other factors also come into play, as shown below, and they are weighted accordingly:

High quality service	(30%)
Highly competent staff	(30%)
Speed of service	(15%)
Price/value for money	(15%)
Location (accessibility)	(5%)
Flexibility/capacity	(5%)

	A H & P	COMP A	COMP B	COMP C
Quality	2.1	2.7	2.1	2.4
Staff	2.1	2.7	2.1	2.4
Speed	1.2	1.2	1.2	1.2
Price	0.9	1.2	0.9	1.2
Location	0.5	0.4	0.5	0.4
Flexibility	0.3	0.5	0.3	0.4
	7.1	**8.7**	**7.1**	**8.0**

We do not compare favourably with our main competitors. We are not sufficiently professional in terms of the quality of work and staff, nor do we have the flexibility/capacity to respond to sudden and unusual requests.

However, we are favourably located and easy to reach, and the speed of our work is not bettered.

(b) *Opportunities and threats*

The main threat stems from potential clients going to larger, more commercially orientated firms. However, to offset this, there are advantages in having local, readily accessible advice – if the quality is right.

Another opportunity is the wider recognition of clients of the potential pitfalls associated with the opening of European markets, and the all-pervading EC law.

(c) *Issues to be addressed*

This work has just evolved in the past and no serious attempt has been made to develop the expertise and capacity, or to make our capabilities known to local industry and commerce. We should be clearer about what we offer, and to whom.

Even within individual client companies, there are different legal requirements according to its different functional departments.

For example:

Functional area	Legal requirements
Finance	Capital and project finance deals Corporate tax
Marketing	Property leasing Covenants Franchise agreements
Product development	Intellectual property (patents and copyright)
Purchasing	Contractual arrangements
Production	Employment issues Safety legislation Environmental issues Compliance
Distribution	Contracts Consumer protection

In addition to these, there are legal requirements associated with diversification, mergers and acquisitions, and international trading.

This wide diversity of potential legal requirements poses additional problems, in terms of:

(i) Should we focus on just one or two legal areas and attempt to develop a reputation as local 'specialists'?

or

(ii) Should we exploit all of our commercial contracts and try to broaden our areas of contact in each one, i.e. become something of a 'one-stop legal shop'?

Either decision can have far-reaching consequences for the way this part of the firm develops.

7 Product portfolio and directional strategy

Considering the firm's main business areas in terms of how they match up with its relative strengths and market attractiveness, it is possible to construct a directional policy matrix as shown below.

The factors which were taken into account in calculating the positions on the matrix are as follows:

● *Relative business strengths*
  – Reputation/successful track record
  – Quality of staff
  – Capacity
  – Personalization of service

- *Market attractiveness*
  - Prospects for continued growth
  - Not unduly price sensitive
  - Geographically close
  - Lacking own legal expertise

The reasons for the projected trends come out of the SWOT analysis:

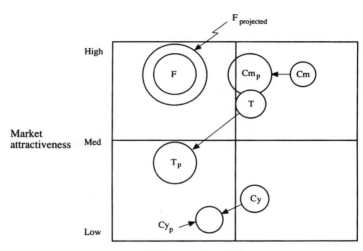

Relative business strengths

Key:		Current % fees	Projected 3 yrs
	F = Family	40%	45%
	T = Trusts, Wills and Probate	30%	25%
	Cy = Conveyancing	22%	15%
	Cm = Commercial	8%	15%

Family	Still a growth area, especially with more proactive stance.
Trusts, wills and probates	Competition from 'authorized practitioners' makes it less attractive.
Conveyancing	Depressed housing market and competition from banks and building societies make the market less attractive.
Commercial	Proactive stance plus improved capability should improve our business strengths.

In terms of generating funds, the directional policy matrix indicates that Conveyancing and Trusts, wills and probate will need to be 'milked' to finance expansion of commercial business.

Family will also need some investment, but will be largely self-financing.

8 Marketing stance and objectives

Broadly speaking, our marketing objectives are concerned with what products/services go to which clients. Therefore, the options open to us can be represented by the following diagram:

Using this framework:

Products/services

	Existing	New
Existing Clients	Least risky option	Medium risk
New	Low risk (exploiting our expertise)	High risk

Wills, trusts and probate	Existing services to existing and new clients
Family	Existing services to existing and new clients
Conveyancing	Existing services to mainly new clients
Commercial (mixture of)	Existing services to new clients and new services to existing clients.

Thus, overall, our marketing objectives do not entail high levels of risk, except for part of the commercial business. However, since this is a relatively new area for the firm, some experimentation, hence risk, is only to be expected. Our safeguard here is the analysis we have applied to this sector, which ensures that our stance is as realistic as possible.

Overall, the objective is to increase fee income by 15 per cent p.a. for the next three years.

Taking the business sector by sector, here is a more detailed record of what we aim to achieve.

(a) *Wills, trusts and probate*

> *Objectives* To manage the sector so that it is contributing 25 per cent of fee income in three years' time. This represents an 8 per cent increase from the current level in real terms.
>
> *Assumptions* There will be no significant changes in either legislation or competition, other than that already mentioned earlier.

Strategy   To gain clients from those who are already using other services of the firm. This will require a selective analysis of clients in order to identify the 'right' ones.

To re-design the brochure for this service, emphasizing client benefits. Have copies prominently displayed in reception.

To contribute articles, advice columns, etc. to local newspapers as a means of advertising.

To distribute brochures to local accountants and financial advisers so that they can recommend us.

To develop/reinforce staff in order to improve the quality of our advice, and hence our competitive position.

(b)   *Family*

Objectives   To manage this sector so that it is contributing 45 per cent of fee income in three years' time. In real terms, this means a 28 per cent increase on today's income.

Assumptions No significant players enter the local market over the strategic time frame.

Strategy   Keep fees at the lower end of the competitive range for divorce matters by reducing costs. This means increasing the number of clients as the main means of increasing income.

This will be achieved by:

(i)   Encouraging satisfied clients to recommend us
(ii)   Local advertising
(iii) Increasing and publicizing our ability to handle new children's legislation
(iv) Maintaining our differential advantage over competing firms.

High fees can be charged for this new children's legislation.

(c)   *Conveyancing*

Objectives   To manage this sector so that it contributes 15 per cent of total fee income in three years' time. With the targeted growth of 15 per cent p.a. overall, this means that, in real terms, fee income has to be maintained at its current level.

Assumptions That the recession in the housing market has bottomed out and will not get worse. Also, that some business will be taken by banks and building societies.

Strategy   To cross-reference suitable clients who are using other services.

To develop/maintain good relationships with local builders and estate agents.

To charge fees at the top end of the competitive range.

To advertise in local newspapers at a modest level.

(d)   *Commercial*

Objectives   To manage this sector so that it contributes 15 per cent of total fee income in three years' time. In real terms, that means that this sector has to increase 23 per cent on the current level.

Assumptions   None of our immediate competitors will develop faster than ourselves. Large commercial law firms will concentrate on high potential earning jobs (which would be too big for us).

Strategy   To target our marketing effort on all small to medium-sized commercial organizations that are successful, within easy reach, and have no 'in-house' legal expertise.

To gain introductions by running half-day seminars about pertinent legal issues.

To develop a brochure and good quality supporting promotional material.

To use cross-referrals from clients using our other services.

To price very competitively to win initial assignments, and then to exploit contacts and other departments in client companies to acquire additional work.

Footnotes

1   *Information systems*

In order to enable cross-referencing and analysis of existing clients to take place, our internal systems need to be modified.

Equally, in order to control costs, it is important to know exactly how staff allocate their time. This means setting up an effective management control system.

Both of these initiatives should begin as soon as possible.

2 *Review*

As this is our first attempt at producing a marketing plan, it is essential that progress after the first year is reviewed critically, and any deviations from the expected are analysed and understood.

By building in such a rigorous review procedure, our future planning will become increasingly accurate.

Steadfast Design Corporation

Background information

SDC is a long established and successful company providing design and purchasing services, mainly to the building industry. It operates in five main building markets: Industrial, Offices, Retail, Private residential and Leisure (sports centres and hotels).

The company originated in the Midlands and has a head office in Birmingham. However, it operates throughout the mainland UK and has regional offices in Birmingham (Midlands and Wales), Stockport (North and Scotland) and Basingstoke (South).

Due to the nature of the business, SDC deals with a wide range of customers, including large public limited companies, banks, building societies, pension funds, local authorities and housing associations.

The company has long been interested in marketing and many of the senior managers have attended courses at Cranfield. Although, traditionally, the building and associated trades and service providers have not been noted for innovation in management thinking, SDC is striving to be an exception to this rule.

What follows is the company marketing plan for the next three years.

Executive summary

1 Financial targets

Year	Income (£m)	Expenditure (£m)	Profit (£m)	Income growth over previous year	Profit growth over previous year
Current	84.00	71.40	12.60	46.1%	85.3%
+1	112.90	95.70	17.20	34.4%	36.5%
+2	132.20	109.40	22.60	16.9%	31.4%
+3	162.60	132.30	30.30	23.2%	34.1%

2 Analysis of customer base

Customer survey	Highly compatible + good business potential	Highly compatible + low business potential	Not very compatible + high business potential	Low compat-ibility + low business potential	No repeat business
Last year	27%	27%	5%	18%	23%
Current year	36%	28.5%	7.5%	16%	12%

This illustrates the beginning of a favourable trend towards having more customers who are compatible and who have good business potential.

However, there must be an effort made to reappraise those customers who are not compatible or who have low business potential in terms of whether they are still worth cultivating or whether they should be allowed to drop from our portfolio.

The reduction in 'no repeat business' is in line with what we hoped to achieve.

3 Regional trends

	Southern	Midland	North and Scotland
National last year	49.5%	30.7%	19.8%
National current year	52.5%	29.5%	18.0%
Relative change	+3.0%	−1.2%	−1.8%
SDC last year	38.0%	35.0%	27.0%
SDC current year	42.5%	30.0%	27.5%
Relative change	+4.5%	−5.0%	+0.5%

This table shows that in the Southern Region we are increasing our share of the business at a faster rate than the national trend. This is true also for the Northern Region. However, in our traditional stronghold, the Midlands, we seem to be doing less well.

4 SWOT analysis

Full details are included in the report but probably the most noteworthy elements are as follows:

Strengths
(a) The size and status of the company
(b) The quality of our staff
(c) Our willingness to innovate (both technically and managerially).

Weaknesses

(a) We have yet to match the company to many of the potential high business potential customers

(b) Continued growth is bringing with it communication problems and a danger that our high standards might be compromised.

Opportunities

(a) Buy out some small quality builders who are strategically placed to improve our national coverage

(b) Government preparedness to increase public spending

(c) EC deregulation.

Threats

(a) Ability to keep key personnel and/or get adequately skilled recruits

(b) Increased marketing sophistication by competitors

(c) EC deregulation

(d) The national economy goes into deep recession.

5 Major objectives over next three years

(a) Increase turnover

(b) Improve probitability

(c) Continue to broaden customer base so that no single customer in any market accounts for more than 20 per cent of the turnover

(d) Maintain high standards of ethics in all our business transactions

(e) Maintain a level of social responsibility in all the building projects we undertake.

6 General progress

The company is moving along the right lines and is stronger than it was a year ago. Broadly speaking our last year's marketing plan was achieved and brought with it the benefits we anticipated.

However, there is no room for complacency. We really need to have more information about our competitors and their activities. We need to explore the potential of new markets. The EC deregulation can be a two-edged sword; it can bring both opportunities and threats. Above all, if the economy should be depressed for too long, the challenge for all of us at SDC to meet our targets will be considerable.

Introduction

This Corporate Marketing Plan incorporates all three operational regions' activities and has been compiled with their assistance.

The layout of this plan is as follows:

Section 1   Situation review

We deal with five different 'business sectors'

- Industrial building
- Office building
- Retail
- Private residential
- Leisure

1   Relative market share

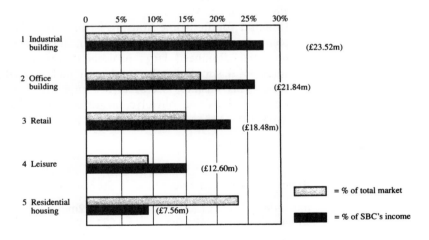

Current review of (relative) market share

Conclusion

Our relative market share (in terms of income) is greater than that for each sector of the building industry as a whole, except for Residential housing.

This can be explained because much of the residential building has been on small sites which are uneconomical for us.

The actual revenue figures are shown in brackets. Total income was £84m.

2 Characteristics of these business sectors

- *Industrial building*
  There is considerable growth in medium to small industrial parks in the south-east and in areas where heavy industry has declined. Also many old industrial buildings are unsuitable for high technology industries. Prospects look good in this sector.
- *Office building*
  In most urban renewal schemes there is considerable scope for office building. Also, property developers can tap cash-rich pension funds and investment houses. Good prospect area.
- *Retail*
  This has been a considerable growth area, with the popularity of shopping precincts either in or out of towns. Possibility of growth slowing down as major retail chains rethink their strategies for a period of high interest rates.
- *Leisure*
  There is still reckoned to be a shortfall in hotel rooms for business and tourism needs. Similarly, more health and recreation centres are required to meet fitness lifestyle needs, either provided by private funding or local authorities.
- *Residential housing*
  Demand for first-time housing is high, but greenfield development opportunities are reducing in those areas with growth potential. We need large projects to separate ourselves from small local suppliers who could not tackle anything on such a scale. This business sector is beginning to look less attractive unless we position ourselves more creatively by redefining our market.

3 Income

Business sector	Last year	Current year	% change
Industrial	£12.40m	£23.52m	+90%
Office	£12.20m	£21.84m	+79%
Retail	£15.00m	£18.48m	+23%
Leisure	£ 9.60m	£12.60m	+31%
Residential	£ 8.30m	£ 7.56m	−9%
Total	**£57.50m**	**£84.00m**	**+46%**

Conclusion

Our income per sector, comparing last year with the current year, confirms our subjective analysis of the characteristics of each of our markets.

4 Distribution of income

Analysis of our current year shows that our customer base of 260 contributed to our income as follows:

% customers	10	20	30	40	50	60	70	80	90	100
Cumulative income	58.3	74.5	83.6	89.6	93.7	96.3	98.0	99.1	99.8	100
Income per %	58.3	16.2	9.1	6.0	4.1	2.6	1.7	1.1	0.7	0.2
Grade	A		B	C		D			E	

This approximates to the conventional Pareto distribution, with our 20 per cent largest customers accounting for 74.5 per cent of our income.

The customer grading bounds are somewhat arbitrary but make it possible to extract more useful data in the customer matrix analysis which follows.

5 Customer matrix

The customer matrix was designed around two dimensions, compatibility with our business and business potential. Each customer was allocated scores using these criteria.

- *Compatibility*

Quality of our relationship with customer	0–3 points (for very good)
Needs complete range of services	0–3 points
Low sensitivity to price	0–2 points
Needs high quality	0–2 points
	10 points max.

- *Business potential*

Customer's business is showing average to high growth	0–3 points
Potential for further business	0–3 points
Potential for high profit projects	0–4 points
	10 points max.

Looking at the total business

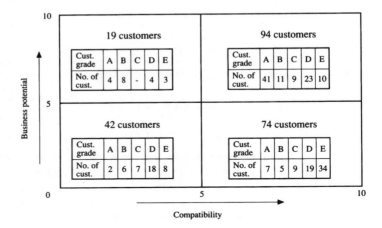

Note: Of the customer base of 260, 31 no-repeat business clients were eliminated from the matrix. The breakdown of these companies by customer grading is:

Customer grade	A	B	C	D	E
No. of customers	–	1	1	12	17

Conclusion

This high compatibility/high business potential quadrant of the matrix contains 76 per cent of Grade A customers, 35 per cent of Grade B and 35 per cent of Grade C.

In contrast, the no-repeat business group was predominantly Grades D and E.

Both of these results are consistent with our previous marketing objectives.

6 *Regional breakdown of customer matrix*

(i) Southern

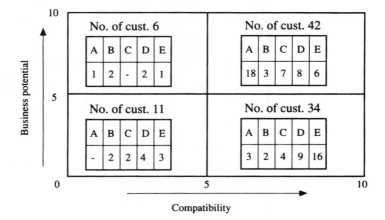

(ii) Midlands

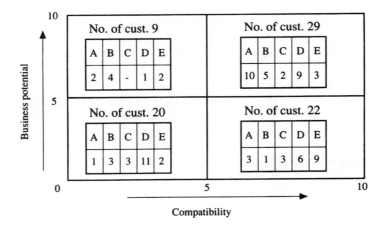

(iii) Northern

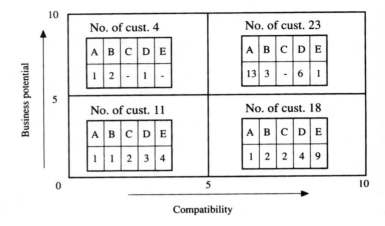

Conclusion

Each region will need to take steps to reduce the number of customers in the low/low quadrant and to increase those in the high/high quadrant. Also in this quadrant: work on B, C, D and Es to win larger contracts where possible.

For high business potential/low compatibility, eliminate the Es and consider how we might adapt our offer to other grades and achieve better matching.

For low business potential/high compatibility, reduce the number of D and E grades and offer consultancy to improve business potential of A and B customers.

7 Sources of funding

Source	As % of total income	
	Last year	Current year
Owner-occupied, industrial	33%	20%
Owner-occupied, non-industrial	7%	18%
Public sector	3.5%	21%
Pension and investment funds	42.5%	34%
Developers	14%	7%
	100%	100%

Conclusion

The biggest increases are in public sector spending and owner-occupied non-industrial projects, with an apparent slowdown in other areas.

8 Environmental review

- *The economy*
  The current balance of payments deficit and the high interest strategy to remedy the situation are sending ripples throughout the economy. Nevertheless, assuming the situation does not deteriorate further, there are some positive signs:
  - Public spending is on the increase again.
  - Work on the infrastructure and urban renewal is being given high priority.
  - There is still a high demand for leisure facilities and from tourism.
  - Foreign companies are coming to the UK and wanting custom-built premises.
  - There is pressure on government to invest more in industry and adopt a regional policy.
  - Forecasts for industrial and commercial premises still show an upward trend, as do those for retail premises in the Southern Region.
- *Technology*
  There is a continued growth in Design and Build and a requirement for fast-build techniques.

  Computerized inventory control and procurement systems should make our operations even more efficient.

  New materials and techniques will have to be continually monitored.
- *Competition*
  Our two nearest competitors are going through a transitionary period and are reorganizing themselves. While this currently acts in our favour, they are likely to re-emerge in a more competitive shape.

  There is a danger if there is a substantial downturn in the economy that a 'price war' will start as everyone scrambles for the little business that would be available. We need contingency plans for such an eventuality, or a refocussing of our corporate objectives.

  Overall we do not know very much about our competitors and their marketing strategies. We have been too busy getting our own house in order. This situation will need to be redressed.

  EC deregulation might present us with new competitors.

Section 2　SWOT analysis

Strengths

- Size and status of the company
- Our experience and track record
- National coverage
- Quality we provide
- Quality of our staff
- Willingness to innovate
- Relationships with customers
- Improved marketing skills
- Computerized services

Weaknesses

- Coordination between regional offices
- Shortage of some key skills
- Inconsistent quality standards
- We deal with too many 'mismatched' customers
- Inexperience of new recruits

Opportunities

- Increase in public spending
- Buy out other builders
- Use some of our services, e.g. quantity surveying, as a separate profit-centre
- Extend regional coverage in South with new office
- Investigate new markets, e.g. private hospitals
- Make better use of our computer systems
- EC deregulation
- Look for a partner on mainland Europe

Threats

- Downturn of the economy
- Loss of key personnel
- Problems in recruiting right calibre people
- EC deregulation
- Material shortages
- Revitalized and more sophisticated competitors
- Continued growth will stretch us too far and lead to inefficiencies
- Changes in key market segments
- Environmental lobby makes it more difficult to get land and/or planning permission

Section 3　Assumptions

Three main assumptions have been made as a backdrop to the thinking behind this plan.

1　The economy will not go into deep recession.
2　We maintain a similar organizational structure over most of the next three years.
3　Any new EC competitor will not make a significant impact in the period under consideration.

Section 4   Marketing objectives and strategies

	Objectives	Strategies
1	Increase turnover by the amounts shown in Section 6	Increase market penetration and customer base Target new customers more accurately Work to develop more business from existing high potential customers Actively market our specific competences Acquire three small existing businesses

Note: As a safeguard, no one customer in any segment is to account for more than 20 per cent of turnover.

2	Improve profitability by the amounts shown in Section 6	Eliminate 'mismatched' unprofitable customers from the portfolio and concentrate efforts on those with high business potential Improve inventory control and logistics

Other objectives and strategies

3	Maintain a high level of social responsibility	Respond to contacts from schools regarding careers talks, etc. Support local charities, etc. Maintain safe working practices Each region to have someone to keep abreast of local environmental issues
4	Maintain a high standard of ethics in all our transactions	An internal 'code of practice', to be developed A video to be made to explain to staff why the directors see this as such an important issue
5	Keep one step ahead	Explore potential of new markets, e.g. hospitals Examine prospects of EC deregulation and/or partnership with Euro-company Explore more attractive employment 'packages' to attract new and keep existing staff

Section 5   Alternative plans and mixes

1   The time is coming for each region to become an individual profit centre and be responsible for its own marketing plan, rather than it being controlled and compiled centrally. However, it is probable that there is not enough marketing expertise throughout the organization to allow that to happen yet.

   Nevertheless, this should be considered as a longer term organizational goal to guide our short-term thinking.

2   Another possibility was to exploit the profit potential of some of our internal services, e.g. quantity surveying, computer applications to the construction industry, project management, etc.

   However, this development was shelved temporarily, for two main reasons:

   (a)   With our relatively rapid growth rate, it is probably helpful if we consolidate as opposed to diversifying and perhaps putting additional pressures on our hard-pressed organization.

   (b)   Such a move might compromise the eventual move of making the regions more autonomous.

3   If the economy goes into a deep recession then much of this marketing plan will have to be reviewed, particularly our growth targets.

Section 6   Targets and programmes

1   Financial targets

Southern

Year	Income (£m)	Expenditure (£m)	Profit (£m)
Current	35.50	30.10	5.40
+1	48.55	41.25	7.30
+2	56.80	47.08	9.72
+3	69.90	56.90	13.00

Midlands

Year	Income (£m)	Expenditure (£m)	Profit (£m)
Current	22.40	19.10	3.30
+1	29.35	24.85	4.50
+2	34.40	28.52	5.88
+3	42.30	34.40	7.90

Northern

Year	Income (£m)	Expenditure (£m)	Profit (£m)
Current	26.10	22.20	3.90
+1	35.10	29.80	5.30
+2	41.00	34.00	7.00
+3	50.40	41.00	9.40

2 Customer base

Targets to be achieved over three-year period:

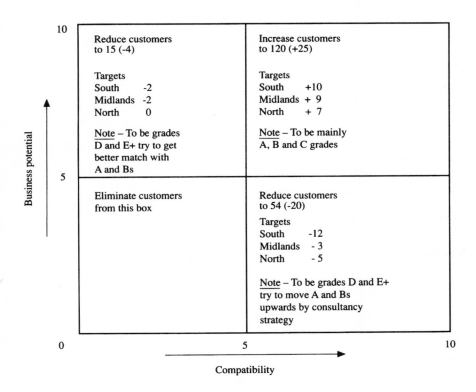

Note: New customers should be selected using the criteria upon which the customer matrix was based (Section 1.5). While these criteria are not meant to override local knowledge, regions will have to present a good case for accepting customers who do not meet them.

3 Advertising and promotion

This will be at the discretion of each regional manager, consistent with the targets and budgets he is allowed.

4 Pricing

Our policy of providing high quality services and pleasing and functional design, plus our reputation of completing projects on time, vindicates our strategy to price at the top end of the market.

Wilcox and Simmonds Project Management Ltd

Introduction

Wilcox and Simmonds have a long and, on the whole, distinguished record of supplying the UK construction industry with a range of specialist goods and services.

The Project Management Division was recently set up to run as an autonomous unit to provide project management services to the construction industry, something which is a relatively new idea in this business sector.

Project management originally developed in the heavy, civil and process engineering industries. It involves taking the responsibility for the overall planning, control and coordination of a project from inception to completion, with the objective of meeting the client's requirements of achieving completion on time, within the target cost and to the required quality standards.

During a construction project a whole range of functional specialists might get involved. Typically these would be architects, structural engineers, service engineers, quantity surveyors and building contractors. Very large projects might also include town planners and civil engineers.

The project manager's task can be to recommend those who can fulfil these roles, or to work with those of the client's choice. Essentially the project manager becomes the 'hub' of a network of interrelated activities, the output of which is dictated by his budgetary planning skills and his ability to influence and cajole everyone to deliver their particular contribution at the required time.

The key benefit for the client is that all progress can be monitored through one person. Equally, if things are going wrong, there is again only one person to deal with. Although a client company might have a department capable in theory to tackle such work, in practice there is often not the required wide range of expertise and experience to sustain the project management role.

Thus the UK construction industry, with its tradition of separating design from construction, and its propensity for developing managers as functional specialists, appeared to be a suitable candidate for an overall, project management approach. It was this opportunity which spurred the company to set up its new division.

So new is project management in the building industry that its role is not yet fully accepted, nor is there an established pricing structure.

It is against this background that the chief executive and his team prepare for the next three years, following an eventful and quite successful first year in business. What follows is the business plan produced by the Project Management Division.

In order to protect identity, all names, locations and values have been changed. However, the integrity of the company's planning process still remains to provide an interesting example of business planning from which we can all learn.

1 Review of first full year's trading

Although financial targets were met, a substantial amount of time was devoted to setting up and staffing our three offices. In addition it was difficult to recruit staff experienced in both project management and the construction industry, therefore a considerable amount of training had to be provided.

However, we now have an administrative base, the personnel and technical procedures. This means that project managers can start to focus on building up the business in a planned and sustained way, rather than chasing work as and when opportunities present themselves.

Financial

£000	Budget	Actual
Income	2352	2573
Expenditure	1970	2052
Profit	**382**	**521**

Personnel

	Actual	Deviation from plan
Professional staff		
Croydon	13	−3
Coventry	14	0
Manchester	5	0
Administrative		
Croydon	7	+1
Coventry	5	−1
Manchester	1	0
Total	**45**	

Analysis of profit

	Turnover	Profit
Project management	£1,750,000	£250,000
Construction management	£860,000	£271,000
Total		**£521,000**

2 Mission statement

Our review of our first year has not caused us to be swayed from our original statement of intent:

To become the leading company supplying project management within the construction industry.

We will achieve this by:

- Establishing a reputation for quality and successful completions
- Having the largest market share
- Being the first choice of clients seeking project management
- Being the first choice of the best candidates in the job market.

Above all, we must be clear about what we are striving to achieve at a time when there are many potential opportunities in the market place.

We believe a key to success is to break our organization into strategic business units.

3 Financial projections

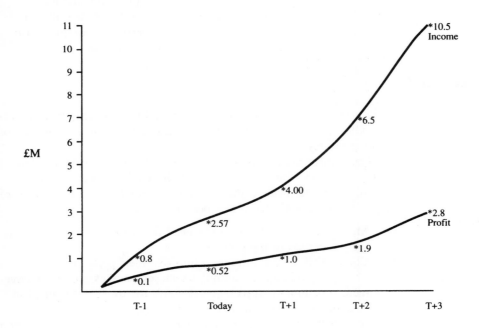

4 Market overview

Competition

There are probably at most only about 40 companies set up to offer a similar service to ours. Of these companies we are one of the largest, in terms of project managers employed.

However, there are a number of other types of competitors who partially compete with us by offering a reduced range of services. These companies fall into the following broad categories:

Organization category	*Services*
1 *Management consultants* These are often parts of major accounting firms	Specialist advice feasibility studies
2 *Management contractors* Usually parts of large building contractors	Management of site work little involvement in design
3 *Civil engineering contractors* (with project management depts)	Tend to stay in civil engineering. Also undertake feasibility studies
4 *Quantity surveyors with PM depts*	Tend to limit their role to providing ongoing information at meetings etc. Some duplicate the work of building contractors
5 *PM depts of client companies*	Do not have the all-round expertise to compete with us on quality

Market trends

The construction industry is a very large, if fragmented, overall market. Over the last ten years it has grown steadily at an average rate of approximately 5.5 per cent.

The project management market we estimate to have a potential value of £120m. Our current market share of this is 2.1 per cent.

However, we believe there will be a rapid increase in sales of project management for a number of reasons:

- More clients will perceive the need for it as it becomes increasingly accepted in the industry.
- Clients seek new solutions to improve their performance.
- The rate of change in building technology makes project management ever more complex and difficult for those not trained in it (the majority of construction managers).
- Architects are failing to fulfil clients' needs in terms of providing value-for-money solutions.

- There is increasing pressure to shorten the inception-to-completion time-span.

Market structure

There are two driving forces for the construction industry:

1 *Property developers and investors who create facilities for sale or lease*
Included in this category are insurance companies, banks, pension funds, investment companies.
2 *Property occupiers who create facilities for their own use*
In this category are firms from the private sector, such as manufacturing, retailing, distribution and leisure. There is also a sizable public sector which includes government ministries, local authorities, public utilities, public transport and health authorities.

Strategic business units

It would make sense to manage our business through five specific business units:

1 *Regional project management*
Managing medium-to-large projects (ideally over £250,000 construction turnover per month) in all principal markets.
2 *Construction management*
Managing fast-track, complex projects (ideally over £1m construction turnover per month) which require a site-based construction team. This SBU would focus on commercial owner occupier/developers in the south-east.
3 *Special projects*
A design and management service to small building projects, operating mainly in the developer, pension fund, owner-occupier markets.
4 *Manufacturing process projects*
Managing manufacturing plans, machinery installations and associated commercial buildings. The principal markets will be industrial and warehousing.
5 *Major projects*
Projects which require a dedicated team and are likely to be in the order of £2m construction turnover per month. The initial market to be targeted will be investor/developer, although this unit will operate in all principal markets.

Note: SBUs 4 and 5 will not come on-stream for another year.

Ansoff matrix

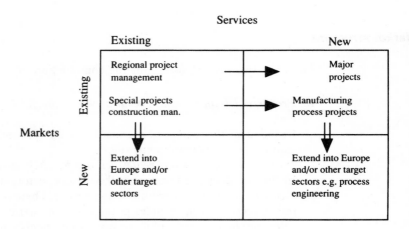

Gap analysis

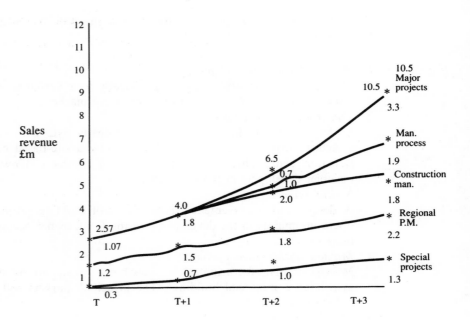

5 SWOT analysis

The following analysis holds true for all the SBUs.

Strengths	Weaknesses
• Reputation of W & S in the construction industry in general • Regional representation in growth areas of UK economy • High expertise in PM of staff • One of the largest companies • Now have a business plan • Wealth of contacts in the industry via W & S • Starting with a 'clean sheet' and can get it right from the start	• Training of new staff needs to be improved, both in quality and duration (too long) • Lack of detailed market information • Need more/better promotional material • We have made mistakes in recruiting PMs. Some do not fit our 'culture'. More attention to selection and better employment package required • PMs are excellent individuals but do not yet function well in teams • To date we have been chasing any work just to meet targets and have not been focused • Technical procedures still need to be improved • Need to establish unique selling points/ selling skills
Opportunities • PM is in its infancy in the construction industry • Large potential market • Expand by acquisition if necessary • Joint ventures, in UK and Europe • Traditional structure of construction industry lends itself to PM • Few serious competitors at present	**Threats** • Interest rates increase even higher, and trigger-off a recession • Entry of new competitors • Large contractors develop their own PM depts • Inability to recruit sufficiently high calibre staff to sustain growth • PM does not really 'catch on' in the construction industry

6 Critical success factors

Regional project management

CSF	Weighting	Score vs competition	Total
1 Staff are perceived by clients as highly professional	3	5	15
2 We provide value for money	2	6	12
3 Our corporate reputation and track record	2	8	16
4 Staff are motivated to win business	3	5	18
	(10)	(out of 10)	**58/100**

Issues to be addressed

1 Improve professionalism and motivation of staff, by training and better field management.
2 Improve service surround to provide better value for money.

Construction management

CSF	Weighting	Score vs competition	Total
1 Early identification of opportunity	3	7	21
2 Demonstrate knowledge of client's business	3	8	16
3 High level of PM consultant teamwork	2	4	8
4 Value for money	2	6	12
5 Track record	1	7	7
	(10)	(out of 10)	**64/100**

Issues to be addressed

1 Improve consultant teamwork.
2 Look for ways to offer more value for money.

Special projects

CSF	Weighting	Score vs competition	Total
1 Close contact with clients	1	6	6
2 Demonstration of early success	3	6	18
3 Flexibility to adapt to changing client needs	3	8	24
4 Value for money	2	8	16
5 Track record	1	6	6
	(10)	(out of 10)	**70/100**

Issues to be addressed

1 Improve contact with clients – establish schedules.
2 Improve and publicize track record.
3 Reappraise staffing levels at front end of projects in order to develop more momentum and hence quicker results.

Manufacturing process projects

CSF	Weighting	Score vs competition	Total
1 Early identification of opportunity	3	5	15
2 Can 'talk clients' language'	4	5	20
3 Value for money	2	8	16
4 Track record	1	7	7
	(10)	(out of 10)	**58/100**

Issues to be addressed

1 Improve intelligence sources.
2 Develop more expertise about client business through recruiting people with different appropriate career backgrounds *or* buy out a suitable company to gain right expertise.

Major projects

CSF	Weighting	Score vs competition	Total
1 Dedicated team of high quality	3	6	18
2 Value for money	2	7	14
3 Swift evidence of impact of services	2	7	14
4 Early identification of opportunity	3	5	15
	(10)	(out of 10)	**61/100**

Issues to be addressed

1 Improve market intelligence.
2 Develop teamwork.
3 Look for ways of demonstrating quick paybacks to client.

7 Assumptions

Underlying all of the foregoing analysis were the following assumptions:

1 The growth rate of the construction industry will continue at its average rate of the last few years (1 per cent).
2 Interest rates will not go any higher.

3 Investor confidence stays reasonably buoyant in the short and medium term.

4 There is a continuing growth in the demand for project management.

5 A change of government (should it happen) will not lead to a significant change in the economic prospects of the construction industry.

8 Portfolio analysis

Within Regional project management it was possible to break down the current and potential business in terms of our competence in dealing with key market segments and their attractiveness. The results are shown here. It is intended to develop this type of analysis for each SBU as data becomes available.

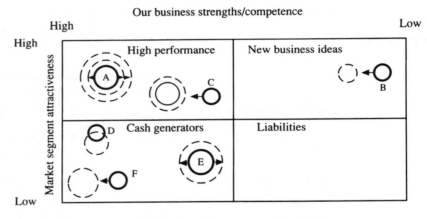

Regional project management portfolio

A = Developer/Investor P.M.   D = Owner Occupier Project Coordination
B = Dev./Inv. Design & Build   E = Owner Occupier Design & Build
C = Owner Occupier P. M.   F = Consultancy Services

Overall comment

The portfolio is reasonably well balanced at present. There are no services in the liabilities quadrant. We will need to start thinking about another new business idea fairly soon in order to keep a 'flow' going. We need more revenue from existing cash generators so that we can invest in the high performers and new business ideas.

The implications are that we review our pricing and look at ways of saving on costs.

9 Marketing objectives and strategies

To increase from £2.57m to £10.5m over the next three years, while at the same time growing net profits from £0.52m to £2.8m. This will come from the following:

Existing business

1 *Regional project management*
   - To increase income from £1.2m to £2.2m over the next three years.
   - To increase average project size by 25 per cent over that period.
   - Each project manager to start two new projects per year.
   - Opening of new regional offices or acquisition of existing company will be reviewed throughout the planning period.
2 *Construction management*
   - To increase income from £1.07m to £1.8m over the next three years.
   - Focusing on commercial owner occupiers and developers in the south-east.
   - One additional project required each year over the total managed in previous year. Average project value to increase by 10 per cent per annum minimum.
3 *Special projects*
   - To increase income from £0.3m to £1.3m over the next three years.
   - Treble the number of contacts made with potential clients each year and improve conversion rate by 25 per cent.
   - Average contract value to increase by 10 per cent per annum minimum.

New business

4 *Manufacturing process projects*
   - To initiate the business by $T + 1$ and to earn revenue of £1.9m over the next two years.
   - Focus on small to medium-sized projects in order to gain quick results and demonstrate a track record.
5 *Major projects*
   - Starting in $T + 1$, to earn revenue of £3.3m over the next two years.
   - Focus on developers and investors.
   - Look for opportunities in public sector.

Long-term strategies beyond the three-year plan

Build on the expertise we will have developed in terms of planning procedures, systems, quality procedures and staff to lead into new growth market segments. These are likely to be:

- Large design and build projects (UK and Europe)
- Direct development of property (UK and Europe)
- Major manufacturing process projects (worldwide).

10 Marketing strategies (i.e. the marketing mix)

	Regional project management	Construction management	Special projects	Manufacturing process projects	Major projects
Market share	Increase	Increase	Increase	Establish	Establish
Promotion	Rely on face-to-face selling skills and developing good personal relationships with clients. Indirect promotion will focus on press releases about success stories, articles in journals and presentations at conferences, etc. Any promotional material will have to be high quality, and consistent with our image				
Price	High end of range	High end of range	High end of range	Competitive for entry	Competitive for entry
Product	Increase product surround and provide added value for money			Experiment with 'most acceptable' product	
Place	Regional representation will be provided whenever possible to establish closeness to clients. This might entail opening new offices in the UK and Europe				
Developments	Develop USPs re value management. Establish better data re costs and prices	Consider use of joint venture approach with suitable partners	Develop USPs re value management	Maximize profile with suitable launch. Sales campaigns into target industries	Maximize profile with suitable launch. Consider acquisition strategy from early days

Note: Ideas for developing value management are attached (Appendix A) and criteria for acquisition are provided (Appendix B).

Appendix A   Developing value management

The project manager's task is twofold: To manage the physical construction chain and to manage the value-added chain.

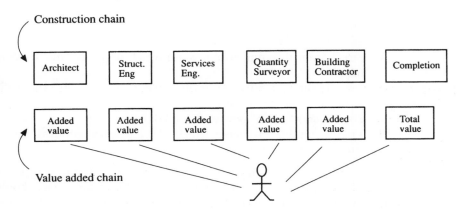

Project manager

It is not from the completion of the project that we earn anything. It is the *total added value* from which we earn our profits and reputation.

Added value will accrue from the project manager's ability to reduce costs (in real terms) and to save time. For example, a day saved at an early stage of the chain might lead to many being saved at the later stages of the project, which in turn could dramatically alter the whole cost structure of the construction, both for the client and ourselves.

There must be regular reappraisals of our current working procedures by all project managers and teams in order that we can improve upon the value-added chain.

Appendix B   Criteria for acquisition

Should the growth of the project management market outstrip our capabilities to meet demand we will need to consider acquiring existing businesses. However, in order to be a genuine asset, such a purchase should meet these criteria.

The company will:

● Have a good reputation in the industry
● Add to our collective experience due to its track-record and/or its contacts
● Provide us with advantageous geographical coverage
● Provide expertise in terms of its operating systems and procedures, and/or staff

- Have the financial resources to share in the investment costs of technical development, sales and marketing, and staff training.

For us to be certain we will be making a good investment we will need to:

- Research and monitor our competition, both in the UK and abroad
- Prioritize the above criteria
- Select from the competition those which best meet our requirements
- Identify the mutuality of our objectives and assess the synergistic potential from acquisition
- Have a short-list of potential candidates
- Plan a suitable campaign which will maximize goodwill and a trouble-free integration.

Note: Acquisition might also be considered as a solution to overcoming skill shortages in the short term. In this instance care should be taken that too much extraneous 'baggage' is not taken on board at the same time.

Moritaki computers (UK) Ltd

Background and information

The company was set up four years ago by the parent organization, which is in Tokyo. In total the group employ just over a hundred people, with approximately half of them based in London.

Between them the two companies provide an international computer consultancy specializing in the installation, enhancement and support of corporate accounting systems. Both units operate virtually autonomously in terms of seeking new business. Territorially, the London office deals with the northern hemisphere and Tokyo the southern.

Primarily the target customers are large, international companies who continually invest in their management information systems. The Tokyo office already has a client base which includes five of the largest Japanese companies.

Although the London office is expected to focus its activities primarily on Europe, it does have a small sales office in New York.

The company specializes in the Cassandra (Comprehensive Accounting Spread Sheet and Revenue Analysis) financial accounting system, which is supplied by the author Genesis Inc. from California, USA. In addition there is a systems development group, and multiuser hardware is also supplied.

The total group turnover is expected to be in the order of £3m this year, with London accounting for about 60 per cent of the total.

However, the Managing Director in London was both pleased about the trading success of the young company and yet worried. He knew that his sales team were good at spotting new opportunities as they arose, but could see that there was a danger of a proliferation of products and markets. Indeed, there seemed to be a general lack of focus for the company. It was tending to be reactive to the market rather than proactive.

This line of thinking prompted the MD to recruit a Marketing Director who was given this initial brief:

1 Define a strategy for the company as it moves through a period of rapid expansion and change.
2 Establish some marketing objectives for the company.
3 Lay down some compatible strategies for all of our products and services within each of the major market segments in which we compete.
4 Design a framework against which the directors can evaluate and sensibly judge a wide range of marketing opportunities which are uncovered by the sales force.

What follows is the three-year marketing plan developed by the new Marketing Director for Moritaki Computers (UK) Ltd.

1 Corporate mission

1 To provide a complete service in the design, enhancement, support and development of corporate accounting systems across the major industrial centres of the world.
2 To seek sustained growth through operating with high margins and reinvesting a substantial part of our profits. Our profit goal should never be less than 12.5 per cent (after tax and interest charges).
3 To provide a professional service which generates quality solutions to client problems and maintains a high level of customer service.
4 To encourage our staff to use their initiative by giving them responsibility and control over their own spheres of work, and rewarding them according to their contribution to the business.
5 To avoid any business activity which is peripheral and not consistent with our core business. In doing this we expect to double our turnover over the next three years.
6 To keep the company privately owned.

2 Situation review

Market review

It is possible to describe several key identifying characteristics which typify Moritaki customers:

- They have high expectations of their systems and demand systems capable of providing comprehensive management information about their business activities.
- They are above average in sophistication in their approach to computerization.
- They are perhaps installing a computerized accounting system for the second or third time.
- They are large companies with specialist financial and accounting functions.
- They are faced with multicurrency or other difficult reporting requirements.
- They consider their investment in information systems in terms of their strategic value to the company as well as cost benefits.
- They demand high quality and superior support services.

The following three market segments would appear to offer us the best opportunities for providing complete business systems, consistent with the above customer profile.

1 *European multinational companies*
These offer the prospect of multiple installations on an international scale.

2 *Large UK firms with complex currency/information requirements*
   Our expertise and ability to enhance the product give considerable scope in this segment.

3 *Japanese multi-national companies who are clients of Moritaki in
   Japan, but with a presence in the northern hemisphere*
   Introductions are easy and logistically it is better to service test
   clients from London rather than Japan.

Competition and company image

A survey was conducted by telephoning a number of existing and
potential client companies.

1 *How well is Moritaki known?* (Sample 20 typical client companies selected at random)

	Percentage
Competitor A	75
Competitor B	95
Competitor C	60
Competitor D	50
Competitor E	65
Competitor F	80
Competitor G	100
Moritaki (UK)	55

Conclusion Compared with our major competitors we are one of
the least well known suppliers (together with Competitor D). In
contrast, everyone has heard of Competitor G.

2 *Quality of the product* (Sample 18 users, scoring 1–10 points,
   10 = highest quality)

	Average score
System W	6.3
System X	5.8
System Y	7.9
System Z	6.7
Cassandra	9.2

Conclusion The Cassandra system is perceived to be superior in
quality to competing systems by users who are in a position to
make a comparison.

3   *Marketing ability*   (Sample 20 companies where we are known, scoring between 1 (low) and 10 (high))

	Average score
Competitor A	5.4
Competitor B	6.2
Competitor C	7.8
Competitor D	4.8
Competitor E	5.0
Competitor F	5.5
Competitor G	9.4
Moritaki (UK)	4.5

Conclusion   Competitor G is seen to have the highest level of marketing ability, whereas we have the lowest average score.

Overall conclusions

Little information is known about competitors, but on the basis of some admittedly rather crude surveys, it appears that:

- We are little known outside our existing bank of clients.
- Our product is the best on the market.
- We are not perceived as having much marketing ability.

This helps to explain why 65 per cent of our business is either from repeat sales or referrals from existing customers. Useful though this is, we will need to be capable of breaking out of our existing customer network if we are to achieve the corporate objectives of doubling our turnover over the next three years.

Market positioning

It is possible to define our existing position and determine our repositioning strategy by using the 'map' shown here.

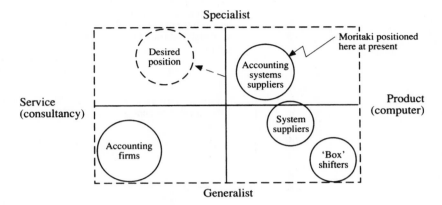

The new position is more consistent with the corporate objective of being a professional, specialist, consultancy company, providing a high level of customer service.

Marketing environment

The foreseeable threats and their potential to damage us are best described in the following table.

Threat analysis

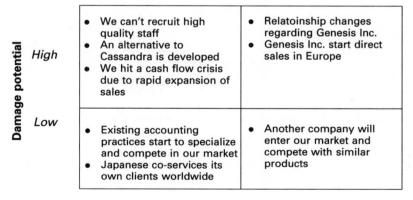

	Low	High
High	• We can't recruit high quality staff • An alternative to Cassandra is developed • We hit a cash flow crisis due to rapid expansion of sales	• Relatoinship changes regarding Genesis Inc. • Genesis Inc. start direct sales in Europe
Low	• Existing accounting practices start to specialize and compete in our market • Japanese co-services its own clients worldwide	• Another company will enter our market and compete with similar products

Damage potential (vertical axis label)

Likelihood of occurrence

Equally there are a number of opportunities, as described below.

Opportunity analysis

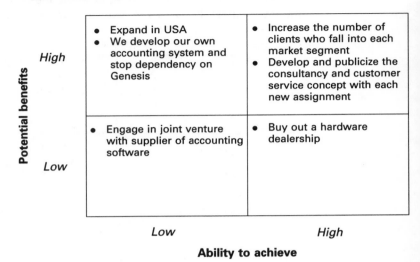

3 Product plans and analyses

The organization could be said to have this configuration:

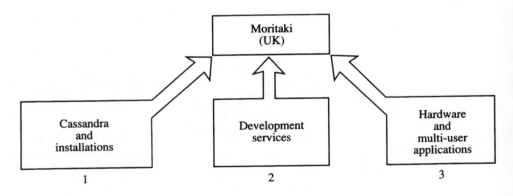

What follow are individual analyses of the three component parts that comprise Moritaki (UK) Ltd.

Cassandra system

- Best available product on the market.
- We have a very high level of experience with this system and a track record of successful installations and satisfied clients.

- Our development staff understand the open architecture of the product and can identify cross-selling opportunities for enhancement services.
- We have a special relationship with the authors, Genesis, who provide us with customer leads.
- It has a life cycle of at least another two years, because of the conservative nature of the client companies and its relative lack of penetration in the market.
- Sales have followed this pattern up to now:

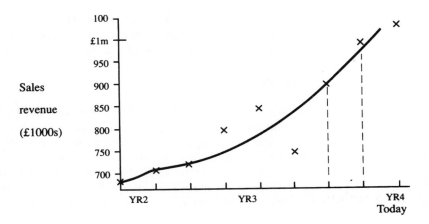

We need to:

- Monitor sales to get better at establishing life-cycle trends
- Monitor competitor activity
- Start thinking about the system to succeed Cassandra.

Critical installation factors which generate success

Ranked in order of importance they are:

1 Ability to provide a complete system including installation
2 Ability to understand the client's needs and talk in their language
3 Demonstrable technical competence, e.g. track record
4 Value for money, e.g. value added or cost savings
5 Ability to customize product to meet special requirements
6 High level of service and customer support.

SWOT analysis

Strengths
  Our technical knwowledge and expertise
  Accounting background
  Track record
  Relationship with Genesis.

Weaknesses

High perceived level of charges
Not well known in market
Dependency on Genesis
Lack of customer service skills/consulting skills.

Opportunities

Expand level of consultancy with each installation
Add other services to enhance system.

Threats

Not getting right quality staff as we expand
Genesis might use own sales team in Europe
Maintaining standards with rapid expansion.

Key issues

- We must focus on our 'customer services' not our 'product'.
- Our high perceived level of fees is because we are associated with 'computer companies', not professional service companies.
- We need to develop selling and customer service skills in installation staff, thereby generating more leads and business.
- We must maintain the high quality of installations.
- We need to keep Genesis out of Europe by persuasion.

Objectives

	Now	*+3 years*
Turnover (£m)	£1.1	£1.98
Contribution (£k)	£105	£175
Growth	×1	×1.8

Key assumptions

- No system superior to Cassandra comes on the market in the next 3 years
- The relationship with Genesis stays cordial
- There is no worldwide trade recession.

Strategies

- Present our range of products and services as a complete corporate accounting system.
- Add as much value as possible to each installation
- More meetings with clients prior to installation in order to:
  - explore all accounting and systems issues
  - create in the customer's mind the distinction between the software and the final completed system.

Pricing

Our current charges are 20–30 per cent higher than our main competitors and have probably inhibited our level of business in the past.

Our proposed market positioning can sustain this price differential, but as an interim measure we will need to carry out some research to find out:

- Customer perceptions about our fee levels
- What the market will bear
- How we can adopt a pricing strategy which will be consistent with our changing image.

Promotional strategy

Get the company better known in general by:

- Getting articles etc. into clients' trade journals
- Running seminars about specific problems which will interest potential clients
- Re-evaluating our existing promotional materials and upgrading where necessary
- Exhibiting at one or two prestigious venues
- Investing in a limited advertising campaign.

Because of our relative lack of experience in the visual impact of designing promotional materials, exhibitions and advertising, outside consultants will have to be used.

Sales strategy

- Recognize that every contact with a client is a sales opportunity.
- Train all installation staff in selling and customer service skills.
- Ensure that installation staff are aware of all other products and services and can sell 'through the range'.
- Develop a client contact plan as a means of improving our relationships with clients before and after a sale.

Product strategy

- Develop installation checklists to ensure consistent standards.
- Standardize pre- and post-installation evaluation checks.

Development services

- Can provide bespoke systems to extend the facilities of Cassandra.
- Use COBOL – the same as Cassandra, hence no additional learning required by clients.
- Provide database requirements for clients.
- Several similar bespoke systems have been amalgamated into specific 'products' which include:
  - 'loans and overdraft' system
  - 'futures investment' system.

Critical success factors for development work

Ranked in order of importance they are:

1 Our services outmatch the client's internal services in terms of charges and completion times.
2 We can talk the client's language.
3 Being able to demonstrate a track record.
4 Availability, when client has a problem.

SWOT analysis

Strengths
- Very high technical skills
- Intimate knowledge of Cassandra system
- Staff have financial background
- Have accumulated a 'portfolio' of bespoke solutions to many client problems.

Weaknesses
- Tend to be more interested in the technical problems than the client's lack of customer awareness
- Lack of coordination regarding similar projects
- Lack of control/project management on large projects
- No promotional material for this service.

Opportunities
- To exploit some of the 'bespoke' systems.

Threats
- Recruiting and keeping quality staff are problems
- Quality will suffer if department is overloaded.

Key issues

- How to get better control and coordination of projects at all stages.
- Getting better customer service skills.

- Recruitment, training and rewards package for development staff to be improved.

Objectives

	Now	*+3 years*
Turnover (£m)	£400	£800
Contribution (£k)	£38	£79
Growth	× 1	× 2

Key assumptions

- There are no crashes in the financial markets.

Pricing strategy

In order that we maximize our profits there are two considerations:

- Our prices are competitive.
- We do not run over the time allowed for each project.

The better the record of delivering on time, the more we can justify above-average prices.

The whole situation regarding prices for development needs reviewing. Current market prices have been distorted by the inclusion of the fees of 'one-man bands' who could not tackle most of the projects we undertake.

Promotional strategy

The main promotional thrust for Cassandra and installations will also publicize our development services.

In addition, staff will be trained in selling and customer service skills.

Product strategy

- Develop a 'house style' in terms of design, coding and testing so that consistent quality and appearance are perceived by clients.
- We must continually take full advantage of the latest developments in both software and hardware.

Hardware and multiuser applications

- Two-thirds of our installations are integrated with some form of PC network.
- New and existing machines can be linked via a network.
- Increasing interest in market re multiuser systems.

- We supply maintenance and support contracts.

Critical success factors

Ranked in order of importance they are:

1 Confidence client places in technical skills and abilities of the consultant.
2 Ability to provide general advice as well as the mainstream topic.
3 Speed of response and back-up services.
4 Prices of products and services.
5 Selling and customer contact skills.

SWOT analysis

Strengths
- Technically astute
- Customer orientated.

Weaknesses
- We are small compared with specialist firms in this part of the market
- Limited on dealerships with major equipment manufacturers
- Outdated promotional material.

Opportunities
- Growing demand for networks
- Our preferred multiuser system is becoming very popular and could be promoted
- Become agent for overseas equipment manufacturer.

Threats
- Larger companies enjoy economies of scale
- Dependent on sales of Cassandra to generate business
- Competition is getting fiercer in this market.

Key issues

- Targets to be set for non-Cassandra work.
- More promotion effort to get known in market.
- Capitalize on growing demand for networks and multiuser applications.

Objectives

	Now	+3 years
Turnover (£m)	£250	£720
Contribution (£k)	£24	£66
Growth	× 1	× 2.9

Key assumptions

- Current growth trends for networks and multiuser systems will continue.
- Sales for Cassandra reach their projected levels.

Pricing strategy

We need to focus on 'added value' not 'cheapness'. We provide very good products, excellent and impartial technical advice, above average installation and maintenance services, a fast response to client problems and a flexible approach.

The product is only part of this 'package', therefore we will avoid discounting as practised by the 'box shifters'.

In the short term (up to one year) prices will stay the same. Thereafter we will push to charge the highest the market will bear, in line with our publicity and company image campaigns.

Promotional strategy

- Develop promotional materials.
- Set realistic sales targets for non-Cassandra linked work.
- Ensure staff can sell 'through the range'.

Product strategy

- Keep abreast of all new developments.
- Standardize as much as possible on configurations, installation checks, pre- and post-installation tests.
- Develop closer ties with major hardware suppliers.

Houston Strategic Marketing Plan*

Market review

Houston is dominated by oil production. At present, it is at the bottom of the recession with full recovery not expected until 1990.

Stability of the economy is very volatile due to the glut of oil in the open market and the fall in the price per barrel. Totally dependent on the oil industry, Houston did not diversify sufficiently in other industries to make up for the deficit of the oil-related activities.

The Industrial Production Index was and still is well above the US average, and used to be above the Texas average until 1980. Now it is in sharp decline, falling from an index of 240 in 1981 to 210 in 1983, and it will continue to fall for the next two years before it is expected to hold.

Rig utilization is down from almost 100 per cent in 1980/1981 to just 50 per cent in 1982/1983. It increased to some 63 per cent last January but dropped again to just over 50 per cent subsequently. Many large contractors have withdrawn their fleets from the field and there are no indications that the coming months will see any improvement. Staff levels and production have reduced accordingly.

Per capita personal income in Houston increased from US$ 4000 in 1971 to US$ 13,000 in 1981. It amounted to US$ 12,500 in 1983/1984 and it may further decline before it holds. It is certainly not expected to grow, as the economy remains unstable and salary levels have dropped.

The number of British subsidiaries in the Houston area rose from 25 in 1974 to a total of 170 in 1981. This number has remained static for the last three years and is expected to hold for the next three years. Here again, the oil-related 'boom' has stopped.

Unemployment in the Houston area did not exceed 4.6 per cent in the period from 1973 until 1981. In 1982 it jumped to 6.7 per cent and in 1983 to 9.3 per cent, which was almost equal to the US average. The latest unemployment figure for July 1985 shows 7.7 per cent for the state of Texas (+1.4 per cent compared with July 1984). In Houston, the unemployment rate over the 12 month period rose from 7.1 per cent to 8.4 per cent.

* Based on a real marketing plan in the airline industry. This study dates back to the 1980s, but we have felt it important to be included because it is a good example of an airline marketing plan. The data and information have been disguised and some parts removed in order to preserve confidentiality. However, although not all extracts chosen relate to each other, sufficient detail has been provided to enable you to appreciate what a complete strategic marketing plan looks like.

Outside influences

We are influenced by the American political involvement in foreign countries more so than by the British involvement. Unfortunately, it often works against us, as in the case of Libya.

Domestic UK problems can also reflect badly, such as the Belgian soccer violence by the English fans and racial disturbances in Birmingham.

The continuous hijacking problem and the recent series of accidents and incidents have hit the airline industry in general.

The First Class market is small and is in decline, while new carriers have moved in – Continental with daily non-stop services to London Gatwick, and Lufthansa non-stop to Frankfurt with a high level of service.

Because of the increased competition, yields declined quite dramatically both for passenger sales and cargo.

Last, but by no means least, the stronger pound versus the weaker dollar will influence the flow of traffic to and from the USA.

Passenger sales

Strengths	F*	J*	Y*
Reputation and high awareness	x	x	x
High standards of service	x	x	
Commision levels and relationship with travel agents	x	x	x
Punctuality	x	x	x
Weaknesses			
Small and declining market	x		
One film against two of competitor	x	x	x
Congested lounge and no identity	x		
Lack of lounge facilities		x	
Departure time, just after main competitor	x	x	x
No frequent-traveller incentive	x	x	x
Seven-abreast seating		x	
Low awareness of BCAL network	x	x	x
Lack of Executive Class Europe/Nigeria	x	x	
Lack of capacity European services			x
Price perception: more expensive than competitor			x
Lack of advance seat selection			x
Opportunities			
Earlier departure, ahead of competitor	x	x	x
Price strategy (2 for 1; winter special)	x	x	
Frequent-flyer incentive (VAT)	x	x	x

	F*	J*	Y*
Small F-Class cabin and six-abreast in larger J-Class cabin	x	x	
Meet and greet chauffeur-driven service	x		
Free helicopter service Houston and destination	x		
Own lounge(s)	x	x	
Complimentary hotel accommodation London	x	x	
New routes to Middle East		x	x
Executive product Europe and Nigeria	x	x	
Hobby airport interline potential and new feed (US Air and Pride Air)	x	x	x
Beyond LGW – European markets	x	x	x
Free rail tickets	x	x	x
Advance seat selection			x
Through check-in facilities	x	x	x
Strong, competitive in-house product		x	x

Threats

	F*	J*	Y*
A continuing decline of the market	x		
Improvement of competitor's product	x	x	x
Competitor's price strategy (2 for 1)	x	x	x
New, larger (747?) equipment by competitor	x	x	x
Limitation of the Houston catchment-area lack of feed	x	x	x
Currency fluctuations			
New carriers to/from Europe (SR, SK)	x	x	x
Accidents/incidents in industry			
Unrest and riots in UK			
London pricing itself out of the market			
Declining London saturation			
Competitors' strong in-house products			

F = First Class; *J* = Super Executive; *Y* = Economy

Objectives and strategies

Objectives

To maintain and increase share of the business travel market segments.

Strategies

With effect from Spring 1986 introduce a Boeing 747-Combi on the Houston route with the following configuration and product enhancement:

A First Class

Objectives To hold/increase market share in declining but attractive market.

Strategies Reduce size of cabin to 16/18 seats

Introduce a 'meet and greet' chauffeur service in Houston	£300,000
Offer complimentary London hotel accommodations – two-night package	£206,000
Advertising and promotions of the above strategies	£75,000
Open BR's own First Class lounge	Capital
Introduce a bonus point system for for frequent FC pax whereby they receive a certain number of points for either gifts or free travel	Corporate
Total cost	**£581,000**

Result
Revenue/FC potential 900 r/t incremental pax increase
plus retention of existing market share: (2.5 pax per
flight) × £2250 RT yield × number of flights (360) =   £2,025,000

F Class gross contribution   **£1,444,000**

B Super Executive Class

Objectives To increase market share in an increasingly attractive market.

Strategies Six-abreast seating

Larger cabin (approximately
40–45 seats)

Offer complimentary London hotel accommodations one-night package 25 × £75 × 360 =	£241,000
Offer use of Continental's lounge	
Total cost	**£241,000**

Result

Super-Executive revenue potential 1260 pax
(3.5 pax per flight) £1428 RT yield × 360 =   £1,799,280

J Class gross contribution   **£1,558,280**

C Economy Class

Objectives Hold/increase share in a declining market

Strategies Introduce advance seating selection

Result

Revenue/Economy potential 900 pax (2.5 pax increase per flight)

Y Class gross contribution	£636,000

Revenue potential

F Class	£2,025,000
J Class	£1,799,000
Y Class	£636,000
Total	**£4,460,000**

Glossary of marketing planning terms

Assumptions   The *major* assumptions on which the marketing plan is based.

Benefit   A perceived or stated relationship between a product feature and the need the feature is designed to satisfy. *See also* Differential advantage *and* Feature.

Business plan   A plan commonly intermediate between a company's strategic plan and its annual marketing plan. The purpose of the business plan is to establish the broad business objectives and strategies to be pursued by the business unit or centre over a time period of as many as five years. In this respect, business plans are similar to strategic plans which concern themselves with equally long time frames. Business plans are like strategic plans in one other respect: usually they deal with such strategic considerations as new product development, product acquisition, and new market development to achieve desired financial goals. Business plans also require extensive marketing input for their formulation and in this respect, they share characteristics in common with marketing plans. However, business plans generally do not include action programmes – a feature typical of marketing plans – but simply spell out intentions and directions. For example, if new product development was among the strategies to be pursued, this would be stated along with appropriate supporting rationale. However, the statement of this strategy would not be accompanied by a new product development plan.

Charter   A statement of the chief function or responsibility of an operating unit within an organization made up of several operating units. *See also* Mission.

Core strategy   A term used in marketing to denote the predominant elements of the marketing mix, selected by marketing management to achieve the optimum match between the benefits customers seek and those the product offers. This process of selection is sometimes referred to as 'making the differential advantage operational'.

Differential advantage A benefit or cluster of benefits offered to a sizeable group of customers which they value (and are willing to pay for) and which they cannot obtain elsewhere. *See also* Feature *and* Benefit.

Distribution A term used in marketing to refer to the means by which a product or service is made physically available to customers. Distribution encompasses such activities as warehousing, transportation, inventory control, order processing, etc. Because distribution is the means of increasing a product's availability, it is also a tool which can be used by marketing management to improve the match between benefits sought by customers and those offered by the organization.

Experience effect It is a proven fact that most value-added cost components of a product decline steadily with experience and can be reduced significantly as the scale of operation increases. In turn this cost (and therefore price advantage) is a significant factor in increasing the company's market share.

Feature A characteristic or property of a product or service such as reliability, price, convenience, safety, and quality. These features may or may not satisfy customer needs. To the extent that they do, they can be translated into benefits. *See also* Benefit *and* Differential advantage.

Gap In marketing terms, the difference between a product's present or projected performance and the level sought. Typically, the gaps in marketing management are those relating to return on investment, cash generation or use, return on sales, and market share.

Gap analysis The process of determining gaps between a product's present or projected performance and the level of performance sought. *See also* Gap.

Growth/share matrix A term synonymous with 'product portfolio' which in essence is a means of displaying graphically the amount of 'experience' or market share a product has and comparing this share with the rate of growth of the relevant market segment. With the matrix, a manager can decide, for example, whether he or she should invest in getting more 'experience' – that is, fight for bigger market share – or perhaps get out of the market altogether. These choices are among a number of strategic alternatives available to the manager – strategic in the sense that they not only affect marketing strategy but determine use of capital within the organization. *See also* Experience effect.

Marketing audit A situational analysis of the company's current marketing capability. *See also* Situational analysis.

Marketing mix The 'tools' or means available to an organization to improve the match between benefits sought by customers and those offered by the organization so as to obtain a differential advantage. Among these tools are product, price, promotion and distribution service. *See also* Differential advantage.

Marketing objectives A statement of the targets or goals to be pursued and achieved within the period covered in the marketing plan. Depending on the scope and orientation of the plan – whether, for example, the plan is designed primarily to spell out short-term marketing intentions or to identify broad business directions and needs – the objectives stated may encompass such important measures of business performance as profit, growth and market share.

Marketing objectives with respect to profit, market share, sales volume, market development or penetration and other broader considerations are sometimes referred to as 'primary' marketing objectives. More commonly, they are referred to as 'strategic' or 'business' objectives since they pertain to the operation of the business as a whole. In turn, objectives set for specific marketing sub-functions or activities are referred to as 'programme' objectives to distinguish them from the broader business or strategic objectives they are meant to serve.

Marketing plan Contains a mission statement, SWOT analysis, assumption, marketing objectives, marketing strategies and programmes. Note that the objectives, strategies and policies are established for each level of the business.

Market segment A group of actual or potential customers who can be expected to respond in approximately the same way to a given offer; a finer more detailed breakdown of a market.

Market segmentation A critical aspect of marketing planning and one designed to convert product differences into a cost differential that can be maintained over the product's life cycle. *See also* Product life cycle.

Market share The percentage of the market represented by a firm's sales in relation to total sales. Some marketing theorists argue that the term is misleading since it suggests that the dimensions of the market are known and assumes that the size of the market is represented by the amount of goods sold in it. All that is known, these theorists point out, and correctly, is the volume sold; in actuality, the market may be considerably larger.

Mission A definite task with which one is charged; the chief function of an institution or organization. In essence it is a vision of what the company is or is striving to become. The basic issue is: 'What is our business and what should it be?' In marketing planning, the mission statement is the starting point in the planning process, since it sets the broad parameters within which marketing objectives are established, strategies developed, and programmes implemented. Some companies, usually those with several operating units or divisions make a distinction between 'mission' and 'charter'. In these instances, the term 'mission' is used to denote the broader purpose of the organization as reflected in corporate policies or assigned by the senior management of the company; the term 'charter', in comparison, is used to denote the purpose or reason for being of individual units with prime responsibility for a specific functional or product-marketing area.

Objective   A statement or description of a desired future result that cannot be predicted in advance but which is believed, by those setting the objective, to be achievable through their efforts within a given time period; a quantitative target or goal to be achieved in the future through one's efforts, which can also be used to measure performance. To be of value, objectives should be specific in time and scope and attainable given the financial, technical and human resources available. According to this definition, general statements of hopes or desire are not true 'objectives'. *See also* Marketing objectives.

Planning   The process of pre-determining a course or courses of action based on assumptions about future conditions or trends which can be imagined but not predicted with any certainty.

Policies   Guidelines adopted in implementing the strategies selected. In essence, a policy is a summary statement of objectives and strategies.

Positioning   The process of selecting, delineating and matching the segment of the market with which a product will be most compatible.

Product   A term used in marketing to denote not only the product itself – its inherent properties and characteristics – but also service, availability, price, and other factors which may be as important in differentiating the product from those of competitors as the inherent characteristics of the product itself. *See also* Marketing mix.

Product life cycle   A term used in marketing to refer to the pattern of growth and decline in sales revenue of a product over time. This pattern is typically divided into stages: introduction, growth, maturity, saturation and decline. With time, competition among firms tends to reduce all products in the market to commodities – products which can only be marginally differentiated from each other – with the result that pioneering companies – those first to enter the market – face the choice of becoming limited volume, high-priced, high-cost speciality producers or high-volume, low-cost producers of standard products.

Product portfolio   A theory about the alternative uses of capital by business organizations formulated orginally by Bruce Henderson of the Boston Consulting Group, a leading firm in the area of corporate strategy consulting. This theory or approach to marketing strategy

formulation has gained wide acceptance among managers of diversi-
fied companies, who were first attracted by the intuitively appealing
notion that long-run corporate performance is more than the sum of
the contributions of individual profit centres or product strategies.
Other factors which account for the theory's appeal are: (1) its usefulness in developing specific marketing strategies designed to
achieve a balanced mix of products that will produce maximum
return from scarce cash and managerial resources; and (2), the fact
that the theory employs a simple matrix representation useful in
portraying and communicating a product's position in the market
place. *See also* Growth/share matrix.

Programme   A term used in marketing planning to denote the steps
or tasks to be undertaken by marketing, field sales and other functions within an organization to implement the chosen strategies and
to accomplish the objectives set forth in the marketing plan.
Typically, descriptions of programmes include a statement of objectives as well as a definition of the persons or units responsible and a
schedule for completion of the steps or tasks for which the person or
unit is responsible. *See also* Strategy statement *and* Marketing objectives.

Relative market share   A firm's share of the market relative to its
largest competitor. *See also* Market share.

Resources   Broadly speaking, anyone or anything through which
something is produced or accomplished; in marketing planning, a
term used to denote the unique capabilities or skills that an organization brings to a market or business problem or opportunity.

Situational analysis   The second step in the marketing planning process (the first being the definition of mission), and reviews the business environment at large (with particular attention to economic,
market and competitive aspects) as well as the company's own internal operation. The purpose of the situational analysis is to identify
marketing problems and opportunities, both those stemming from
the organization's internal strengths and limitations, and those external to the organization and caused by changes in economic conditions and trends, competition, customer expectations, industry
relations, government regulations and, increasingly, social perceptions and trends. The output of the full analysis is summarized in
key-point form under the heading SWOT (strengths, weaknesses,
opportunities and threats) analysis; this summary then becomes
part of the marketing plan. The outcome of the situational analysis
includes a set of assumptions about future conditions as well as an
estimate or forecast of potential market demand during the period
covered by the marketing plan. Based on these estimates and assumptions, marketing objectives are established and strategies and programmes formulated.

Strategy statement   A description of the broad course of action to be taken to achieve a specific marketing objective such as an increase in sales volume or a reduction in unit costs. The strategy statement is frequently referred to as the connecting link between marketing objectives and programmes – the actual concrete steps to be taken to achieve those objectives. *See also* Programme.

Target   Something aimed at; a person or group of persons to be made the object of an action or actions intended, usually to bring about an effect or change in the person or group of persons, e.g. our target is the canned food segment of the market.

Index

Books in the series

Below-the-line Promotion
John Wilmshurst

Creating Powerful Brands
Leslie de Chernatony and Malcolm H. B. McDonald

How to Sell a Service
Malcolm H. B. McDonald

International Marketing Digest
Edited by Malcolm H. B. McDonald and S. Tamer Cavusgil

Managing your Marketing Career
Andrew Crofts

Market Focus
Rick Brown

Market Research for Managers
Sunny Crouch

The Marketing Book
Edited by Michael Baker

The Marketing Dictionary
Edited by Norman A. Hart and John Stapleton

The Marketing Digest
Edited by Michael J. Thomas and Norman Waite

Marketing Led, Sales Driven
Keith Steward

Marketing Plans
Malcolm H. B. McDonald

Marketing to the Retail Trade
Geoffrey Randall

The Marketing of Services
D. W. Cowell

Marketing-led Strategic Change
Nigel Piercy

The Practice of Advertising
Edited by Norman Hart

The Practice of Public Relations
Edited by Wilfred Howard

The Principles and Practice of Export Marketing
E. P. Hibbert

Professional Services Marketing
Neil Morgan

Profitable Product Management
Richard A. Collier

Relationship Marketing
Martin Christopher, Adrian Payne and David Ballantyne

Retail Marketing Plans
Malcolm H. B. McDonald and Chris Tideman

Solving the Management Case
Angela Hatton, Paul Roberts and Mike Worsam

The Strategy of Distribution Management
Martin Christopher

The Chartered Institite of Marketing/Butterworth-Heinemann Marketing Series is the most comprehensive, widely used and important collection of books in marketing and sales currently available worldwide.

As the CIM's official publisher, Butterworth-Heinemann develops, produces and publishes the complete series in association with the CIM. We aim to provide definitive marketing books for students and practitioners that promote excellence in marketing education and practice.

The series titles are written by CIM senior examiners and leading marketing educators for professionals, students and those studying the CIM's Certificate, Advanced Certificate and Postgraduate Diploma courses. Now firmly established, these titles provide practical study support to CIM and other marketing students and to practitioners at all levels.

 The Chartered
Institute of Marketing

Formed in 1911, The Chartered Institute of Marketing is now the largest professional marketing management body in the world with over 60,000 members located worldwide. Its primary objectives are focused on the development of awareness and understanding of marketing throughout UK industry and commerce and in the raising of standards of professionalism in the education, training and practice of this key business discipline.